# *Words of Love*
## Volume 2
### *Radio Sermons*

*A BOOK OF SERMONS BY:*

## J. WAYNE McKAMIE

First Edition
Published By
Robinson Digital Publications
P.O. Box 2634
Weatherford, TX 76086

For additional copies contact:
Gary Robinson
P.O. Box 2634
Weatherford, TX 76086
parables@sbcglobal.net

# *Table of Contents*

# *Preface*

If I had the ability to over-estimate the importance of the Word of God in our lives, I would try. The authenticity and authority of God's Word are assailed on every hand. As a result, multitudes of unsuspecting individuals are being deceived. Indeed, "if the foundations be destroyed, what can the righteous do" (Psalm 11:3)? One thing is sure: the theories of mankind will not awaken a soul from the sleep of sin. It is only God's Word that can accomplish that feat, and His voice must be heard!

This work is an attempt to bring all who will listen face to face with the Word of God that will abide forever and ever.

J. Wayne McKamie

# Sermons

# *According to the Pattern*

Good morning, everyone. Our lesson today concerns itself with Paul's statement "that we should do all things according to the pattern." When we begin a discussion of patterns, we are discussing something that is common knowledge and that we all have a clear understanding of what we are talking about. Every time you see a large beautiful building, you are surely aware of the fact that some architect used his talent in designing and planning every minute detail that made that structure all it is. The construction was left to men who could follow the plan drawn by the architect. This same principle is found in other lines of work. The designer plans the mold in which the foundry worker pours the molten metal. The die is cut by which the machinist fashions the metal. A lady who is about to cut out a dress first lays down the pattern by which she plans to cut the cloth, then she follows the pattern.

In matters of religion, God is the designer. It is God who designed and made the universe in every part and every detail. When we single out man whom God made, we are caused to marvel at the completeness of God's design. We join the psalmist as he says to God, "I will praise thee; for I am fearfully and wonderfully made: marvellous are thy works; and that my soul knoweth right well" (Psalm 139:14). As God made man, He designated man's purpose and also designed the work man was to do. He gave man a pattern for his life. This plan has been true for man both in the general sense as well as for every special work God has assigned to different men throughout the generations. God's directions have always been specific. For every work that God has given to man to accomplish, He has given the opportunity to carry it out by His plan. And God has never asked the impossible. God has granted to each one the ability that is commensurate with the task assigned. Then, of man, He has required the faith to obey the pattern God has given to him. The inevitable conclusion is that God has always abundantly blessed the obedient and He has abundantly cursed the disobedient. The failure has always been the result of man's lack of faith in God and in his failure to follow God's plan.

Probably two of the most notable examples in the Bible are Cain and Abel. The Bible teaches they were the sons of Adam and Eve. Of them, God required a sacrifice. We are sure God spoke to them, for Hebrews 11:4 states, "that by faith Abel offered unto God a more excellent sacrifice than Cain." Romans 10:17 says, "So then faith cometh by hearing, and hearing by the word of God." Abel's faith called him to obey God as he brought the firstlings of his flock and the fat thereof (Genesis 4:4). Abel's sacrifice was accepted, and the Lord had respect unto Abel and to his offering; but God did not accept Cain and his sacrifice—that is, He had no "respect" for Cain and his offering. We are not to conclude that Cain misunderstood the instruction God gave to them or that each of the boys didn't have the ability to carry out God's plan. Or that Cain could not have come up with the proper offering. God's demands are not unjust or impossible. The failure of Cain was because of his lack of faith to obey. God says to him in Genesis 4:7, "If thou doest well, shalt thou not be accepted? and if thou doest not well, sin lieth at the door." The Bible tells us that sin is a transgression of or a neglect to obey the law of God (1 John 3:4; James 4:17). So Cain sinned; and in his anger, he killed his brother. He could not escape the consequences of his sin nor hide his guilt. You recall he paid dearly for his failure to obey God's plan for him and I will assure you that it has ever been from then until now.

I want you to think for just a moment about Noah's salvation from the flood. Noah lived in a time of much evil. Genesis 6:5 tells us that God saw the wickedness of man was great in the earth and that every imagination of the thought of his heart was only evil continually. But Noah was a just man and perfect in his generation, and Noah walked with God, verse nine. God proposed to destroy the wicked and to save Noah because of his righteousness and because of their sinfulness. You recall that God gave Noah the plan for the ark to be made of gopher wood. The length was to be three hundred cubits, the width fifty, the height thirty. It was to have three stories and one window and one door. Animals of all kind were to be taken into the ark. Of the unclean, there were to be two of each kind, male and female. Of the clean, he was to take in seven pairs. Noah worked long and hard to build it according to God's plan. Thus, Genesis 6:22 says, "Thus did Noah; according to all that God commanded him, so did he." When the waters covered the earth and the wicked were all destroyed, then Noah and his family were saved because Noah had enough faith in God to do what He asked. He followed God's pattern in building the ark, and thus he was saved. He is an example to every one of us today, showing us that we must follow the commands of God so that we may be saved. Our salvation is not from the flood, but we are to be saved from eternal destruction by fire that shall come upon the wicked.

May I point you to another example? That Moses obeyed Jehovah. God gave to him the commandments and ordinances by which the nation of Israel should be governed and by which they should worship God. In particular, God gave a detailed pattern for the tabernacle that was to be built saying, "And let them make me a sanctuary; that I may dwell among them. According to all that I shew thee, after the pattern of the tabernacle, and the pattern of all the instruments thereof, even so shall ye make it" (Exodus 25:8-9). The tabernacle itself was to be built thirty cubits long and ten cubits high and ten cubits wide. There were to be two parts: the Holy Place and the Most Holy Place where the Ark of the Covenant and the Mercy Seat were to be placed. In the Holy Place should be the table of shew bread, the golden candlestick, and the altar of incense. Outside the tabernacle, but within the court, were to be the altar for their sacrifices and the lavor of brass where the priest could bathe before they ministered before God. Specific instructions were given for every part and for every one of its instruments. Moses followed the pattern of God and the tabernacle was built. The Bible teaches the glory of God's presence was made manifest in that because he did as he was commanded. Exodus 40:16 states, "Thus did Moses: according to all that the Lord commanded him, so did he."

God blessed Moses for his faithfulness in following the pattern that He had given to him. You recall the Bible goes on to state that Solomon built a Temple for God, and God gave the plan for it to David. David says, "The Lord made me understand in writing by his hand upon me, even all the works of this pattern" (1 Chronicles 28:19). You recall David was not permitted to build the tabernacle or the Temple. God says, "Thou shalt not build a house for my name, because thou hast been a man of war, and hast shed blood" (1 Chronicles 28:3). But David gave the pattern of God to Solomon, his son, and charged him, "Take heed now; for the Lord hath chosen thee to build an house for the sanctuary: be strong, and do it" (verse 10). Solomon built a magnificent Temple according to the plan of God.

May I point out to you that Jesus Christ came into this world to carry out the pattern or the plan of God. God had prophesied that the church should be established. Of it, Isaiah had prophesied in Isaiah 2:1-5. Daniel also pointed to its coming in Daniel 2:44, as he interpreted the vision of King Nebuchadnezzar. John the Baptist spoke of it saying, "Repent ye: for the kingdom of heaven is at hand" (Matthew 3:2). Jesus says after John had died and as he talked with the apostles in the coast of Caesarea Philippi, "Upon this rock I will build my church" (Matthew 16:18). The plan for the church of our Lord was designed, and the Lord Jesus Christ established the church on Pentecost according to Acts 2. Christ became its builder and Christ was its foundation. 1 Corinthians 3:11 says, "For other foundation can no man lay than that is laid, which is Jesus Christ." "God hath made that same Jesus, whom ye have crucified, both Lord and Christ" and thus, God made Him the anointed ruler or King over the kingdom of God, the church (Acts 2:36).

In Ephesians 1:22-23, the church is spoken of as the body of Christ and we are told how God put all things under His feet and gave Him, Christ, to be the head over all things to the church, which is His body the fullness of Him that filleth all in all. Thus, God gave the perfect plan for the church, Jesus Christ is the head of the church, and He has been given all authority over the church as His body. As well, Jesus is the savior of the body, the church (Ephesians 5:23). All the saved are added to the church by our Lord (Acts 2:47). There are no saved ones outside the church. As each individual obeys the Gospel of Christ and thus is born again, he becomes the child of God by faith in Christ Jesus and by a burial with the Lord in baptism (Galatians 3:26-27; Colossians 2:12). Paul tells us in 1 Corinthians 12:13, "For by one Spirit are we all baptized into one body, whether we be Jews or Gentiles, whether we be bond or free; and have been all made to drink into one Spirit" and the church is that one body (1 Corinthians 12:12; Ephesians 4:4-5).

We can no more be saved outside the church than we can be saved without the Lord Jesus Christ, who loved us and shed His blood for the remission of our sins (Matthew 26:28). I would like to point out to you today that as God had a pattern for everything from the beginning, so His pattern for the church today is complete. He has given us the manner of worship to be found in the church. God's people or His children are to sing praises onto Him, and in so doing to teach and admonish one another (Ephesians 5:19; Colossians 3:16). Christians are to pray to God (Acts 2:42). They are to teach or edify one another (1 Corinthians 14:26). Upon the first day of the week, they are to eat the Lord's Supper (Acts 20:7; 1 Corinthians 11:23-24). The Bible teaches upon the Lord's Day that His people are to lay by in store, that is, to contribute of their means as God has prospered them (1 Corinthians 16:2). This is God's pattern for worship. We are no more at liberty to change this plan, either by addition, subtraction or substitution, than was Solomon in building the Temple according to God's pattern or was Moses in building the tabernacle according to God's pattern or was Noah in erecting the ark to save them from the flood. God expects of us the same obedience by faith that was commanded in each of these noble characters of the Old Testament.

Actually, we have a greater building. We have a greater plan, the church of our Lord, a greater system in which to worship God. We must follow God's pattern if we hope to be pleasing in God's sight and to be blessed of Him. Certainly, the congregational organization of the church is also part of God's perfect plan. The scripture so decreed that each congregation is to be independent and autonomous. Each congregation where men are qualified is to have its own elders and deacons. Each one is to carry on its own work before God to whom they are directly responsible.

There is no larger organization or governing body than the local church and, likewise, no outside organization is to interfere with the work of the local church. We must respect God's plan. The name of the church of Jesus Christ is to be honored. The name of Christ Himself is to be honored, for His name is above every name (Philippians 2:9-11). Paul refers to the churches when he says, "The churches of Christ salute you" (Romans 16:16). He addresses his letter to the church of God, which is at Corinth (2 Corinthians 1:1). To the Thessalonians, he writes, "Unto the church of the Thessalonians which is in God the Father and in the Lord Jesus Christ" (1 Thessalonians 1:1). Certainly, these are divine names or descriptions for the church and should be adequate terms to use today. Denominational or sectarian names help to do nothing but divide the people of God into conflicting groups. The Lord prayed for the unity of the people of God (John 17:21).

Let us use scriptural terms in referring to the New Testament plan. Let's be sure that we do all things, as he puts it in Hebrews, "all things according to the pattern." Today the question is: Are you following the pattern that God is given for your life? Have you today obeyed the gospel of Jesus Christ according to the New Testament pattern? Are you today making your plans to go to worship God according to the New Testament pattern? All of these things you will find in the congregation that is supporting this broadcast. Please rest assured that they stand ready and willing to assist you in learning the pattern that God has given and how to render obedience to that pattern.

# *Matthew 4:4*

Good morning, everyone, I am very happy that you decided to join us as we study together another portion of the Holy Bible. If you have your Bible, let us turn to Matthew 4:4, noticing that Jesus says "It is written, Man shall not live by bread alone, but by every word that proceedeth out of the mouth of God." Following the baptism of Jesus, we read in Matthew 4:1, "he was led up of the Spirit into the wilderness to be tempted of the devil." In the New Testament, we read, "For we have not an high priest which cannot be touched with the feeling of our infirmities; but was in all points tempted like as we are, yet without sin" (Hebrews 4:15). Jesus was tempted in order that He might understand the temptations we have—that He might make intercession for us at the throne of God.

Jesus was hungry following a forty-day fast, but He refused to yield at Satan's suggestion to satisfy His hunger by turning stones into bread. In resisting temptation, He quoted from the words of Moses found in Deuteronomy 8:3, that man does not live by bread alone but by every word which proceeds out of the mouth of God. These words quoted by Jesus need to be studied again and again in our day. We are living in a day when too many have allowed the material to crowd out the spiritual. Too many today prefer cash to character. Too many of our day have forgotten that time is not as important as eternity and our souls are worth more than all the world. Thus, in our lesson, we will try to explain that the things of earth cannot satisfy us fully—that man descends to the level of a mere animal if he lives primarily on the physical plain of bread alone.

Therefore, we come to this all important principle: man shall live by the word of God. We must live by every word that proceeds out of the mouth of God. God's word contains food for the soul. God's word is not just a luxury. It is an absolute necessity! My soul and your soul must feed upon the word of God or else our souls shall die. The statement that Jesus quotes to Satan (Deuteronomy 8:3) is what God said to the Israelites many centuries before when they bitterly complained of hunger in the wilderness. God allowed them to hunger that they might know there are some things more important in true living than sustaining the physical man. In sending manna to the hungry Israelites, God taught them that their true source of life was from heaven.

When the tempter sought to test Jesus by daring Him to change stones into bread, Jesus refused to yield to the tempter's challenge. To make bread out of stones, contrary to God's will, would have been in obedience to Satan. It was for this reason that Satan tempted Him to do it. Jesus chose to trust God to supply His temporal needs. He honored God's word; and it sustained Him, just as it will sustain us when we live in faithful obedience to it.

When Jesus says that man shall live by God's word, He means living their little span of years by being concerned with far more than their eating and drinking and pleasure and getting gain upon this earth. In this statement, Jesus asserts the fact of immortality. If that assertion is not true, then the idea of life after death is not true. Then let us eat and drink for tomorrow we die. It should behoove us to listen to Jesus in this text and rise to a real or true conception of life. When do we have a different standard of value from that of the mere bread standard, we are concerned with what we get, what we accumulate, what we feed upon instead of what makes us pure and good, strong and faithful, making our life worthwhile. We are to live by everything that comes from the mouth of God; that is, all that God gives, not merely to the body, but especially to the soul. Job says, "I have esteemed the words of his mouth more than my necessary food" (Job 23:12).

Every word of God contains a revelation and a commandment from Him. His words give us life that is life indeed, the life without end. Solomon says he taught him also and said to him "let thine heart retain my words: keep my commandments, and live" (Proverb 4:4). He is to live this high life and is to be obedient to the word of God. Obedience is actually the secret of life with God. The supreme duty of every man is that he should study to learn these words and obey them. Man is blind and foolish if he lives from day to day, from week to week, from month to month, from year to year without any concern for the word of God, hoping that after being unconcerned about it, even rebellious to it, he will at last slip into some happy state.

Self-control and a willing humiliation of self to the will of God is man's first and hardest lesson. Such a spirit will drive a man hungering and thirsting for every word that proceeds out of the mouth of the Lord. To such, the Lord makes this promise: "Blessed are they which do hunger and thirst after righteousness: for they shall be filled" (Matthew 5:6). It was by obedience that Jesus proved His Sonship. Paul says, "Though he were a Son, yet learned he obedience by the things which he suffered; And being made perfect, he became the author of eternal salvation unto all them that obey him" (Hebrews 5:8-9). God has bidden me to be His son here. The life of a son is the life of obedience. I must prove my sonship by a life of obedience to Him. And, Jesus is our only source of true spiritual life. He says, "I am the way, the truth, and the life: no man cometh unto the Father, but by me" (John 14:6). Again, the Lord says of Himself, "I am that bread of life. Your fathers did eat manna in the wilderness, and are dead. This is the bread which cometh down from heaven, that a man may eat thereof, and not die. I am the living bread which came down from heaven: if any man eat of this bread, he shall live forever" (John 6:48-51).

In the words of the Apostle Peter, "Lord, to whom shall we go? thou hast the words of eternal life" (John 6:68). No one else can offer us the best here. No one else can offer us anything hereafter. He alone can offer the abundant life, now, and certainly He alone can offer us eternal life hereafter. It is most evident that man shall live by the word of God. Thus, we have the question, where may this wonderful food be found that is needed to nourish our souls? We believe that God's word may be found in the Bible, and we believe it is the word of God. Concerning the scripture, the apostle says, "All scripture is given by inspiration of God, and is profitable for doctrine, for reproof, for correction, for instruction in righteousness: That the man of God may be perfect, thoroughly furnished unto all good works" (2 Timothy 3:16-17). The scriptures, therefore, are entirely adequate for supplying the spiritual needs of man. They do not furnish partially, but completely, the man of God unto every good work. Our need for today is not some new religion or some new revelation. Just as the food that God has given us still satisfies man's physical hunger, so the word of God will still satisfy man's spiritual hunger.

The Bible is not just a book among Books. It is "THE" Book. It is the only book that can tell us of our origin; that is, that we came from God. It is that which can tell us of our duty—that we are here to serve God and our fellow man; and it is certainly the only book that tells us of our destiny—to dwell with God throughout eternity. Man may see evidence of the Creator in nature, but he cannot know the nature of our Creator without knowledge of the Bible. In reality, all that anyone knows or needs to know about God is found in the Bible. Furthermore, all that anyone knows or needs to know about Christ may be found in the Bible. All that anyone knows or that he needs to know about the plan of salvation may be found in the word of God, and this is true about heaven or hell or any other subject that we need.

I would like to point out to you this morning, that in the churches of Jesus Christ, you will find a group of people earnestly striving to exalt the Bible in both our worship and our teaching. It is our aim, not only to live by some of the word of God; but as Jesus says, "By every word that proceeded out of the mouth of God." While keenly conscious of our weaknesses and our failures as individuals, we believe the Bible, as our guide, is a perfect standard. If you would like to be associated with a group of Bible-believing and Bible loving people, we would be happy for you to investigate our plea and to study with us the word of the Lord.

In His word, the Bible, you will find that you are to "Believe in Christ"—"Believe on the Lord Jesus Christ, and thou shalt be saved, and thy house" is the admonition in Acts 16:31. You will also find in this book, that you are to repent of your sins. "I tell you, Nay: but, except ye repent, ye shall all likewise perish" (Luke 13:3). You will find that you are to confess the Christ. "Whosoever therefore shall confess me before men, him will I confess also before my Father which is in heaven" (Matthew 10:32). You will also read that you are to be baptized. "And now why tarriest thou? arise, and be baptized, and wash away thy sins, calling on the name of the Lord" (Acts 22:16). With a faith in your heart, which leads you to obey the commands of our Lord, you will be a Christian. As a Christian, follow these words of Peter "As newborn babes, desire the sincere milk of the word, that ye may grow thereby" (1 Peter 2:2). If any of you who are listening now to the call of the gospel—and you are not a Christian—if you have been living by bread alone, and have an appetite for the bread of life, then please turn to Him who can give you both peace and happiness here and eternal blessedness in the great hereafter.

# *Justification*

Good morning, everyone. Today, we invite your attention to a special study—a study that is most important. Certainly, it is one that is contained within the Holy Scripture and one that is vital for the salvation of your soul. We invite you today to study with us justification by faith.

The study of justification by faith has been challenging the attention of Bible students all down through the ages. It should be a matter of primary importance to every one of us. The sinner who has never turned from his sin should be interested because God's plan for his justification is his only hope of salvation. The man who is burdened with sin should be concerned about how to get out from under the condemnation of sin, to be released from its penalty, and to be justified in God's sight. The Christian should continuously rejoice in God's provision for him. He can rejoice with Paul, who says, "Therefore being justified by faith, we have peace with God through our Lord Jesus Christ: By whom also we have access by faith into this grace wherein we stand, and rejoice in hope of the glory of God" (Romans 5:1-2).

God's plan by which the Christian is made just, means peace to him each day that he lives. It means peace with God. It means peace of mind in knowing that he is free from the guilt of sin that would condemn his soul. It is a peace that the world cannot possibly give (John 14:27). Many people are confused on the subject of justification. So many theories about justification by faith have been taught by the religious teachers, that the average person does not know what the Bible actually teaches about this important matter. You may ask yourself the question as to whether you really know what the Bible says about justification by faith.

Some years ago, in the last of a series of articles titled "Religion in America" the United Press International writer, Lewis Cassel, had pointed out the lack of understanding along these lines and upon this subject. Writing under the heading "Justification by faith, doctrine of Luther found in Paul's letter" in the *Alabama Journal*, August 25; Mr. Cassel began by asking,

> Do you believe in justification by faith? Spring that question on a typical Protestant today and you'll draw a blank stare. Four centuries ago, Protestants shed blood, their own and others, in defense of the doctrine Martin Luther expounded in the name of justification by faith (Cassel, *Alabama Journal*).

Like any such articles, this one did not correctly represent the teaching of Luther or the teaching of the Bible. It showed the lack of understanding of Luther and the teachings of God's word, the lack of understanding that so many have in regard to all of these things. It should also call attention to the need for more complete teaching so that we can know and we can understand what the Bible says.

Martin Luther was a man of considerable learning and of great courage. This, I think no one would deny. He recognized the errors in the teaching of the Roman Catholic church, and he had the courage to speak against those errors, even though it endangered his own life. He spoke against the corruption of the Roman church in their selling indulgences, in the doctrine of purgatory, in the so-called masses for the dead, and of many forms of immorality in the Roman church. His teaching stirred the people of his day, and they were protesting against these errors and advocating breaking away from the Roman Catholic church.

But Martin Luther himself erred in his understanding of God's plan of justification by faith. In his study of Romans 1:17, he came to the conclusion that faith only was sufficient to justify. He took his pen in hand and wrote in the margin of the text an extra word, where Paul says, "The just shall live by faith," Mr. Luther added the word "alone" making the passage read, "The just shall live by faith alone." Thus, Luther illustrates the common misunderstanding of how men are justified by faith.

I would like to emphasize today, that man cannot—cannot—be justified by faith alone. The second chapter of the book of James beginning with verse 14 shows clearly that both faith and works are necessary for man to be justified. James says, "Ye see then how that by works a man is justified, and not by faith only" (James 2:24). James concluded his reasoning saying, "For as the body without the spirit is dead, so faith without works is dead also" (James 2:26). But many denominational doctrines have been based on the idea of justification by faith alone. Thus, men are often taught that they can be saved the very moment they believe, that obedience has nothing to do with salvation, that the Lord's command to believe, to repent, to be baptized in order to be saved, is not necessary. On this same false premise is based many of the arguments that a man does not have to be a member of the Lord's church in order to go to heaven.

To point out God's plan of justification by faith as the Bible teaches it, is to couple faith with works. It is to show the real meaning of faith and how true faith will always cause men to obey the gospel of Christ. It means that men will obey from the heart that form of doctrine which God has given us, as we read in Romans 6:17. The importance of such obedience is seen in the next verse. Paul says, "Being then made free from sin, ye became the servants of righteousness" (Romans 6:18). Freedom from sin can be realized only when a man obeys from the heart the form of doctrine of the death, the burial, and the resurrection of Christ as pictured by Paul in Romans 6. It means a faith that will cause a man to become dead to sin, even as Christ died upon the cross for his sin—a faith that will cause that man to be buried with his Lord in baptism, even as Christ was buried in Joseph's tomb. And a faith that will cause him to arise from the waters of baptism to walk in newness of life. It is this obedient faith by which a man can be justified and by which he can live for Christ, even as Paul says in Romans 1:17: "The just shall live by faith."

Now this teaching does not mean that a person can be saved by his own deeds apart from God's grace or apart from faith in God's plan of salvation. Surely, no one could justly jump to such a conclusion; however, false teachers sometime charge such conclusions upon those who insist that the Bible teaches the necessity of obedience to salvation. Charles Spurgeon once wrote, "I do not remember ever meeting with a person who absolutely professed to be at peace with God as a result of his own endeavors." To this, I agree. Job says, "If I justify myself, my own mouth shall condemn me" (Job 9:20). But with a little reflection, any person can see that he is not perfect. Certainly, the Bible says that: "There is none righteous, no, not one" (Romans 3:10). Again, "For all have sinned, and come short of the glory of God" (Romans 3:23). Isaiah says, "All we like sheep have gone astray" (Isaiah 53:6). The result of sin is plain. Ezekiel says, "The soul that sinneth, it shall die" (Ezekiel 18:4). In Romans 6:23, Paul says, "The wages of sin is death."

The gospel of Christ is "the power of God unto salvation to every one that believeth." "For therein is the righteousness of God revealed from faith to faith: as it is written, The just shall live by faith" (Romans 1:16-17). The gospel of Christ has revealed God's plan of righteousness by which we can be justified. Some power had to be brought to bear on the sinful lives of every person, to point out his lost condition, to show how he could be saved. Man is not righteous because he lived a good life but because he accepts and obeys the gospel of Christ. It is God's power that will save him from his sinful state so that he can be released from the penalty of sin, which is eternal death.

Now the next question—please follow me—the next question must follow logically. What are the terms of the gospel of Christ? Now the gospel of Christ is the power of God unto salvation to everyone. What are His terms? What are the conditions stated in that gospel whereby we can be justified? Let's list them and examine ourselves accordingly.

One, faith is the foundation. We are justified by faith (Acts 13:39). The just shall live by faith (Romans 1:17). We cannot be saved without faith in Christ. Every unbeliever, whoever he may be, the heathen or the uninformed, is condemned because of his unbelief. Jesus says he that believeth not is condemned already because he has not believed in the name of the only begotten Son of God (John 3:18). In order to be justified, we must believe. God is the justifier of him who believes in Jesus (Romans 3:26).

Secondly, repentance must follow. Jesus says, "Except ye repent, ye shall all likewise perish" (Luke 13:3). Acts 11:18 says, "Then hath God also to the Gentiles granted repentance unto life." Peter says, "Repent, and be baptized everyone you in the name of Jesus Christ for the remission of sins" (Acts 2:38). Surely no one can be saved in rebellion against God. Repentance is essential to our justification. It is the expression of faith in Christ that brings men to repent.

Thirdly, men must confess Christ. Romans 10:10 says, "For with the heart man believeth unto righteousness; and with the mouth confession is made unto salvation." The believer should be ready and happy to confess his faith in Christ, who is able to free him from sin.

Fourth, baptism is essential to salvation. Christ says, "He that believeth and is baptized shall be saved" (Mark 16:16). How can a man expect to be saved if he refuses to obey the Lord's command to be baptized? How can he possibly expect the reward of salvation? In obedience to the Lord in baptism, the believer is baptized into Jesus Christ (Romans 6:3; Galatians 3:27). Here he comes into the body of Christ, the church. 1 Corinthians 12:13 states, "For by one Spirit are we all baptized into one body." No man can be justified by faith in Christ if he or she refuses to come into Christ. No man can be in Christ who has never been baptized into Christ. Man's redemption is in Christ (Ephesians 1:7). To be in Christ, means to be in His body, the church.

When a person is saved, the Lord adds him to the church (Acts 2:47). Therefore, justification by faith means justification in and through Christ. It means that the justified are in the church, that they are members of the Lord's church. It means that we can be justified by faith in obedience to the gospel of Christ, and as members of the church of our Lord Jesus Christ. These commands and these proofs surely are so plain that we cannot misunderstand them. To refuse to accept them means to refuse the Lord's plan of justification by faith in Christ.

I would like to say just this word about being in Christ. We are justified by faith. We have peace with God through our Lord Jesus Christ (Romans 5:1). We are justified by His blood. "Being justified freely by his grace through the redemption that is in Christ Jesus" (Romans 3:24). In 1 Corinthians 6:11, we are told, "Ye are washed, but ye are sanctified, but ye are justified in the name of the Lord Jesus, and by the Spirit of our God." In Christ, we can live for Christ, we can worship God, and we can discharge all of our Christian duties, both to God and to our fellow man. In Christ, we can share the blessings of being the sons of God and we can be heirs of God and joint heirs with Christ and be glorified with Him when He comes again (Romans 8:16-18). All of these blessings can be ours by being justified by faith in obedience to the gospel of our Lord Jesus Christ.

Would you refuse—please listen to me—would you refuse all of these blessings? Would you ignore the fact that a man is either justified or he is condemned now before God? Would you forget that death is coming to you one of these days? When the Lord comes, "we must all appear before the judgment seat of Christ; that every one may receive the things done in his body, according to that he hath done, whether it be good or bad" (2 Corinthians 5:10).

We shall give an account in judgment for every unforgiven sin, for every act of unrighteousness, for every deed and thought of ungodliness from which we have not been justified through Christ, our blessed Lord. So, may we beseech you today in the name of Christ, to turn from sin and to obey the gospel of Christ that you might be justified by faith in Jesus Christ? You can be saved today—today—the Lord invites you today, whosoever will may come, today!

# *Appeal of Haggai*

Good morning, everyone. We are indeed grateful for the privilege of coming into your home one more time upon the Lord's Day for the purpose of studying with you the word of God. Today we invite your attention to a subject we might simply call "The Appeal of an Old Prophet." It had been a long time since Haggai made his first appeal to the people of Israel. His message was forceful and pointed. The book of the Old Testament that he wrote contains only two chapters, consisting of only thirty-eight verses. Yet it gives us both a summary of his message and an account of the results obtained.

We know nothing of the parentage or the background of Haggai. He was the tenth of the minor prophets in the order of the time of their prophesies. His prophecy was spoken seventeen years after the Jews returned from Babylonian captivity, a period of time in which Jehovah chastened His people because of their sins. Haggai stated the time of his work began in the second year of Darius, the king. He was joined two months later by the prophet Zechariah, who came to confirm his message. Haggai was a very successful preacher. His work brought almost immediate response. In only twenty-three days from the time of his first prophecy, the people began to rebuild the Temple of God. It had been destroyed when the Jews were carried away to Babylon. Upon the return, they laid the foundation of the Temple but then neglected their work for about fifteen years. It was Haggai's task to stir up the people so that God's house of worship would be finished. That he did by speaking to them the word of the Lord. Thus, the Lord, through this prophet, stirred up the spirit of the leaders and of the people. His words were the message God wanted them to hear, and they regarded them as the voice of God. Therefore, we are told in verse 12 of the first chapter, they "obeyed the voice of the Lord their God, and the words of Haggai the prophet, as the Lord their God had sent him, and the people did fear before the Lord."

It would be encouraging if all the preaching of God's word could always bring such immediate results. But sometimes it takes years for God's word to win the hearts of people. As Haggai points out, God does not want any to perish. He wants all to come to repentance (2 Peter 3:9). The gospel of Christ is the power of God to salvation to everyone who believes (Romans 1:16). Sometimes it falls on deaf ears. Sometimes it takes a long time for people to come to an understanding of the truth, especially with the many false teachings in the world and with the prejudice that exists. It takes a lot of teaching and considerable study of the Bible to clear away prejudice and misunderstandings so that man can come to a knowledge of the the truth and be saved. Some refuse to hear God's word. They will not listen as it is preached either in the pulpit, over the radio, or on television. Their minds evidently are closed. It was so in the days of Christ's ministry. On one occasion, He says, "And ye will not come to me, that you might have life" (John 5:40). It is not new, therefore, to find men who will not hear nor study the Bible and who will not accept Christ so that they might be saved. Let us remember, however, there are others who have open hearts and open ears. God's word is powerful (Hebrews 4:12). God says through Isaiah, "So shall my word be that goeth forth out of my mouth: it shall not return unto to me void, but it shall accomplish that which I please, and it shall prosper in the thing whereunto I sent it" (Isaiah 55:11). If we do not receive it so that we can be saved, others will receive it and be blessed. Those who reject His word shall be lost, and those who obey Him to the end shall be saved. Each person must decide for himself.

Obedience to God brings rejoicing! Ezra records the joy that came to Israel in the days of Haggai; they kept the special feast seven days with joy: "For the Lord had made them joyful" (Ezra 6:21-22). Those who obey the Lord will be joyful. The Psalmist referred to it as "the joy of thy salvation" (Psalm 51:12). When the Lord came, of whom Haggai prophesied, it was He, Jesus, who caused this Temple to have great glory. The prophet says, "The glory of this latter house shall be greater than the former, saith the Lord of hosts: and in this place will I give peace, saith the Lord of hosts" (Haggai 2:9). Christ brought joy and peace to men according to Luke 2:14. The preaching of Jesus by His disciples is referred to as "glad tidings of good things."

When Peter preached Christ for the first time after His resurrection and ascension, his preaching (on Pentecost) struck deep into the heart of his hearers. They cried out saying, "Men and brethren, what shall we do?" Then Peter says, "Repent, and be baptized every one of you in the name of Jesus Christ for the remission of sins, and ye shall receive the gift of the Holy Ghost" (Acts 2:38). Then he says, "They that gladly received his word were baptized" (Acts 2:41). These happy followers of Christ "continuing daily with one accord in the temple, and breaking bread from house to house, did eat their meat with gladness and singleness of heart, Praising God, and having favour with all the people" (Acts 2:46-47). They obeyed Christ as soon as they learned what to do, and they continued rejoicing. Their response had been even more immediate than it had been with the people of Haggai's day. They obeyed the Lord the same day. It took the appeal of Haggai three weeks to stir up the people in his time.

The prophet's appealing message actually falls into four distinct parts. First, he rebuked the people for their neglect. The Lord's house was laying in waste. Only the new foundation had been laid. They had permitted their enemies to discourage them and to weaken their hands (Ezra 4). Later, their enemies hired counselors and wrote letters to the king to stop the work; but if they had been disposed to work at the time when they started building, they would have been successful, regardless of these things. Too often we allow others to discourage us from what is right. So, the people of Israel needed the rebuke Haggai gave them. They had neglected the Lord's house, but they built their own houses. They neglected the Lord's business, but they continued sowing and reaping, eating and drinking, and having their own activities. God should always come first. Jesus says we are to "seek first the kingdom of God, and his righteousness" (Matthew 6:33). Israel should have placed God's house first. They were not condemned for having houses and for working but for stressing the wrong thing by neglecting God's house. Neglecting God has always had its penalty. Israel's neglect caused their eating not to satisfy their hunger and their drinking not to fill them and their clothes not to warm them. The prophet says, "He that earneth wages, earneth wages to put it in a bag with holes" (Haggai 1:6). God withheld the dew, the earth did not give her fruit, and there was drought throughout the land. All of these were the penalty for their neglect. People of our day need to learn this same lesson. Paul says, "Be not deceived: God is not mocked: for whatsoever a man soweth, that shall he also reap" (Galatians 6:7). The prosperity of a nation or an individual will never satisfy when God is neglected. When our point of emphasis is self interest and God is forgotten, then all we have or ever will have will not suffice. Let us not deceive ourselves into thinking that times have changed or that God will overlook our neglect. Compare the condition of Israel in Haggai's time with the condition of America. We need to hear again the words of God's messenger: "Be sure your sin will find you out" (Numbers 32:23). The Hebrew writer says, "How shall we escape, if we neglect so great salvation?" (Hebrews 2:3). God must come first, or we must pay the penalty for our neglect. Let us be warned by this prophet who wrote almost 2,500 years ago.

Secondly, their obedience brought God's encouragement as He spoke through His prophet saying, "I am with you, saith the Lord" (Haggai 1:13). They were stirred in their spirits and obeyed God. So it will be today when we are stirred in our thinking and obey God's teaching for us. God speaks to us now through the message of Christ contained in the gospel (Hebrews 1:1-2). We must hear Christ (Matthew 17:5). We must believe in Christ and be baptized (Mark 16:16). We must live for Christ as members of the Lord's church; and, in so doing, we may have the same assurance, "I am with you," saith the Lord of hosts, and "I will never leave thee, nor forsake thee" (Hebrews 13:5).

Thirdly, think of God's building. They were discouraged in Haggai's day because they compared the new Temple with the magnificence of Solomon's Temple; but their Temple would be greater because Jesus would, by His coming, bring far greater glory than Solomon's Temple ever did. Today we have the Lord's church, the true Temple of God, to enjoy. As Christians, we can say with Paul, "Know ye not that ye are the temple of God, and that the Spirit of God dwelleth in you?" (1 Corinthians 3:16). Each one of us can, by becoming a child of God, become a part of a Temple far more glorious than either Solomon's or Zerubbabel's. God's blessings are great and abundant in the Lord's Temple, that is, the church that Christ built. It should make us happy to think how God has given us the opportunity to become living stones and to be "built up a spiritual house, an holy priesthood, to offer up spiritual sacrifices, acceptable to God by Jesus Christ" (1 Peter 2:5). Such a thought should cause all to want to be Christians and thus be added to the church of our Lord (Acts 2:47). Finally, Haggai called the people to repentance. He pleaded with them to get rid of the unholiness in their lives, for it defiled their work and robbed them of God's blessing. The prophet led them to repentance; therefore, God blessed their labors.

Jesus still bids men to repent: "Except ye repent ye shall all likewise perish" (Luke 13:3-5). Let the goodness of God call you to repent (Romans 2:4); be baptized into Christ and be faithful to Him every day of your life. You can be a member of the Lord's church, the greatest Temple the world has ever known.

# *Acts 6*

Good morning, everyone. We are grateful for the privilege of coming to you one more time with a message from the word of God. We invite your attention to a study of several happenings that occurred in the sixth chapter of Acts of the Apostles. Specifically, there are three points of particular significance in this chapter: the selection of the seven to be over the business of serving tables, the increase in the number of disciples, and the stringent opposition to the preaching of Stephen. This chapter is a relatively short one, so we should be able to notice most of these points.

The scripture begins very plainly, very humanly, that there arose a murmuring over the occasion of the selection of seven men to be over the daily administration. This murmuring came as a result of the increase in the number the disciples and as a result of the neglect of the Grecian widows in the daily ministration. The scripture states, "And in those days, when the number of the disciples was multiplied, there arose a murmuring of the Grecians against the Hebrews, because their widows were neglected in the daily ministration" (verse one). We have noticed in the teaching of Acts 2:44-47 and in Acts 4:32-37 an intense spirit of sharing that was manifested in the early disciples. The scripture declares they brought the proceeds from the sale of possessions and laid them at the feet of the apostles and distribution was made to each as anyone had need (Acts 4:35).

The murmuring evidently arose as a result of something neglected in this distribution. It was not intentional. It was rather the consequence of increase in the number of disciples. I am persuaded it was the natural development. The remedy was natural also, as the apostles dispositioned this matter recorded by Luke, "Then the twelve called the multitude of the disciples unto them, and said, It is not reason that we should leave the word of God, and serve tables. Wherefore, brethren, look ye out among you seven men of honest report, full of the Holy Ghost and wisdom, whom we may appoint over this business. But we will give ourselves continually to prayer, and to the ministry of the word" (verses 2-4).

Many members of the Lord's church need to heed the lessons that are indicated here: the work of caring for the needy and the work of ministering in the word are important. All business of the Lord is important and should be handled in the most efficient way. God has revealed the pattern for the church, and it should be recognized as a serious and important business. The first recorded words of our Lord, "Wist ye not that I must be about my Father's business?" (Luke 2:49). The American Standard Version reads, "Know ye not that I must be in my Father's house?" The Greek literally denotes "of the things of my father." I think the point is clear. We should give proper attention to the things of God.

This episode in the early church recorded here by Luke shows us how this matter was handled. There was just cause for the Grecian Jews to complain, the matter was corrected, and then we hear no more about it. There is no further reference to it in Acts anywhere. Sometimes today when one cause of murmuring is corrected and removed, the murmurers turn their attention to other murmurs. Some, it would appear, are chronic murmurers; but such was evidently not the case in the early church, according to Luke. A proper grievance may be properly expressed and corrected and then forgotten.

Paul's words to the Philippian church should be heeded:

> Do all things without murmurings and disputings: That ye may be blameless and harmless, the sons of God, without rebuke, in the midst of a crooked and perverse nation, among whom ye shine as lights in the world; Holding forth the word of life; that I may rejoice in the day of Christ, that I have not run in vain, neither laboured in vain (Philippians 2:14-16).

Following this instruction will prevent many disturbances in the church. There is no excuse for constant grumblings and complaints from those who call themselves Christians. Proper and decisive action on the part of leadership and corresponding reception on the part of disciples will always result in harmony and progress for the cause of Christ. It did in the beginning. It will today. Those busy and devoted in the Lord's work will be happy and contented; and the church, the Bible declares, will increase in number.

We learn from this account that the apostle gave instructions for the selection of the seven. They designated the qualifications of the men to be chosen and called on the multitude of disciples to make the selection among themselves; then the apostles appointed them over this business. I want you to notice the orderly formula for any group of disciples to follow in selecting those who will oversee the work of the church.

For example, the qualifications for elders are given by inspiration in 1 Timothy 3 and Titus 1. Disciples in every place can follow with confidence the example given here for the selection of specific individuals for a given task. When that same respect for biblical authority is followed in all situations and the same spirit manifested, the work of the church will be accomplished efficiently.

Speaking of the spirit that prevailed, it perhaps should be observed that the apostles were not arbitrarily separating themselves from the task of serving tables because of any aversion to the work or because of any feeling of superiority in ministering in this service. They were obligated to other things: the ministry of the word. And they were giving themselves wholeheartedly to it. Of these seven men named here, two of them are more familiar in the history that follows than the other five:

> And the saying pleased the whole multitude: and they chose Stephen, a man full of faith and of the Holy Ghost, and Philip, and Prochorus, and Nicanor, and Timon, and Parmenas, and Nicolas a proselyte of Antioch: Whom they set before the apostles: and when they had prayed, they laid their hands on them (Acts 6:5-6).

In verse seven, we have an interesting expression, "And the word of God increased; and the number of the disciples multiplied in Jerusalem greatly; and a great company of the priests were obedient to the faith" (verse 7). The expression, "The word of God increased" indicates that the spread of the gospel, the preaching of the word, resulted in the growth of the number the disciples even the reaching to a great company of the priests. The word the apostles preached is "the Faith." Jude writes:

> Beloved, when I gave all diligence to write unto you of the common salvation, it was needful for me to write unto you, and exhort you that ye should earnestly contend for the faith which was once delivered unto the saints (verse 3).

Obedience to the faith is necessary for salvation. Paul makes such instruction clear in several places, including the book of Romans:

> But God be thanked, that ye were the servants of sin, but ye have obeyed from the heart that form of doctrine which was delivered you. Being then made free from sin, ye became the servants of righteousness (Romans 6:17-18).

> Therefore we are buried with him by baptism into death: that like as Christ was raised up from the dead by the glory of the Father, even so we also should walk in newness of life. For if we have been planted together in the likeness of his death, we shall be also in the likeness of his resurrection: Knowing this, that our old man is crucified with him, that the body of sin might be destroyed, that henceforth we should not serve sin. For he that is dead is freed from sin (Romans 6:4-7).

Now those priests, whom we read about in Acts 6:7, were obedient to the faith, meaning they had accepted the word of the Lord and turned from unrighteousness to righteousness. So, it was undoubtedly a great cause of rejoicing to those who were already in the faith; but the thing that concerns us is this: it increased the animosity and the opposition of those who were determined to reject the word of the gospel. Evil men who were unwilling to believe and obey and who were unable to meet the power of the word resorted to foul means in restraining the message preached.

The scripture says:

> And Stephen, full of faith and power, did great wonders and miracles among the people. Then there arose certain of the synagogue, which is called the synagogue of the Libertines, and Cyrenians, and Alexandrians, and of them of Cilicia and of Asia, disputing with Stephen. And they were not able to resist the wisdom and the spirit by which he spake (verses 8-10).

Notice what they did when they could not meet the word fairly and honestly:

> Then they suborned men, which said, We have heard him speak blasphemous words against Moses, and against God.

And they stirred up the people, and the elders, and the scribes, and came upon him, and caught him, and brought him to the council, And set up false witnesses, which said, This man ceaseth not to speak blasphemous words against this holy place, and the law: For we have heard him say, that this Jesus of Nazareth shall destroy this place, and shall change the customs which Moses delivered us (verses 11-14).

These charges were not only misrepresentations, they simply were blantantly false. They were designed to prejudice and to inflame the base instincts of the people in the guise of religious fervor. Such is often the path followed by those who are unable to meet the truth of God's word. Certainly, this behavior is not right. It was not right then, nor is it right now. In this case, however, their end was achieved: the death of Stephen—but not before he delivered the defense, which is recorded by Luke in Acts chapter seven.

The scripture declares that Stephen stood before them to speak to them the words of Life. Among those others, I think that none are more galant and courageous or more like their Savior in spirit and strength and suffering. In fact, in verse 15 it states, "And all that sat in the council, looking steadfastly on him, saw his face as it had been the face of an angel." Stephen is arrayed before his accusers, and he is determined to preach to them the story of the cross.

Sometimes when the story of the cross is preached, it ends in salvation. Sometimes it ends in destruction. This particular sermon was destined; it seemed, to end in destruction for Stephen because they could not resist the words that he spoke. Certainly, it is the Lord's will that one should yield himself to the teaching of the Holy Spirit in full obedience to the gospel of Jesus Christ rather than resisting the Holy Spirit as Stephen said these did.

We plead with you today to think of these accounts that are handed down to us, these true accounts that teach us what the Lord would have us to be and how He would have us act.

If you hear the message today, would you believe it and make the decision to give yourself to the Lord Jesus Christ. He has done so much for us—He has given Himself. And all that He asks is that you obey the gospel of Christ through faith, through repentance for your sins, through confession of your faith in the Lord, and then through baptism, allowing yourself to be immersed in His dear name for the remission of your sins? Would you please feel free to call upon us, upon those who support this program, to study with you and teach you the things that God would have you to do?

# *Expression of Faith*

Good morning, everyone. We are privileged one more time, to come into your home and study with you the word of God. We indeed appreciate this privilege, and we trust that we would never violate the confidence you have placed in us to allow us to come into your home to study the word of God. Our study today concerns itself with faith and its expression. The Bible was given to man by Jehovah, the only true and living God. We have continually emphasized that the Bible is God's message for man. Indeed, all scripture is given by inspiration of God (2 Timothy 3:16). As Peter, directed by the Holy Spirit, says, "For the prophecy came not in old time by the will of man: but holy men of God spake as they were moved by the Holy Ghost" (2 Peter 1:21). That revelation of God is complete:

> According as his divine power hath given unto us all things that pertain unto life and godliness, through the knowledge of him that hath called us to glory and virtue: Whereby are given unto us exceeding great and precious promises: that by these ye might be partakers of the divine nature, having escaped the corruption that is in the world through lust (2 Peter 1:3-4).

The Bible is true and reliable and merits our faith. The more we can learn of God as our Creator and loving Father, the more we know of His great blessings and love. From God's truth, we can understand how Christ came to live, to suffer, and to die for us. As we accept Him as our Savior, we can experience the joy and happiness of His constant companionship. The gospel of Christ is the power of God to salvation to everyone who believes (Romans 1:16). Therefore, we need to read the Bible by day and meditate on it by night and live it in our lives. Our faith should be real. It should be the active principle of our lives, a real source of our spiritual strength. It should cause us to obey our Lord and to trust in His great promises. Every part of our lives should be directed by its force. It is to be the foundation upon which we build our whole spiritual relationship (Hebrews 11:1). But, we cannot stop with the foundation alone. It is upon a foundation that we must build. So, we are saying today, that our faith, the foundation, must express itself in the infrastructure of a Christian life.

God has told us through James, "What doth it profit, my brethren, though a man may say he hath faith, and have not works? can faith save him?" Again, he says:

> Even so faith, if it hath not works, is dead, being alone. Yea, a man may say, Thou hast faith, and I have works: shew me thy faith without thy works, and I will shew you my faith by my works. Thou believest there is one God; thou doest well: the devils also believe, and tremble. But wilt thou know, O vain man, that faith without works is dead? (James 2:14-20).

It is by works that faith is made perfect. Verse 24 says, "Ye see then how that by works a man is justified, and not by faith only." And verse 26 says, "For as the body without the spirit is dead, so faith without works is dead also." This is a principle that is true in all of the God's word and in all of life. We cannot deny it; therefore, we must not over look it. Our faith must express itself if we want to be saved. We cannot, the Bible states, we cannot be saved by faith alone. The Bible does not teach that we are saved the moment that we believe, notwithstanding all of men's statements on this matter. Remember even the devils believe and tremble, but certainly they were not saved because they had not obeyed the Lord.

When Christ was teaching in His ministry, John tells us:

> Nevertheless among the chief rulers also many believed on him; but because of the Pharisees they did not confess him, less they should be put out of the synagogue: For they loved the praise of men more than the praise of God (John 12:42-43).

Surely no one would contend that the cowardly rulers were saved, even though they believed on Christ. And so it is with many people in our world today: many believe in Christ, but their faith has never been expressed through obedience to the will of Christ. Therefore, they remain in a lost condition before God. Jesus says, "Not everyone that saith unto me, Lord, Lord, shall enter into the kingdom of heaven; but he that doeth the will of my Father which is in heaven" (Matthew 7:21).

God's word, the Bible, plainly tells us what we must do, how our faith must express itself, so that we might be saved. First of all, the Bible teaches that faith must express itself in repentance of sins. Jesus says, "Except ye repent, ye shall all likewise perish" (Luke 13:3). Jesus came to call sinners to repentance (Matthew 9:13). He sent out His apostles to teach His will, and they preached that men should repent (Mark 6:12). After His resurrection, Christ said that repentance and remission of sins would be preached in His name among all nations beginning at Jerusalem (Luke 24:47). Thus, on the day of Pentecost, when the first sermon was preached by the apostles, after His ascension and when men were convinced that Jesus, whom they had crucified, was now made both Lord and Christ, they cried out saying, "Men and brethren, what shall we do?" Then Peter says unto them, "Repent, and be baptized every one of you in the name of Jesus Christ for the remission of sins, and you shall receive the gift of the Holy Ghost" (Acts 2:37-38). God wants all men everywhere to repent. The Bible states He is "longsuffering to us-ward, not willing that any should perish, but that all should to repentance" (2 Peter 3:9). Paul points out that God now commands all men everywhere to repent (Acts 17:30). In Acts 11:18, we read that God also to the Gentiles granted repentance unto life.

Jesus also taught, "that likewise joy shall be in heaven over one sinner that repenteth, more than over ninety and nine just persons, which need no repentance" (Luke 15:7). Again, He says, "There is joy in the presence of the angels of God over one sinner that repenteth" (Luke 15:10). Think of how the repentance of each of us can cause rejoicing in heaven and among the angels of God, and thus we can accomplish God's will. But again, what causes people to repent? What will cause you, today, to repent of your sins? The Bible teaches that repentance is the result of faith, faith in God, faith in eternal judgment. In Romans 2:4, we read, "Or despisest thou the riches of his goodness and forbearance and long-suffering; not knowing that the goodness of God leadeth thee to repentance?" Think how good and merciful and longsuffering God has been to you. Think how He has loved you and suffered His son Jesus to die for your sins. Consider how He has blessed you and lengthened your life to this hour. Count all the blessings you have and then look up to the great God from whom they have come. Remember that He wants you to be saved. Don't forget that Jesus Christ came into this world to suffer and die for you. That He came to teach you to repent and not perish. That He bore all those things—the pain, the suffering, and the death of Calvary—for your salvation. Then stop to consider the sins you committed against God.

The Bible states that "all have sinned and come short of the glory of God" (Romans 3:23). Sorrow should fill your heart today, because sin is an offense against God. "Godly sorrow worketh repentance to salvation not to be repented of: but the sorrow of the world worketh death" (2 Corinthian 7:10). Surely the realization of God's goodness and the realization of your own sins will move you to repentance that you would never regret as long as you live, now or at the bar of God's eternal judgment. Without repentance, you cannot be saved neither now nor in eternity. What greater incentives could we possibly find than these? If these do not move you to repentance, then there can only remain the fear and the dread of eternal punishment. God has done all that is possible to cause you to repent of your sins.

Let's notice a little further the meaning of repentance. It is a change of mind that leads to the change in action or change of life. Jesus illustrated it with the story of two sons in Matthew. He says:

> A certain man had two sons; and he came to the first, and said, Son, go work to day in my vineyard. He answered and said, I will not: but afterward he repented, and went. And he came to the second, and said likewise. And he answered and said, I go, sir; and went not (Matthew 21:28-29).

Then Jesus asked the question, "Whether of them twain did the will of his father?" Of course, the answer is quite obvious. The first repented and went. The change of his mind is expressed in the word repent. Then he went to work in the vineyard as his father had said. It is quite evident, then, that repentance carries the idea of a fixed purpose to reform the life.

Paul says to bring forth fruit meet for repentance, that is, fruit in keeping with the change in mind to serve God. When Jonah preached repentance to the ancient city of Ninevah, they understood what he meant. They turned from their evil ways (Jonah 3:10). It should not be difficult for us to understand what repentance should mean to us. Paul preached that all men "repent and turn to God, and do works meet for repentance" (Acts 26:20). Repentance leads to an humble return to God. This principle is illustrated in the story of the prodigal son. When he realized his condition, he came to himself. He felt how unworthy he was and what a terrible plight was his. So, he says, "I will arise and go unto my father, and will say to him, Father, I have sinned against heaven, and before thee, And am no more worthy to be called thy son: make me one of thy hired servants" (Luke 15:17-19). Notice our Lord pictures an humble return of the sinner to the Heavenly Father, who went out to welcome him home.

Repentance must be real and genuine and complete. There are some who profess Christianity but are not saved because they have never truly repented. They want to hold onto sin, instead of leaving it. They want both God and men to forgive them without ever doing the will of God. Let's stop and think and ask ourselves the question: Have I believed in Christ to the extent that I have repented of my sins, all of my sins? Every one of us who would be saved must be able to answer in the affirmative and without reservation. We must repent or perish. I would also like to point out that our faith must express itself in confessing Jesus Christ:

> Wherefore God also hath highly exalted him, and given him a name which is above every name: That at the name of Jesus every knee should bow, of things in heaven, and things in earth, and things under the earth; And that every tongue should confess that Jesus Christ is Lord, to the glory of God the Father (Philippians 2:9-11).

The time has come when this scripture will be completely fulfilled, because in eternity, after this life is over, all men will recognize the greatness of Jesus Christ as God's Son. But God wants men to confess Christ now, in this life, so that they might be saved. If you don't confess Him now, you cannot be saved. In Romans 10:10, the scriptures say, "With the heart man believeth unto righteousness; and with the mouth confession is made unto salvation."

I would like to express last of all today, that our faith must express itself in baptism. The Apostle Peter says, "Repent and be baptized every one of you in the name of Jesus Christ for the remission of sins" (Acts 2:38). Jesus says, "He that believeth and is baptized shall be saved" (Mark 16:16). The kind of faith that Jesus wants us to have will cause us to be baptized. To be baptized, we must acknowledge the teaching of a burial in baptism for the remission of our sins.

It is our prayer today that you will obey these commands—commands of our Savior just as He has taught in the New Testament, and to do so while we have the opportunity. This faith, expressed thusly, will lead us to live as Christians. Every day will be a day of life for Christ.

As we live in the faith and walk by faith, our faith will grow and bear fruit to the glory of God and for our eternal happiness. May I ask in closing, what kind of faith do you have? Is it the faith that is based on the New Testament? Is it the faith that will save you through obedience to the will of Christ, that God's grace may be yours? It is for those who will do so that we close with this prayer, that God may help us all. Believe His word and so act and so obey Him that we can be saved now and for all eternity!

# The Things That Really Matter

Good morning, everyone. We are extremely grateful for the privilege that we have today, to come into your home to study with you the word of God. We are very pleased to speak on behalf of the congregation that supports this program. We bid you to listen carefully to the announcements: the meeting times and the worship times of this congregation. Today, we invite your attention to the subject: "The Things That Really Matter." We live in a busy world, and I am sure this is no news to anyone who hears me today. There are so many things that are clamoring for our attention. There are so many things that we want to do and so little time in which to do them. If we are not careful, we may find ourselves fully engrossed in the affairs about us; and we may overlook the most important things—the things that really matter. Ask yourself, today, the question: What does really matter to me? What are the most valuable things in life so far as I am concerned? What do you want to get out of life more than anything else? Stop to think about the question. Turn it over and over in your mind. What are the things that really matter?

If it will help you, take your pencil and paper and make a list of the interests you have in life. Write down your secret aims and ambitions. Select the most important one of all and place it at the top of your list; then arrange in the order of importance about a half-dozen or more of those things that you have listed. Consider each one seriously; then take a look at your activities for the day or for a week to see if you are gaining from life the things that really matter. But you may be asking How can I determine the most important things? How can I determine the things that really matter?

There are many ways of weighing the relative value of activities and the ambitions of life. Sometimes we use the wrong standard for this measurement. Question: What kind of standard do you use? May we suggest to you today that the Bible is the standard for judgment? God's book is the book by which we will all be judged in that last and final Day of Judgment. Jesus says, "The word that I have spoken, the same shall judge him in the last day" (John 12:48). It is best to hold in our minds the statement of 2 Corinthians 5:10, "For we must all appear before the judgment seat of Christ; that every one may receive the things done in his body, according to that he hath done, whether it be good or bad."

Let us examine those things again that we have listed as important. Let us consider them in their relationship to these three questions: (1) How important will they be when I come to die? (2) How important will they be when I stand before Christ in judgment? (3) How important will they be in eternity? These are most sobering thoughts for me. I suspect they are for you, too. Too often, we forget these thoughts or we neglect them when we are determining what is really valuable in life. They need to be reiterated frequently. Death is certain; there can be no doubt about that. I have never met a man who did not believe in death. Those of us who believe the Bible know, too, that judgment is coming. The Bible says, "It is appointed unto men once to die, but after this the judgment" (Hebrews 9:27). Eternity is a long, long time. Where we spend eternity, whether in God's presence in heaven or in the suffering of eternal torment, will depend upon these choices that we are making today. I mean the choices that we are making at this moment, and that we are making day by day by day—these will determine where we will be for all eternity.

Many people give little attention to these truths. Even the children of God sometimes forget. We all need to be reminded of them from time to time, do we not? If we are not reminded, we may spend eternity in regret that we did not have them before us when we were selecting the things that really matter. May God help us to make the right decision. One thing is sure, God knows what is best for me. God knows what is best for you. God sees for all eternity, and He is all-wise. The wisdom of men, as we can evidence for ourselves, is often short sighted. But God has given us the Bible to direct us in making the right decisions. He has recorded some examples for us—some to warn us and some for us to follow. Let us notice God's teaching, and we will find the right answers; then let us examine our lives accordingly.

The immediate appeal often determines the value we place on anything. It seems so much easier to decide for the thing before us, that is, the things we can see or what we want, right now. Something else may have had many advantages, but the urgency of the present has influenced many a choice. I propose to you that the urgency of the present is a real danger. Esau illustrated this thought. He came in from the field hungry and faint. He wanted something to eat, so he said to Jacob, his brother, "Feed me, I pray thee, with that same red pottage; for I am faint." That food before him seemed so important that he sold his birthright to obtain it (Genesis 25:30-34). He forgot for the moment the honor, the authority, the blessings, and the double inheritance that were included in the birthright. He bargained all those things away for something to eat. However hungry he might have been, it was a dear price to pay for a mess of pottage. In Hebrews 12:17, we are told that he could not change the matter and recover his inheritance, even though he sought to do so with many tears.

The world has had many who are like Esau. The appeal of something to eat or something to drink has been stronger to them than all the great and more important things. Such an attitude has caused men to the bargain away their opportunities to be God's children. It has led to many a crime and has cost the life of many a person. Unfortunately, there are still thousands and thousands of people more interested in something to eat or in satisfying their worldly desires than in all the important values of life. Men are still selling their birthrights for the satisfying of their physical appetites.

Material possessions have a strong appeal to many in our world  Jesus once told a story about the rich man whose land brought forth plentifully. The man confidently said to himself:

> I will pull down my barns, and build greater; and there will I bestow all my fruits and my goods. And I will say to my soul, Soul, thou hast much goods laid up for many years; take thine ease, eat, drink, and be merry (Luke 12:18-19).

This man is typical of many a man who has thought that all that really mattered was getting more abundance of this world's goods or of increasing his business. Houses and land and cars and clothes and money and material wealth have obsessed and possessed many a soul. To eat, drink, and be merry have become the aim of many a person. The sad part is that the warning in the story of this rich man has been forgotten by many. God says, "Thou fool, this night thy soul shall be required of thee: then whose shall those things be, which thou hast provided?" (verse 20). Jesus spoke the parable to illustrate the truth that a man's life consists not in the abundance of the things that he possesses.

There is something more important than riches—please understand me—there is something more important than riches. The scripture says:

> For we brought nothing into this world, and it is certain we can carry nothing out. And having food and raiment let us be therewith content. But they that will be rich fall into temptation and a snare, and into many foolish and hurtful lusts, which drown men in destruction and perdition. For the love of money is the root of all evil: which while some coveted after, they have erred from the faith, and pierced themselves through with many sorrows (1 Timothy 6:7-10).

It was the fact that he had great possessions that caused the young ruler to turn away from Jesus and not take up his cross and follow Him. Think of the multitudes of those who through the years have done the same thing for far less of this world's wealth. The rich man of Luke 16 passed by the gate of the beggar who desired to have crumbs that fell from his table. He showed no interest in his brothers or in the things of eternity until it was far too late. When in hell, he lifted up his eyes, being in torment. He then thought of those things. May we not make the same mistake today.

But another question: What about position and popularity? The comparative position in keeping up with others has seemed all that mattered to so many. What others have and what others do and the desire to be like their neighbors and their friends has been the downfall of untold numbers of men and women and boys and girls. To be popular is more important to them than to be right. To have the praise of man has meant more than the praise of God (John 12:43). It is indeed sad to see anyone make such grave mistakes. But it seems so much more so when parents lead their children into such positions and influence them to eternal condemnation of their souls.

Worldy pleasures tempt many. The appeal to engage in even morally good things has caused some to neglect the things that really should matter. Parties and entertainment and various programs and sports may have their place, but anytime they cause us to neglect our duties to God, to forsake the assembly of the saints, or to take them into associations that are not right for us or are not compatible with Christian influence, the Christian should beware. The fleeting desire for a few minutes of worldly pleasure has meant the condemnation of many a soul. The social drinker would endanger the purity of his life and dull the senses of the body, which should be the Temple of God's Holy Spirit. The Christian is taught by John, "Love not the world, neither the things that are in the world. If any man love the world, the love of the Father is not in him." He insists that any person who loves Him cannot love this world. Any person who loves the world does not have the love of the Father in him. He insists these material things will pass away, but he who does the will of the Father will abide forever (1 John 2:15-17).

I want you to consider with me, Paul's example. He had many things that seemed important to him. He listed them in Philippians 3. He was circumcised the eighth day of the stock of Israel, of the tribe of Benjamin, a Hebrew of the Hebrews. As touching the law, a Pharisee. Concerning zeal, persecuting the church. Touching the righteousness that is in the law, blameless. We must be familiar with these expressions to appreciate fully the value of all of them to Paul who was taught and trained to place emphasis upon those matters. They showed his family background. They reflected his training, and they showed his zeal and his devotion to what he had valued most of all. Paul laid them all aside—please hear me—the Apostle Paul laid them all aside. He says that what things were gain to him, those he counted loss for Christ.

Paul had been convinced of something else that was more important. It was to live for Christ. In Philippians 1:21, he says, "For me to live is Christ." He realized that the most important thing in life was to live for the Master. He desired that the Philippians would follow his example. He would have us to say, "For me to live is Christ." Further the apostle says, "This one thing I do, forgetting those things which are behind, and reaching forth unto those things which are before, I press toward the mark of the prize of the high calling of God in Christ Jesus" (Philippians 3:13-14). Here was the only thing that really mattered to Paul. He wanted to live for Christ. He wanted to be with Christ in heaven. He knew that to die is gain. It would be gain to receive the blessings of God's mercy and grace in the presence of the Lord and His saints.

Question today: Would you be like Paul? He says, "Be ye followers of me, even as I also am of Christ" (1 Corinthians 11:1). In order to do so, you must learn to place the proper emphasis upon the things that Paul counted most important. You must learn to become a

Christian, baptized into Christ, like Paul (Romans 6:1-4). You must then consecrate your life to the service of Christ. You must learn to share the same hope of eternal life that he had. The things that really matter are the things of God, the salvation of our souls, and our preparation for eternity. All of the other things in life are relatively important as they bear, and only as they bear, upon these important values.

To impress these upon your thinking, let me ask these questions please. (1) Are you a Christian? (2) Do you place Christ and His kingdom first in your life? (3) Are you living like Christ and for Christ? (4) Does heaven mean all to you? Do you really want to go to heaven? Do you want to go to heaven above every other desire in life? Have you subjected every other desire to this one great aim? These questions should stir up your thinking and help you have before you the things that really matter!

# *Psalm 1*

Good morning, everyone. We invite your attention today to the first Psalm that David ever wrote. I think we should begin by saying that the world has many great libraries with millions upon millions of volumes. But where can you find in all of them any book to compare to the word of God? Think about what has been written down through the years; yet in all the writings of men nothing can be found that reflects the basic needs of man like the Bible. God gave us the Bible and directed the writers, who were chosen men, selected and directed to give us the greatest book in all the world. Peter describes them, saying, "Holy men of God spake as they were moved by the Holy Ghost" (2 Peter 1:21). The Apostle Paul says, "All scripture is given by inspiration of God" (2 Timothy 3:16); therefore, God through the Holy Spirit inspired men, holy men, to write the Bible for the good of everyone. From the story of the beginning, as recorded by Moses in Genesis, to the unfolding of the things that shall be hereafter by John in the book of Revelation, every part of the Bible is important.

Please consider with me today, this first Psalm, written by David, who penned many of the one hundred and fifty psalms. David, king of Israel, lived on thousand years before Christ was born. Perhaps there were other writers besides David, but all of them together gave us the psalms of praise and psalms of devotion to God that should refresh our souls. This first Psalm seems to introduce the entire book and sets forth the general theme of all of them. It declares the true delight of the man of God. The book has many parts but one great end: the understanding of the happiness that can come to those who serve God.

The first Psalm is one of the most familiar. Many of you can repeat it from memory. It has been recited by both old and young alike. But it never grows old to the one who is acquainted with the depth of its meaning. It begins actually with a benediction, or an exclamation: "Blessed is the man." He is describing the man who has chosen God's truth. As Mr. Adam Clark has pointed out, the word "the" is emphatic. The man, the one among a thousand, who lives to accomplish the end for which God created him. This beginning reminds us of the Lord's sermon recorded in Matthew 5:3-11. Jesus begins that sermon with the beatitudes. He says, "Blessed are the poor in spirit; for theirs is the kingdom of heaven." Then, He gives all of these great qualities that are so essential to man's true happiness.

I would like to emphasize today that God made man to be happy. God gave man all the things necessary for his happiness; and further, God has given man the teaching that can lead him to the realization of that happiness if he will only listen. Every man has the desire to be happy. Everyone would like to turn from the things of misery and sufferings and trouble, but many seek happiness where it cannot be found and they want to obtain it in ways that God has not given. It must be remembered that God knows what is best for man; and only God's way can bring the proper end, the happiness and the salvation of man.

Let us learn the plan of God, let us become acquainted with the kind of man whom God says is blessed or happy. Then, let us seek diligently to apply the divine plan to our lives so that the multiplicity of the Lord's blessings may be ours. Will you please notice with me now that perhaps you have turned to Psalm 1, the negative side is first given. The Psalmist David says, "Blessed is the man that walketh not in the counsel of the ungodly, nor standeth in the way of sinners, nor sitteth in the seat of the scornful." This verse actually contains a triple climax. One, the progressive positions: that walketh not, nor standeth, nor sitteth. Two, the progressive nature of it: that walketh not in the counsel, nor standeth in the way, nor sitteth in the seats. Three, the progressive kind of the characters themselves: the ungodly, the sinner, the scornful.

The ungodly are without reverence toward God. The sinners are not only without piety toward God but transgress the law of God. The word sin means literally to miss the mark, to pass over the prescribed or the prohibited limits, to transgress the law. 1 John 3:4 says, "For sin is the transgression of the law." As the sinner exceeds the ungodly, so the scorner is even worse. He ridicules the things of God, scorns the divine nature of man and the mortality of the soul, and makes light of God's grace for man's salvation. Each time the warning is stronger. The ungodly, the sinner, and the scorner—sin is progressive, as taught here. It gradually grows in confirming the position of those who are inclined to its influence. It leads by its counsel, takes men into its way, and eventually settles them in deceit of the confirmed of its disciples. Let us beware of such influence.

Please notice, sin is that which hardens men (Hebrews 3:13). Sin blinds men (2 Corinthians 4:4). The progressive nature of its development has deceived many, as to its real or genuine character. Many have been, as the old proverb says, about the gradual yielding to sin: first to pity, then to endure, and then to embrace.

Sin always brings unhappiness; it brings unhappiness to the individual himself and to those about him. It carries its curse with it. Therefore, this negative warning is given first and the meaning of it, as we bear in mind, the negative approach, cursed be the man who walks in the counsel of the ungodly and stands in the way of sinners and sits in the seat of the scornful. We must be warned against the bad—we must desire to take the wiser and better counsel, to seek the divine way for our feet to trod, and to take our position among those who love God.

Please consider this happy man, the man who has God's benediction and is described as having his delight is in the law of the Lord. This is the fountain from which his happiness comes. This is the key to his joy, his pleasure, and his delight. The law of the Lord is his meditation, day and night; it is the rule of his life. He delights to read it by day and to meditate upon it in still watches of the night. In Psalm 119, we find expressions of such devotion and delight—read it again—read his wonderful statements of regard and reverence and learn to say with David, "O how I love thy law! it is my meditation all the day" (verse 97). Think of verses 127-128, "Therefore I love thy commandments above gold; yea, above fine gold. Therefore I esteem all thy precepts concerning all things to be right; and I hate every false way." God's truth shows us how to be happy both for time and eternity. It is a mirror for our souls into which we can look to see our imperfections and, thus, learn to cleanse ourselves of the evil practices of sin (James 1:25). We can see there the divine examples of faith and learn how to obey the Savior of our souls. The Bible admonishes us, to make God's word our delight and learn what it can mean to you. It will tell you a man's divine origin. You will learn of your true nature. It will come to understand the justice and the mercy of your very being. You will come to know the fullness of the love of God for your lost soul.

You have so much more than the Psalmist had. You have the teaching of the New Testament and the love God in Christ our Lord. You have the precious teachings of Christ and His gospel; you have the grace of God explained in the story the Cross of Calvary. You can become a

Christian, and can be a member of the Lord's church. You can repent of your sins and be baptized into Christ and learn to experience in your life the great blessings that could be found only in Christ (Mark 16:16; Galatians 3:26-27; Ephesians 1:3-7).

Those who have a desire to know and understand God's word can do so. The reason many people get so little good, and thus so little delight, from God's word is that they give little thought and little study to its teaching. Study will open the doors of God's truth. Meditation will be the index of your spiritual strength. It will fashion the jewels of divine truth and the treasure of your own heart. Learn to study the Bible every day you live. Jesus says, "Search the scriptures," not just pick them up—He says, "Search the scriptures; for in them ye think ye have eternal life: and they are they which testify of me" (John 5:39). Again, we are admonished in 2 Timothy 2:15, "Study"—not just read—"Study to show thyself approved unto God." The Lord says, "Man shall not live by bread alone, but by every word that proceedeth out of the mouth of God" (Matthew 4:4).

The Bible teaches, here in the first Psalm, that the godly man shall not only delight in the word of the Lord but he will be fruitful. He shall be like a tree planted by the rivers of water that brings forth his fruit in his season. His leaf also shall not wither, for whatsoever he does shall prosper. The godly life has a purpose. It is not by accident. He is like the tree planted in a good place, by the rivers of water, in a location that will be for his life and for the end desired. He is to bear fruit. Jesus says, "Herein is my Father glorified, that ye bear much fruit; so shall ye be my disciples" (John 15:8). The fruit of the godly man is the fruit of Christian living, "But the fruit of the Spirit is love, joy, peace, longsuffering, gentleness, goodness, faith, meekness, temperance" (Galatians 5:22-23). It is the fruit to be found in abundance throughout the whole season of his life. There is to be no fading, no withering, and no dying. The godly man shall be a fruitful man. In fact, he has a marvelous promise that whatsoever he does shall prosper.

The godly man has both reason and revelation to assure him of true success. The prosperity that he is to desire is not the outward material prosperity, but the prosperity of his soul. God has promised to make him prosper, and God will not fail. There may be times of trials, but they are often for the development of the soul. James says, "Knowing this, that the trying of your faith worketh patience. But let patience have her perfect work, that ye may be perfect and entire, wanting nothing" (James 1:3-4). The very thing that seems worst may be the thing that is eventually really the very best for the fruitfulness of our souls. Mr. Spurgeon once wrote, "There is a blessing concealed in the righteous man's crosses, losses, and sorrows. The trials of the saints are a divine husbandry, by which he grows and brings forth abundant fruit."

Please notice also in the first Psalm, David says, "The ungodly are not so." The ungodly man's life is worthless like the chaff that the wind drives away. The chaff is only to be destroyed. The ungodly are not prepared to stand in the Day of Judgment and sinners will have no place in the congregation of the righteous. Sinners will have no place in heaven. They would be out of place in the midst of the righteous, their way shall perish (Matthew 25:31-46). The eternal curse of God is all that the ungodly do not have the hope for hereafter. In the Day of Judgment, they shall be condemned to the everlasting fire prepared for the wicked.

Let us be warned, the way of the ungodly shall perish. He may seem to prosper now, for a little season, but Judgment Day is coming.

> In Proverbs 24:1, Solomon says, "Be not thou envious against evil men, neither desire to be with them."
>
> Remember the words also of Proverbs 5:21: "For the ways of man are before the eyes of the Lord, and he pondereth all his goings." The Bible says that the Lord knows the way of the righteous—the righteous are continuously under the eyes of divine providence.
>
> 1 Peter 3:12 says, "For the eyes of the Lord are over the righteous, and his ears are open unto their prayers." God sees, and God knows, and God understands all of our motives, our purposes, and our works. He will provide the thing that is best in all of our circumstances as we endeavor to live for him. An eternal happiness in His presence in heaven shall be our everlasting reward.

So, if today, you desire to be happy, may we point you to the word of God. Make it your delight and your meditation. Let it direct you in becoming a Christian and give your life in service to Christ and His body, the church. May your life always be fruitful in the service of the Master. May you learn the real meaning of happiness and experience it every day that you live. You will then understand so well why he says, "Blessed is the man that walketh not in the counsel of the ungodly, nor standeth in the way of sinners, nor sitteth in the seat of the scornful," but rather he will be the person who delights in the law of the Lord. That is God's man!

# *Sin of Denominationalism*

Good morning, everyone. We appreciate your listening today to this study we title "The Sin of Denominationalism." This term is used to indicate the theory of Christianity that asserts that the church is not necessarily or constitutionally, one, but that it may be divided into a number of churches, each independent of the other. This belief was quite popular in the Protestant world for centuries after the Reformation of Martin Luther. It led to practical anarchy in the Christian world and was responsible for endless bickerings and jealousies among individual Christians. The spirit of partisanship was developed by the presence of sectarian divisions in the church. The whole idea of genuine brotherhood was largely destroyed.

The effect of this jealous and sectarian spirit among the followers of Christ was altogether detrimental to Christianity. People outside the church could justly criticize the distinctions and divisions among different groups that claimed to be Christian; and as a result, the gospel made little progress. It was this situation that served as the occasion for calling into existence the movement that was initiated in the early part of the nineteenth century. Denominationalism is a sin and has, beyond any question, worked great harm in the religious world. In the reaction against the despotism of the medieval church, it was only natural that those who protested against the existing evil should go to the opposite extreme as we as humans tend to do.

Denominationalism was the natural result of this reaction. It embodied the idea of freedom; but unfortunately, it utterly destroyed the idea of unity. It could be explained quite naturally upon historical grounds, but this fact does not justify its continuance or its perpetuation. Unquestionably, it was necessary for the church to secure freedom, even at the cost of destroying the false unity of the medieval church. But having secured freedom, it is now just as necessary that it should again secure unity. This unity must not sacrifice the freedom that has been gained at so great a cost, but it must safeguard and perpetuate that freedom. Now, I propose to you today that this is the past that lies before us.

Many New Testament passages teach against denominationalism. For example, Paul emphasizes in 1 Corinthians 1:10-17 that there are to be no divisions. Many other passages teach the same principle (Ephesians 4:4-6, Romans 15:5-6, Colossians 2:2, etc.). All attempts to prove that Paul's figure of the body and its members in 1 Corinthians 12:14-28 teach denominationalism are simply not correct.

I am glad to see it is now being recognized that the New Testament does not present a church made up of rival denominations. It teaches the unity of the church, and it admits no sectarian interpretation. This teaching is especially true in Jesus' prayer in John 17. All attempts to reconcile this prayer with the modern theory of denominationalism are unsuccessful. The denominational theory must inevitably go over board when Christians begin to understand that we must fairly and honestly accept the scripture as the final course of appeal.

Several points of biblical teaching show that the Lord's church does not fit with the concept of denominationalism. The Lord's people are designated by various names, and yet they refer to only one group. For instance, the Lord's people have an undenominational designation the "church" as in Matthew 16:18 where Jesus says, "Upon this rock, I will build my church." When the Lord's people are called the church, they are distinguished from people of the world because church means "the called out." The Lord's people are the called out. They have been called out darkness into light, out of sin into righteousness, out of the kingdom of Satan into the kingdom of God's dear Son. The term church, in the aggregate, embraces all people who have been so called out.

As for another case of an undenominational designation, the Lord's people are called "the kingdom of God" (Mark 1:15), emphasizing the government feature of the Lord's people under their Lord. Jesus Christ is King, and His people are His subjects. His kingdom is an absolute monarchy—Christ is the King and the will of the King is the law. Every citizen in His kingdom is under divine obligation to obey that law. Ignorance of the law does not constitute a defense for the violation of the law or for a failure to comply with the law.

Thirdly, the Lord's people have an undenominational designation as "the body of Christ" (1 Corinthians 12:12-31). This designation points to the unity feature of the Lord's people—their relationship with each other and with Christ. The term, body of Christ, emphasizes the relationship of the Lord's people, as a body, to their head, Christ. The term also emphasizes the unity and the concern each member must hold for all other members. The body is to be directed by its head, Christ, and there is to be no schism in the body. Christians, therefore, must respect Christ and also cooperate with each other and exercise the proper sympathetic care for one another. They must recognize and respect the right of every person to membership in the body, whether rich or poor, educated or uneducated, white or black. They must also recognize and respect the function of each member.

As for a fourth undenominational designation, the Lord's people are called "the house of God" (Isaiah 2:1-4; 1 Timothy 3:14-15). This designation shows the familial-type relationship the Lord's people to God and to each other as children of God. God is their father and Christ is their elder brother (Hebrews 3:1-6). The Lord's people, therefore, should look in full confidence to God as the divine, merciful, and loving Heavenly Father. There are only two families of men on earth, God's family and Satan's family (John 8:44). Every accountable person is either in God's family or he is in Satan's family. The wonderful and sustaining relationship the people of God enjoy as His children is a never-failing source of peace and comfort in dark days of trouble and heartache, days that are certain to come.

As for a fifth case of an undenominational designation, the Lord's people are called "the Temple of God" (1 Corinthians 3:16). This designation indicates the dwelling place feature of the Lord's people since an abode of the Father-Son-Holy Spirit is emphasized. God, Christ, and the Holy Spirit indwell both the church and the individual Christian. Thus, the church is called the Temple of God (1 Corinthians 3:16) and the Christian's body is also referred to as a Temple or sanctuary of the Holy Spirit. When a person's physical body becomes over much diseased, his spirit will no longer dwell in his body. Death is the result of the departure of a person's spirit from his diseased body. In like manner, when a church or individual Christian becomes over diseased with sin, God, Christ, and the Holy Spirit will have no dwelling place in that church or in that individual Christian, as the case may be.

As for a sixth case of an undenominational designation, the Lord's people are referred to as "the vineyard of God" (Matthew 20:1-16). When they receive this designation, the work feature of His people as members of the church is emphasized. The Christian has been employed to work in God's vineyard, the church. In God's employment, every employee must be a worker. There is absolutely no place for the slacker or sluggard. No employee is allowed to work part-time or at night in another vineyard. The wages of God's employees are much beyond all other wages paid, the spiritual blessings as bestowed from day-to-day and in the end, eternal life.

These designations and others that could be given serve to emphasize clearly and unmistakably, the simplicity and the undenominational character of the Lord's people. Without a full and complete understanding of the varied designations that apply to the Lord's people, the Christian is likely to sink to the level of sectarianism with all of its evil propensities of religious pride, party spirit, and bitter division. This danger is ever present, and it becomes intensified when the characteristics of undenominationalism are only infrequently stressed or are not even stressed at all.

I think we must think carefully as we look to the future and contemplate the church and denominationalism and the way the Lord wants things to be. One thing is sure, the church must return to its pristine spirit of brotherhood and unity if it is to serve the needs of the world. I have often wondered, had it not abandoned those early ideas, civilization might have skipped the Dark Ages and reached the degree of progress we can only dimly imagine. But, having paid the price of apostasy, the one hope that remains is to get back to the original basis of Christianity as is contained in the New Testament. Unless the church does this, and does it speedily, its candlestick could well be taken out of its place and be given to another. We thank you for listening today as we studied the sin of denominationalism, the party spirit. We trust this study will engender some questions, statements or comments or even criticism. But, most of all, we ask you to be like the ancient Bereans and search the scripture daily whether these things are so!

# *How Do You Read?*

Ladies and gentlemen, we appreciate the opportunity of coming into your home one more time for the purpose of learning more of the Master's will. Today, we invite your attention to the question: How do you read the Bible? This may seem to be a simple but superfluous and question. But I think actually it is the key to many, many things. So, we invite your attention to the study.

The book of Luke contains the interesting story of a lawyer who came to Jesus asking him the question: "Master, what shall I do to inherit eternal life?" (Luke 10:25). May we point out the importance of this question? The quest for eternal life should be the controlling desire of every one of us; and to this end we should bend every purpose in every effort of our lives here upon this earth. Our days here are few in number, we know that; and eternity is forever. The blessings of eternal life are great and abundant and of such a nature that nothing we might achieve in this life can be rightly considered as of comparable value. The great question of our hearts should always be, Master, what shall I do to inherit eternal life? Let us notice the Lord's answer. In Luke 10:26, Jesus asks the lawyer, "What is written in the law? how readest thou?" As a student and teacher of the law of God, it was the lawyer's duty to be acquainted with His teachings. At that time, the New Testament had not been written, but the lawyer had access to the revelation of God in the Old Testament.

The Old Testament contains many teachings concerning eternal life and how Jehovah wanted His people to be heirs of the blessings it would afford. That is why our Lord asked him "What is written in the law?" The second part of the Lord's question was "How readest thou?" calling on the Lord lawyer for his own understanding, what he personally thought. What he considered as the true meaning of what was written in the law of God. Here is an important thought: All too frequently, people are familiar with what the scripture actually teach and can repeat or quote the words of various portions of it, but their difficulty is one of failing to understand the meaning of those words and their application in everyday living.

The importance of the second part of the Lord's question can readily be seen when we stop to consider it. The lawyers answer, according our Lord, was correct. He says "Thou shalt love the Lord thy God with all thy heart, and with all thy soul, and with all thy strength, and with all thy mind; and thy neighbor as thyself" (verse 27). Therefore, the Lord says "Thou has answered right: this do, and thou shalt live." But did the lawyer properly read or correctly evaluate the meaning of those words? Notice in verse 29, "But he, willing to justify himself, said unto Jesus, And who is my neighbor?" The tendency so often is to let our own ideas and practices and our own prejudices become the controlling standard of our interpretation of scripture. People are prone to read into the scripture some ideas by which they can do as this lawyer, who wished to justify himself.

There is much to consider in this thought. How readest thou? Then we ask each of you listening today, as you consider the teachings of God's word, what is written and how readest thou? How do you read the Bible? Do you read it with a desire to understand its teachings and to apply them to your life so that you may inherit eternal life? Or do you read the Bible only occasionally, in time of trouble. Or when some great problem has so shaken you that you feel a real need for some greater power or wisdom than you possess? Or, do you, like so many others, just read here a little, there a little, without any real comprehension of what the Lord's message in the Bible really is? Or, do you approach the Bible with the idea that you think it is entirely beyond your understanding, that it is something supernatural beyond the grasp of ordinary people? Search your own life, actually at this moment. Please answer the question for yourself. How do you read the Bible? Hold this thought in your mind today.

God intended that those things He has revealed should be understood. The secret things He did not reveal belong to God (Deuteronomy 29:29). God intended that men should read His revelation and know and understand and obey the commands that He made applicable to us. Further, God has placed upon each of us the responsibility of properly reading the scripture and of doing the things that He wants us to do so that we may be the recipients of eternal life. Our obedience to the gospel of Christ does not make void the grace of God, but to the true believers of the Bible, that obedience becomes the demonstration of their personal faith in and reliance upon the greatness of the grace that God would bestow upon man. None of us can fully know the blessings of God's grace apart from such obedience. The proper understanding of the Bible can be ours only through diligent study and by a devout application of the Lord's teachings in our lives. We must come to know by our own experience what it means to love God and to love our neighbor as ourself. The parable of a man who fell among the thieves must become a living principal applied by us in helping our neighbors, even as the Samaritan, and not as the Priest and the Levite who passed by on the other side and left the man stripped of his clothing and wounded and half dead.

The Bible is not just the book from which to draw proof texts for arguments or sermons. It is the doctrine of God to be applied in the lives of men. It should be so read as God's message to us in this twentieth century. I found through the years that there are many "methods" of Bible study, and most of them are actually incorrect methods; but we should make ourselves at least acquainted with what they are and why they are correct or incorrect. Please, for just a few moments, consider some of them with me.

First of all, there is a method of Bible study called the mystical method. This method has maintained that no man can understand and interpret the Bible unless he possesses some miraculous power— some special communication from God to help him understand. This idea has had the effect of removing the Bible from the masses and of hindering people going to the Bible for the instruction they need. By considering the Bible as a mystery to be known only by inspiration directly, they have failed to learn its evident truths. As a result, false teachers claiming they have special powers have led away multitudes of innocent people. They have conceived many and often contradictory doctrines that would attempt to shroud the Bible and promote the mystery of theories that create sects and parties that are so entrenched with their fancy ideas that they really care little for the most fundamental teachings of our Lord.

Secondly, there is a method called the allegorical method. This method treats the Bible as one great riddle, a combination of many allegories or stories. Those who hold to such ideas do not seek to understand the text but to find some meaning to thrust into the different verses; that is, the interpreter's own ideas. Each interpreter places his thoughts beside the Bible words, and he claims greater importance for his own interpretations than for the text itself. To him, the mention of even a word suggests some theory or some allegory.

To illustrate, one writer would make the eagle mean robbery, the hawk to suggest injustice, and the raven to represent greed. So also, the double meaning that he sees, are as many of the figments of his own imagination.

Thirdly, there is what is called a spiritual interpretation. It is similar to the mystical theory but is even more extensive. To such persons who hold the spiritual method, all of the passages have some special spiritual application. With those teachers there is, not what the Lord has said that is important, but the hidden spiritual application that they claim has been revealed to them. They consider themselves as limited by no laws of interpretation and think that everyone should be wafted into inexpressible ecstasies by their spiritualizing.

Fourthly, there is the hierarchical method. It differs from the others in the assuming of the authority to both express their views and of comparing others to conform to them. This method declares that the church is the custodian and the only true exponent of the scripture. It would make the chosen ecclesiastics or church officers or priests the infallible proclaimers of the meaning of any given portion of the scripture. Such a method is exemplified in the Roman Catholic church and is also adhered to by most Protestant groups today. They claim their power by compelling men to bow in submission to catechisms and creeds, to their articles of faith and to their books of order for the churches. This method has made the interpretations of men or of groups of men of greater importance than any word our Lord spoke Himself. The advocates of this method declare what they consider as essential and what they deem as nonessential, whether it be our Lord's command to be buried in baptism for the remission of sins or the eating of the Lord's Supper in worship to God. They have decreed that instruments of music should be used, even if the New Testament church did refuse to use them. There is no limit to the exercise of their power and to their violation to the rights and liberties of the individuals who profess to be Christians. This is probably the most dangerous evil of all the methods of handling the Holy Scripture.

Fifthly, there is what is called a rationalistic method. It would subject every verse of scripture to the rule of human reasoning. It would exalt the mind of man above the mind of God. It would say to the individual that his reasoning powers are greater than those of God and that anything that he could not grasp with his own power to reason should be considered as either untrue or nonessential. The rationalistic method would reject the miracles of the Bible and would take away the principal of faith in God. It would assert that the individual had better knowledge, even than the God who made us. Now this school of thought was particularly popular in Germany more of a century ago. It is the field of the hyper-critic and the atheist; however, it has become—it actually is—the cornerstone of the so called modernist and the professedly liberal thinkers of our time. Let us remember this—let's remember the teaching of the Apostle Paul, he says, "We walk by faith, not by sight" (2 Corinthians 5:7). Jehovah is greater than the limited minds of sinful men. Just because we cannot reason a thing out to be in complete accord with our feeble minds is no basis for our choosing to close our minds to the facts of God's truth.

Further, many other false methods could be pointed out. But these are sufficient to set before us some of the attitudes of the multitudes of professed religionists of our day. Also, such methods as the dogmatic and the literal interpretation, Matthew dwelt upon at length. But these all have the same general effect upon the minds of the rank and file, of both Catholic and Protestant religionists. All these methods destroy the value and the work of the scripture and they rob the person who follows them of the divine conception of the nature and of the dignity of man as an individual person, whom our Lord valued as a greater work than all the riches of this old world.

How do you read your Bible? Please read your Bible, so as to understand its great value. Read it with the assurance that you are God's creation, made to be like God and one whom God has addressed in His book, the Bible, as an intelligent individual. As God has given you ability, use it. Read with understanding. Read with application to your life, an application that will enrich your soul. That method will give you salvation through Christ our Lord. It will provide you with strength against evil that will comfort you in your sorrows. It will assuage your griefs and lift your heavy burdens and place them upon the Lord.

I would like for us to close by noticing these rules. Here are some rules that we ought to apply in understanding the Holy Scripture.

1.  Observe who wrote the part of the Bible you are reading.
2.  Notice the individual or individuals to whom it was written; and their history, education, customs, and circumstances in relation to sin and temptation.

3.  Give attention to the setting of the sentence at hand. The Bible records the words spoken by the devil but does not sanction them. Job's wife wanted him to curse God and die, to be out of his misery and suffering, but he didn't. Job's professed comforters accused him of great sin, but he was not guilty.
4.  Make your aim to know the proper meaning of the passage. Do not read into it your personal prejudices. Do not strain for hidden meanings and special deep interpretations that violate the true purpose of Bible study.
5.  Remember that all truth is harmonious. Truth never contradicts truth. The Bible contains no contradictions when properly understood.
6.  Understand difficult passages in the light of plain and evident truth. Never try to overdraw or ignore a plain truth to establish some theory concerning another one you do not actually understand.
7.  Observe the proper division of the Bible. Recognize the different periods of God's dealings with men: in the early days of the Old Testament, God dealt with the family through the father or Patriarch. Then God gave His chosen people of Israel the law of Moses, the Old Testament; and taught them through prophets and inspired teachers. That law remained until Christ died on Calvary (Colossians 2:14; Galatians 3).

The gospel of Christ—listen—the gospel of Christ, the perfect law of liberty, is the law to tell us what to do to be saved today and how we may inherit eternal life. Christ is our everlasting Savior, our Priest, and our King. We are taught to believe in Him as God's Son, to repent of our sins, to confess our faith in Him and to be buried with Him in baptism for the remission of our sins (John 3:16; Mark 16:16; Acts 2:38; Romans 10:10).

The New Testament will teach us to live like Christ, how to worship God acceptably, how to serve our fellowman, and how to be good citizens, good neighbors, good companions in marriage, good parents to our children, and good children to our parents. Let us read the Bible. Let us read in such a way, so as to understand it. Let us read it, to apply it and to reap its benefits and its conclusions. We thank you for listening today. Please remember the question: How do you read your Bible?

# *Preaching of Philip*

Good morning, everyone. Today, we invite your attention to a study of the preaching of Philip, found in Acts 8:1: "And at that time there was a great persecution against the church which was at Jerusalem; and they were all scattered abroad throughout the regions of Judaea and Samaria, except the apostles." You recall that the Lord had ordered them in Acts 1:8 to remain in Jerusalem until they received power from on high. They did so; and as a result of their preaching, the church grew and abounded. Then, the Bible tells about the tremendous persecution in Acts 8. This persecution served God's will in scattering the disciples. It did not destroy the church.

Devout men buried Stephen and made great lamentation over him, even as the young man Saul laid waste the church, entering into every house and dragging men and women, committing them to prison. This eighth chapter of Acts is a brief commentary of some of the activities of Philip. He is not Philip, one of the apostles, but rather one of the seven chosen in Acts 6 to be over the daily ministration. Acts 8:5 says, "Then Philip went down to the city of Samaria, and preached Christ unto them." And he was effective in his preaching.

Verse 12 reads, "But when they believed Philip preaching the things concerning the kingdom of God, and the name of Jesus Christ, they were baptized, both men and women." Then, Luke describes Philip's preaching to the man of Ethiopia (Acts 8:26-40); in verse 35, he says, "Then Philip opened his mouth, and began at the same scripture, and preached unto him Jesus." Such preaching was successful then, and it will be today when we preach the same thing.

Unity will prevail when the word of God is respected. To many people, this portion of the book of Acts is quite familiar, and has been studied again and again. Individuals heard the gospel of Christ preached and were persuaded to become His disciple.

Samaria was the province just north of Judea; the city by the same name within that province was the seat of government in that part of

Israel. Long before, it had split off from the tribes of Judah and Benjamin after the death of Solomon. Under the leadership of Jeroboam, the ten tribes set up places of worship designed to keep the people from returning to Jerusalem. It was a governmental rebellion that turned to the worship of idols and false religion. When Samaria fell to the invaders from the north, and the Assyrians left to hold rule over the Israelites, they married their subjects and created this mixed breed of people. These descendants were called the Samaritans. They were held in complete and utter disregard and contempt by the Jews, both racially and religiously. It was a triumph of understanding and obedience to the will of the Lord that Philip preached the gospel to those in Samaria. Multitudes heeded the things spoken by Philip when they heard and saw the signs he did, according to verse six.

The power that Philip possessed enabled him to confirm the message he preached. He cast out many unclean spirits and healed the palsied and lame, causing much joy in that city. He also interacted with a man named Simon:

> But there was a certain man, called Simon, which beforetime in the same city used sorcery, and bewitched the people of Samaria, giving out that himself was some great one: To whom they all gave heed, from the least to the greatest, saying, This man is the great power of God. And to him they had regard, because that of long time he had bewitched them with sorceries. But when they believed Philip preaching the things concerning the kingdom of God, and the name of Jesus Christ, they were baptized, both men and women (verses 9-12).

The preaching of the good tidings concerning the kingdom of God, in the name of Jesus Christ, resulted in these Samaritans accepting that preaching; and they were baptized both men and women. In verse 13 we read, that Simon "believed also: and when he was baptized, he continued with Philip, and wondered, beholding the miracles and signs which were done."

Several pertinent lessons come from these verses. "Now when the apostles which were at Jerusalem heard that Samaria had received the word of God, they sent unto them Peter and John: Who, when they were come down, prayed for them, that they might receive the Holy Ghost: (For as yet he was fallen upon none of them: only they were baptized in the name of the Lord Jesus.)" (verses 14-16). From this account we learn they became disciples through belief and obedience and not by the Holy Spirit falling upon them. In the next verse, we learn how they received the Holy Spirit; the apostles laid they their hands on them, and they received the Holy Spirit.

It is of more than a passing interest to observe that though Philip, the evangelist, was a man full of the Holy Spirit who could perform signs, heal the palsied and the lame, and cast out unclean spirits, it took an apostle to lay hands on these people so that they could receive the gift of the Holy Spirit. It is this power—the power to transmit, the ability to perform wondrous signs—that Simon wanted to purchase. Notice verses 18-19, "And when Simon saw that through the laying on the apostles' hands the Holy Ghost was given, he offered them money, Saying, Give me also this power, that on whomsoever I lay hands, he may receive the Holy Ghost." There is no doubt that he was guilty of a serious error but not of an unpardonable error as we see from the words of Peter in verses 20-21, "Peter said unto him, Thy money perish with thee, because thou hast thought that the gift of God may be purchased with money. Thou hast neither part nor lot in this matter: for thy heart is not right in the sight of God." Having stated his condition, Peter then proceeds to tell him what he must do about it. Listen—"Repent therefore of this thy wickedness, and pray God, if perhaps the thought of thine heart may be forgiven thee. For I perceive that thou art in the gall of bitterness, and in the bond of iniquity" (verse 22-23). Notice he does not say that Simon is in the gall of bitterness, as you may have heard it read, for the purpose of implying that Simon had not obeyed the gospel and had never been saved from his past sins. Such is a futile effort that some use to deny the validity of his faith and his obedience. But Peter does not tell Simon to repent and be baptized—he had already been baptized. He does tell him positively to repent and pray for forgiveness.

Simon's attitude is seen in his response to Peter in verse 24, "Pray ye to the Lord for me, that none of these things which ye have spoken come upon me." The beloved Apostle John writes in 1 John 1:8-10, "If we say we have no sin, we deceive ourselves, and the truth is not in us. If we confess our sins, he is faithful and just to forgive us our sins, and to cleanse us from all unrighteousness. If we say that we have not sinned, we make him a liar, and his word is not in us." James writes, "Confess your faults one to another, and pray one for another, that you may be healed. The effectual fervent prayer of a righteous man availeth much" (James 5:16). In James 5:19-20, "Brethren, if any of you do err from the truth, and one convert him; Let him know, that he which converteth the sinner from the error of his way shall save a soul from death, and shall hide a multitude of sins." Such was Simon's error: he had believed and had been baptized but then erred. Peter tells him to pray. He in turn asks Peter to pray for him.

Luke now writes in chapter 8:25, "And they, when they had testified and preached the word of the Lord, returned to Jerusalem, and preached the gospel in many villages of the Samaritans." This verse is in reference to Peter and John. In the remainder of this chapter of Acts, Luke tells of the remarkable interest of the Ethiopian officer in the prophecy of Isaiah 53, reading it aloud and wondering of whom the prophet was speaking, of himself or some other. Philip, you recall, was nearby having been directed by the angel of the Lord to the way that leads from Jerusalem to Gaza. It should be noted that the one searching for the truth was not aware of the interest of heaven manifested by the angel (verse 26) and the Spirit (verse 29). This communication was made to the evangelist, Philip. Being invited into the chariot with the man, he had a unique teaching situation. Here is an honest inquirer, one who was trustworthy; that is, he was a man of great authority and one over the treasury of Queen Candace of Ethiopia. He wanted to know of whom the prophet was speaking.

> Philip opened his mouth, and began at the same scripture, and preached unto him Jesus. And as they went on their way, they came unto a certain water: and the eunuch said, See, here is water; what doth hinder me to be baptized? And Philip said, If thou believest with all thine heart, thou mayest. And he answered and said, I believe that Jesus Christ is the Son of God. And he commanded the chariot to stand still: and they went down both into the water, both Philip and the eunuch; and he baptized him. And when they were come up out of the water, the Spirit of the Lord caught away Philip, that the eunuch saw him no more: and he went on his way rejoicing. (verses 35-40).

The beautiful simplicity of the gospel of Christ is illustrated vividly in this chapter of Acts. Philip, the evangelist, preached the good tidings concerning the kingdom of God and the name of Jesus Christ, and sincere honest searchers for truth accepted the word and were baptized. It is that simple. It is that grand. That whosoever will believe and obey may be saved.

# *The Lord Is Our Helper*

Good morning, everyone. We are grateful for the privilege we have today to come to you and study with you for a little while the word of God. It certainly is wonderful to live in a place where we can freely discuss the Holy Scripture. We can think upon the things that are divine. We can worship the Lord, today, as we believe the Bible teaches.

Today, we would like to turn your attention to the subject "The Lord is Our Helper." I would like for us to begin by taking note of the fact that there is a great difference between the devout Christian and a man who has never known the Lord. The Christian has so many things to make him happy that the non-Christian has never experienced. He has so many things for which to be thankful. He has strength for every day that gives him great confidence. His faith in God has that strong foundation of eternal truth, which the forces of evil can never destroy. The Christian has God as his helper. The Christian can confidently say "the Lord is my helper" (Hebrews 13:6). No matter what may be the circumstances of his life, the Lord is always on hand to be his helper in every time of need.

This is one of those exceeding great blessings that only devout Christians can really appreciate. God has always been with His people. His presence has been their strength in all ages. He has blessed them in their prosperity, He has sustained them in their trials, and He has given them victory over their enemies. The psalmist says: "Lord, thou hast been our dwelling place in all generations. Before the mountains were brought forth, or ever thou hadst formed the earth and the world, even from everlasting to everlasting, thou art God" (Psalm 90:1-2). Paul says, in speaking of God, "For in him we live and move and have our being" (Acts 17:28). Indeed, He is the eternal God who made us, who sustains our very being. It is from the bounty of His great hand that all of our many blessings flow. It is even as James says, "Every good gift and every perfect gift is from above, and cometh down from the Father of lights, with whom is no variableness, neither shadow of turning" (James 1:17).

All men need God's help, regardless of what their state may be or what they may think about it. Even the strongest of people will sooner or later come to that time when they must realize their strength is not sufficient. There is coming that inevitable time that Solomon wrote, when "the strong men shall bow themselves ... man goeth to his long home ... then shall the dust return to the earth as it was: and the spirit shall return to God who gave it" (Ecclesiastes 12:3-7). That hour of death is coming to us all. God's word says, "It is appointed unto men once to die" (Hebrews 9:27). In that time, if never before, every man shall realize his own weakness and insufficiency. The tragedy is that so many people ignore their need of God. They strive to convince themselves of their own strength. They pride themselves in their own wisdom and ability when all goes well. Oh, but it takes the troubles and the trials of life to bring them to their senses, to make them realize there is something more to life than their selfish pursuits, and to awake them to the fact that the arm of flesh is not sufficient.

We need to realize our need of God's help. In the 37th Psalm, God has given us these words, "But the transgressors shall be destroyed together: the end of the wicked shall be cut off. But the salvation of the righteous is of the Lord: he is their strength in the time of trouble. And the Lord shall help them, and deliver them: he shall deliver them from the wicked, and save them, because they trust in him" (Psalm 37:38-40).

Now, the Psalms that David wrote teach us to trust in God. I am persuaded we should read them often. The Psalms can tell us of the greatness of our God and help us to trust in Him. Let us think of some of these remarkable passages.

> Trust in the Lord, and do good; so shalt thou dwell in the land, and verily thou shalt be fed. Delight thyself also in the Lord; and he shall give thee the desires of thine heart. Commit thy way unto the Lord; trust also in him; and he shall bring it to pass. And he shall bring forth thy righteousness as the light, and thy judgment as the noonday. Rest in the Lord, and wait patiently for him: fret not thyself because of him who prospereth in his way, because of the man who bringeth wicked devices to pass. Cease from anger, and forsake wrath: fret not thyself in any wise to do evil. For evildoers shall be cut off: but those that wait upon the Lord, they shall inherit the earth. For yet a little while, and the wicked shall not be: yea,

thou shalt diligently consider his place, and it shall not be. But the meek shall inherit the earth; and shall delight themselves in the abundance of peace. (Psalm 37:3-11).

In the 31st Psalm, we read:

In thee, O Lord, do I put my trust; let me never be ashamed: deliver me in thy righteousness. ... For thou art my rock and my fortress; therefore for thy name's sake lead me, and guide me. ... But I trusted in thee, O Lord: I said, Thou art my God. My times are in thy hand: deliver me from the hand of mine enemies, and from them that persecute me. ... Oh how great is thy goodness, which thou hast laid up for them that fear thee; .... Blessed be the Lord: for he hath shewed me his marvelous kindness. ... O love the Lord, all ye his saints: for the Lord preserveth the faithful, and plentifully rewardeth the proud doer. Be of good courage, and he shall strengthen your heart, all ye that hope in the Lord (Psalm 31:1-24).

I think that one only needs to read these lovely psalms to be convinced that David was a man who believed in God and who trusted in God. The wonderful faith and feeling of these Psalms may be found in many other of the wonderful Psalms that David wrote, and he would need to read them and read them often. We need to have the same great trust to fill our hearts. We need to learn to say, "I will lift up mine eyes unto the hills, from whence cometh my help. My help cometh from the Lord, which made heaven and earth" (Psalm 121:1-2). This great faith will make us realize with David, "The Lord shall preserve thee from all evil: he shall preserve thy soul. The Lord shall preserve thy going out and thy coming in from this time forth, and even for evermore" (verses 7-8).

The God of the Psalms—please be reminded of this—the God of the Psalms is the God of our salvation today. He rules the universe now; He still occupies the universal throne. His power has not diminished, and His grace yet abounds. His love has been even more fully demonstrated through Jesus Christ our Lord; the provisions of His mercy for His children today even exceed those of the days in which the psalmist extolled the praises of God. Certainly, if in that day, God would be their helper, I will assure you that today God will be our helper now. He would have us to realize that we are weak and sinful creatures. He wants us to know His wisdom far exceeds that of man.

62

God has taught us, "I will destroy the wisdom of the wise, and will bring to nothing the understanding of the prudent" (1 Corinthians 1:19). Man's wisdom leads away from God. The Bible declares, "The foolishness of God is wiser than men; and the weakness of God is stronger than men" (1 Corinthians 1:25). "It pleased God by the foolishness of preaching to save them that believe" (1 Corinthians 1:21). "For the preaching of the cross is to them that perish foolishness; but unto us which are saved it is the power of God" (1 Corinthians 1:18).

We need to learn the lesson of Jeremiah, as he says, "O Lord, I know that the way of man is not in himself: it is not in man that walketh to direct his steps" (Jeremiah 10:23). We need the Lord to direct us. Jesus says, "I am the way, the truth, and the life: no man cometh unto the Father, but by me" (John 14:6). We need the Lord to direct our paths if we would ever enter heaven. We need His help now. We cannot depend upon our own wisdom. Man's own ways only lead to death (Proverbs 16:25). I think we should be reminded occasionally that man cannot save himself. Each of us stands helpless before God. Each of us has sinned. "There is none righteous, no, not one" (Romans 3:10). "For all have sinned, and come short of the glory of God" (Romans 3:23).

We cannot, by ourselves and within ourselves, remove the guilt of our sins. It is even as the words of the old song, that we used to sing and still sing:

> What can wash away my sins? Nothing but the blood of Jesus. What can make me whole again? Nothing but the blood of Jesus.
> Oh, precious is the flow that makes me white as snow, no other fount I know, nothing but the blood of Jesus.

The Bible says, "Without shedding of blood is no remission" (Hebrews 9:22). It took the sacrifice of Jesus, the shedding of His blood to supply the way for our salvation. Christ shed His blood so that our sins might be remitted. We must humble ourselves in our recognition of our sins and accept the Christ as our Savior. We must believe in Him and the cleansing power of His blood. We must repent of our sins (Luke 13:3). Peter says, "Repent, and be baptized every one of you in the name of Jesus Christ for the remission of sins" (Acts 2:38). There is no other way for us to have the blessings of that cleansing blood of our Savior. We must humbly ourselves in obedience to Christ if we would have His help to free us from the awful guilt of sin.

Please be reminded that God's grace is sufficient. Paul learned this lesson. I don't suppose that anyone has suffered more for Christ. In addition to all the trials and the hardships and the persecutions that Paul endured, he had also a thorn in the flesh. Paul prayed that the Lord would remove that thorn from his flesh, but the answer came straight from God. "My grace is sufficient for thee: for my strength is made perfect in weakness" (2 Corinthians 12:9). Paul's dependence upon that wonderful grace of God led him to say, "Therefore I take pleasure in infirmities"—let me read that again—"Therefore I take pleasure in infirmities, in reproaches, in necessities, in persecutions, in distresses for Christ's sake: for when I am weak, then am I strong" (2 Corinthians 12:10). This is a lesson that every Christian must learn. God's grace is sufficient to help in every trial.

Temptations and trials become a means of blessing to the Christian. James says, "My brethren, count it all joy when you fall into divers temptations; Knowing this, that the trying of your faith worketh patience. But let patience have her perfect work, that you may be perfect and entire, wanting nothing" (James 1:2-4). Further, he says, "Blessed is the man that endureth temptation: for when he is tried, he shall receive the crown of life, which the Lord has promised to them that love him" (James 1:12). Trials and troubles and hardships cause the man that was non-Christian to fall, to become hardened and cynical and resentful. But the Christian can find and be given the opportunity to know the Lord is his helper.

A good question for us at this moment: Have you allowed trials and troubles and hardships to get you down? Are you becoming hardened and cynical and resentful? Please remember, that though the trials and the hardships come, when you find yourself growing hard and cynical and resentful, you are following the course of an individual who is not a Christian. When the trials and the troubles come, you should find in them an opportunity to know "the Lord is your helper" and become stronger than you ever have been. In dependence upon the Master, the Christian can overcome the temptations. God has provided for him a way of escape from Satan's snare (1 Corinthians 10:13). Like Paul, the genuine Christian can say, "I can do all things through Christ which strengtheneth me" (Philippians 4:13).

If adversities and sickness and disappointments befall you today, if you are a Christian, you don't have to bear these things alone. The Lord says "I will never leave thee, nor forsake thee. So that we may boldly say, the Lord is my helper, and I will not fear what man shall do unto me" (Hebrews 13:5-6). Please remember the Lord notices the fall of the sparrow, and He numbers the very hairs of our head (Matthew 10:29-30). He knows the needs of our hearts as His children, and He can provide what is best. The Lord has taught us not to be anxious and not to worry about the things around us. If we serve Him and seek first the kingdom of God and His righteousness, we may know that the Lord will not forsake us. He says:

> Is not the life more than meat, and the body than rainment? Behold the fowls of the air: for they sow not, neither do they reap, nor gather into barns; yet your heavenly Father feedeth them. Are you not much better than they? Which of you by taking thought can add one cubit unto his stature? And why take you thought for raiment? Consider the lilies of the field, how they grow; they toil not, neither do they spin: And yet I say unto you, That even Solomon in all his glory was not arrayed like one of these. Wherefore, if God so clothe the grass of the field, which to day is and to morrow is cast into the oven, shall he not much more clothe you, O ye of little faith? (Matthew 6:25-30).

May I read the last verse of the sixth chapter of Matthew, from Mr. Williams' translation of the New Testament? It reads, "So never worry, so never worry about tomorrow. For tomorrow will have worries of its own. Each day has even enough of its own."

Let us remember, that as the Lord can help us and provide for us today as His children, so surely He can provide for tomorrow, when and if it comes. This is the faith that our Lord wants us to possess, so that our days may not be filled with worry. God helps us when we pray. The Lord is near, and we should be ever mindful of this fact. We, then, should live as if we are mindful of these things. Remember, the Lord is your helper. Without Him, you are lost. Without Him, you can do nothing. Without Him, you cannot be saved. Without Him, you cannot overcome the trials and temptations of life. Without Him, you cannot face the things that you must face; but with Him Paul says, "I can do all things through Christ which strengtheneth me." Won't you today please remember those words: The Lord is my helper!

# *Finding the Book of the Law*

Good morning, everyone. We are indeed grateful to be here today and to have you in our listening audience. It is a genuine pleasure to be able to come to you on this Lord's Day with a study from the Master's word. We would like to invite your attention to those things that were written aforetime. Paul states in Romans 15:4 that they were written for our learning and admonition. I would like to invite your attention to the statement that was given to us in 2 Kings chapters 22 and 23 where the Bible declares the effects that the reading of God's book had on a young king by the name of Josiah. Also, we are told of the extensive reforms that he made among the people, after having heard the law of God read. This was indeed one of the good periods in the midst of the evil days of God's people more than 2,500 years ago. May I suggest to you that you very carefully read 2 Kings 22 and 23?

Josiah became king as a boy. He was only eight years old when he began to reign. He reigned for thirty-one years in Jerusalem. He was fortunate to have good tutors and faithful advisers who kept him from the evil ways of his father, Amon. It was said of Josiah, "And he did that which was right in the sight of the Lord, and walked in all the way of David his father, and turned not aside to the right hand or to the left" (2 Kings 22:2). He desired to do God's will that called him to repair the Temple of God in Jerusalem where the worship of God was to be conducted and the sacrifices to be offered. This task was done in the eighteenth year of king Josiah (verse 3). It was here that they found the book of the law. It had been lost in the Temple, in the very place where it should have been considered most precious and most holy. It was in the Temple where God's name was recorded; and from which the knowledge of the law of the Lord should have gone forth among the people. But there the book of the law had been lost. Had the book been covered with rubbish or had it been hidden by someone who did not want to follow His teaching or be disturbed by its warnings? Or had it been so neglected that its presence had just been ignored or overlooked? The Bible does not answer these questions, so far as I know, but it does tell us how that Hilkiah, the high priest, said unto the scribe, Shaphan, "I have found the book of law in the house of the Lord" (2 Kings 22:8).

God's people had lost His law. The Jews were His chosen nation. They were the ones to whom God committed the oracles of His wisdom (Romans 3:2). They should have been its most ardent caretakers. They should have been reading it regularly. Their nation and their lives should have been governed by what it taught, but they lost the law of Jehovah in the house of Jehovah, of all places. I will assure you that the Bible teaches that loss was a costly one. Their failure to know and do the law of the Lord had resulted in all kinds of sin.

Idolatry had filled the city of Jerusalem and had been brought in the very Temple that had been built for the worship of the true and living God. As one sin inevitably leads to another, so all kinds of sin, even the very basest and most corrupt, was found everywhere. Their kings had become evil, the people were corrupted, and the wrath of the Lord's judgment was about to be poured out upon the city of Jerusalem and all the children of Judah. Only a few of the people had retained in their memories some of the teachings of God—only a few had retained only a part. This is a place we ought to stop to take a lesson. Only a part is simply not enough! They needed the whole law of God. They needed its commands, and they needed its warnings and its promises.

When they found God's law, the scribe Shaphan brought it Josiah and read it before the king. Then we are told, "And it came to pass when the king had heard the words of the book of the law, that he rent his clothes" (verse 11). He was greatly disturbed by what he had heard. He wanted to do something about it at once. He says, "Go ye, enquire of the Lord for me, and for the people, and for all Judah, concerning the words of this book that is found: for great is the wrath of the Lord that is kindled against us, because our fathers have not hearkened unto the words of this book, to do according unto all that which is written concerning us" (verse 13). The prophetess, Huldah, sent the king the message, "Because thine heart was tender, and thou hast humbled thyself before the Lord, when thou heardest what I spake against this place, and against the inhabitants thereof, that they should become a desolation and a curse, and hast rent thy clothes, and wept before me; I also have heard thee, saith the Lord" (verse 19).

The Bible declares that Josiah proceeded to make a covenant. It was (1) with the Lord and (2) I quote him "to walk after the Lord, and to keep his commandments and his testimonies and his statutes with all their heart and all their soul, to perform the words of this covenant that were written in this book." Then we are told "And all the people stood to the covenant" (2 Kings 23:3). So, Josiah began his reformation, and it was indeed a reformation. He put down idolatry, its priests, its temples and groves and the evil worshipers that carried on these corrupt and sinful practices. Even the altars and high places that had been built in the 350 years before, in the time of Solomon, were destroyed. The altar of Jeroboam, at Bethel, was torn down and completely destroyed. In so doing, Josiah fulfilled the prophecy of the young prophet from Judah who had spoken of the things about three hundred and thirty-three years before (1 Kings 13:2).

It was no easy task. It never is. It was no easy task to rid the people in the land of all the evil that had become so deeply increased among them. But all of these abominations Josiah put away that he might perform the words of the Lord that were written of the book that Hilkiah, the priest, found in the house of the Lord. They kept the Lord's Passover feast. It was such a Passover that it was said, "Surely there was not holden such a passover from the days of the judges that judged Israel, nor in all the days of the kings of Israel, nor of the kings of Judah" (2 Kings 23:22).

Josiah was indeed a great man, and of Josiah it was said, "And like unto him was there no king before him, that turned to the Lord with all his heart, and with all his soul, and with all his might, according to all the law of Moses; neither after him arose there any like him" (2 Kings 23:25). Josiah was a great man. He accomplished so much in the short life that he lived. When you consider this young man who lived less than forty years, you must admire his faith in God, his respect for the law of God, his great courage and doing what the Lord wanted done. He should be remembered by every one of us as the great reformer, Josiah, whose reformations were brought out because they found the book of the law in the Temple of God.

The book or the law of God was lost not only in the days of Josiah. The Lord's book has been lost at other times, also. For example, it was lost in a sense in the early history of the church. The New Testament was written by men who were chosen as inspired men to write down those things that God wanted men to know concerning

Christ and His church and the gospel as being the power of God unto salvation. But some lost it by either ignoring or by perverting its teachings. The New Testament was given as God's total, complete revelation. It contained all that pertained to life and godliness, as Peter says, "through the knowledge of him that hath called us to glory and virtue" (2 Peter 1:3).

The curse of the Lord, rests upon any person—every person—who perverts its teaching (Galatians 1:8-9). Concerning the book of Revelation, in particular, and all the New Testament teaching, in general, the warning was given for no man to add to or take from the things that God had given (Revelation 22:18-19). The New Testament is God's inspired word that was given for the salvation of sinful man. But men lost the knowledge of the Lord's word. They permitted other things to hide the New Testament truth from their eyes and no longer to be cherished as the truth. Jesus spoke all when He said, "And ye shall know the truth, and the truth shall make you free" (John 8:32).

The Apostle Paul had often expressed the fear that such a time would come. He says in 2 Corinthians 11:3, "But I fear, lest by any means, as the serpent beguiled Eve through his subtilty, so your minds should be corrupted from the simplicity that is in Christ." In 2 Corinthians 4:4, he spoke of how "the god of this world hath blinded the minds of them which believe not, lest the light of the glorious gospel of Christ, who is the image of God, should shine unto them." Such a condition soon began to develop within the early church. The traditions of man and the idolatrous ways of those who failed to separate themselves completely from such things, when they professed Christianity, soon began to corrupt the thinking of the people.

It was like the people of Judah before Josiah was born. Judah copied their neighbors' idols and bowed down before them; and by the fifth and sixth centuries, the people who professed to be the church of our Lord had very little knowledge of New Testament teachings, and then came the dark ages. The Bible was chained to the pulpits. It was kept from the masses of the people. It was soon hidden in monasteries and convents; and for hundreds of years, the New Testament was hidden from the masses in what one time had been the Temple of God, that is the church on earth. The church of our Lord became the corrupted workings of the man of sin and the mother of harlots. It was the dark ages indeed, made dark by the absence of the knowledge of God and by the prevalence of sin.

But there came a reformation. Soon after the beginning of the sixteenth century, a young man named Martin Luther read a dusty copy of the New Testament in an old library. As he studied the Bible more, he began to be impressed with the great sins that were being practiced in the name of religion; and the more he read God's word that had been so long hidden by the traditions and the corruptions of the Roman church, the more he realized that something must be done. Martin Luther began to lecture in the protest against the evils of his day. Like Josiah, he thought that something must be done. His purpose was that of Reformation. On October 31, 1511, he nailed his Ninety-Five Theses to the church door at Wittenburg. His work met with tremendous opposition, and the breach began to widen between him and the Roman church. In 1521, he was summoned to the council of Worms, where he was demanded to repent or recant. Rather, he says, "Here I take my stand. I cannot do otherwise, so help me God. Amen." Then came the work of the New Testament into the hands of men. Luther published his German translation of the New Testament in 1522, and the people began to have the opportunity to read again the word of the Lord. There were others who began to join the work. John Calvin began his work in Geneva, Switzerland in 1536. John Knox, the intrepid reformer of Scotland, soon began his work in that country. Many others began to join in the work since printing had been invented. The Bible was set in type, and copies of new translations in German and English were distributed widely. The tide of persecution was tremendous, but the lost book of God's eternal truth had been found; and men were ready to give their own lives to translate and distribute the Bible to all who would read it—then came the restoration.

Men in England and Scotland and in America began to look beyond reformation to restoration, the complete restoration of the Bible to its rightful place of authority on all matters of religion. The restoration of the New Testament church, in its congregational independence and unity, and the restoration of the gospel plan of salvation as the way of redemption through Christ, and the restoration of the New Testament pattern of worship. All of these became the teachings of men whose desire was to go back to God's book, the Bible, as the only book of truth and authority in the entire world. Men everywhere began to say, "let us go back to the Bible, let us go back to the Bible, and where the Bible speaks we will speak and where the Bible is silence we will be silent." This is the plea of the churches of Jesus Christ today! This is the plea of the congregation who is supporting this broadcast today and the congregations in this area who will be announced, who are indeed supporting this broadcast.

Today, let us go back to the Bible. This is what we are saying. Let us go back to God's plan for man's salvation and teach sinners about Christ and how they should repent and confess their belief in Christ, as God's Son, and be baptized for the remission of their sins. Let us go back to the Bible plan for the church in its name, its work, its organization, and its teaching for the unity that the Lord desires for all the children of God. Let us go back to the Bible pattern of worship. The New Testament church in the beginning had five parts to its worship: the singing and making melody in their hearts, that was without the accompaniment of mechanical instruments of music; the edifying of one another through teaching and prayer; then upon the first day of the week, they ate the Lord's Supper; and they contributed of their substance for the Lord's work (John 4:24; Ephesians 5:19; Acts 2:42; Acts 20:7; 1 Corthinians16:2).

So today, we should want to go back. Let us go back to the real meaning of patterning our lives after the example of Christ and making our lives devout, humble, obedient examples, and telling others what Christ means to us as Christians. God help us today to share together the biblical hope for the eternal happiness of all God's children, which is the hope of heaven through Jesus Christ our Lord. Don't let the Bible become a lost book to you.

May the church today stand and declare all the words of this life. May we never be ashamed to stand up and tell the world, here is the gospel of Jesus Christ; and if reforms are demanded by that book, in the church or in our lives, then let it be. Let us proceed to the task that lies before us. We have found the book of the law. We have found the good news of the kingdom of God; and may the Lord help us to share it with others, first of all, by the lives we live and also by the words we preach. We want to thank you for listening today. We trust that this subject is one that will inspire you to a greater study, and we do suggest that you very carefully read 2 Kings 22 and 23. Until this time next Lord's Day, we bid you a very pleasant good day.

# *Prejudice*

Good morning, everyone. We are very grateful for the privilege of studying with you the word of God. Today, we invite your attention to the book of John and the story that we are told about Nathaniel to whom Philip went to tell about Jesus. Philip told him, "We have found him, of whom Moses in the law, and the prophets, did write, Jesus of Nazareth, the son of Joseph" (John 1:45). You recall that Nathaniel did not wait to hear anymore about Jesus. One thing in Philip's story impressed him above all other things. Jesus was from Nazareth. So, Nathaniel answered, "Can any good thing come out of Nazareth?" Nathaniel expressed the attitude of the people about him in judging the Master by the town from which He had come, without further hearing any evidence in regard to Jesus.

This passage points out something that seems to be a common thing in the world. We are so prone to react precisely as Nathaniel did. We tend to speak too soon; we tend to pass judgment without full knowledge of the person or the matter under consideration. It is much easier to judge carelessly and not put forth the time or the effort to investigate. The decision frequently rests upon the surface appearance. Many a good man has been rejected because of some little thing that some unthinking person may have said. The place in which a man is reared, or something about his background, is often allowed to close the minds of others against Him. That he likes and dislikes or has feelings against something without good reason is permitted to shut out any further evidence.

We are grateful the story about Nathaniel did not stop with his first reaction. You recall that Philip answered his question with an invitation. Philip had learned about Jesus, and now he wanted to share the blessings of his knowledge. He told Nathaniel simply, "Come and see." I suppose that is one of the most practical and yet one of the best approaches that could possibly have been used then, and in many cases the very best approach now. Simply he told Nathaniel, "Come and see." He wanted him to see for himself. Philip seemed confident that first hand and complete knowledge would convince Nathaniel.

Philip was right. Jesus saw them coming and spoke to Nathaniel saying, "Behold an Israelite indeed, in whom is no guile!" (verse 47). Nathaniel said to Him, "Whence knowest thou me?" Jesus answered and said unto him "Before that Philip called thee, when thou was under the fig tree, I saw thee." Nathaniel answered and said to Him, "Rabbi, thou art the Son of God."

The world needs more like Philip today, first, because of his own knowledge of Jesus and, next, because he wanted to share that knowledge with his friend. He wanted someone else to have the blessing he had experienced in knowing Jesus, the Son of God. What wonderful blessings can be ours through our Lord and our Savior. There are friends and acquaintances all about us, surely with whom we would like to share the knowledge and the blessings of our Christian faith. You recall that Philip chose the best way to acquaint Nathaniel with the Master. He says simply, "Come and see."

First-hand knowledge is always better than all manner of tiring arguments. Experience is a wonderful teacher. Arguments have little effect on the prejudice of men. If only it were possible to get most of the world about us to see the real value of Christian living, to learn the true happiness and the joy of Christian service, to taste indeed as the prophet says, "That the Lord is gracious." What a wonderful thing all of that would be. There just simply is no way to know the flavor of an orange without tasting it. There is no way to know the real value of our Christian happiness without tasting of the grace of our Lord. Philip's method should be ours. Whether we can ever preach a gospel sermon or whether we can ever lead a public prayer or whether we can ever lead a song or whatever, we can do what he did—we can say to others, "Come and see." We should invite others to the influence of our own faith and our godliness—we should ask them to come and see for themselves the real truth of Christianity.

Philip was like Andrew, who brought his brother Simon to see the Christ. Simon became the great Apostle Peter.

The woman of Samaria, about whom we read in John 4, went to her own people of Samaria and told them about Jesus. The record says, "And many of the Samaritans of that city believed on him for the saying of the woman, which testified, He told me all that ever I did" (verse 39). She caused a greater company to hear the teachings of the Lord for themselves and then believe on Him.

John 4:41 says, "And many more believed because of his own word." But prejudice often hinders. Many who heard the teachings of Jesus and beheld His miracles, did not accept Him. Why? Simply because of prejudice. Concerning them, Jesus says:

> For this people's heart is waxed gross, and their ears are dull of hearing, and their eyes they have closed; lest at any time they should see with their eyes, and hear with their ears, and should understand with their heart, and should be converted, and I should heal them (Matthew 13:15).

They did not rise above their prejudices as Nathaniel did. Some of them said of Jesus:

> Is not this the carpenter's son? is not his mother called Mary? and his brethren, James, and Joses, and Simon, and Judas? And his sisters, are they not all with us? Whence then hath this man all these things? And they were offended in him. But Jesus said unto them, A prophet is not without honor, save in his own country, and in his own house. And he did not many mighty works there because of their unbelief (Matthew 13:55-58).

Their prejudices had bad consequences. The various signs that should have convinced them and helped them to see the truth of the Lord's teaching were the signs that caused them to be hardened in their unbelief. There He came to expose and to rebuke them, leading to their abandonment of the Lord. He then went to other places to do His teaching and to perform His mighty works.

The apostles later experienced the same feelings of prejudice among their hearers in Jerusalem and, in fact, in many other places. The Jesus they preached was likened to the stone the builders rejected—He then became the head of the corner (Acts 4:11). Paul was followed from city to city by Jews who stirred up the prejudices of people against him, simply because he was preaching Christ to the Gentiles. Demetrius appealed to the idolatrous prejudices of those worshipers of Diana and caused the mob to create a demonstration in Ephesus that lasted for two hours. There is no appeal that will more readily create the reaction of violence then the appeal to the offended prejudices of man, especially—listen—especially when those prejudices are deeply rooted in the traditions of a people.

Prejudice is opposed to truth. The word itself, prejudice, means a judgment or an opinion or an overt leaning without just grounds and before sufficient knowledge. Literally, it means to judge before or to prejudge, that is, to judge before one obtains full evidence or facts or knowledge; and in so doing the mind of the individual becomes closed to the truth or the facts in the matter. This statement is true in anything, certainly not simply in matters of religion.

Prejudice may be the result of many things. For instance, it might be the result of fixed opinions that draw on a person's training or family background, or the tradition by which he is accustomed to thinking, or by which he is accustomed to living. Prejudice has been opposed to truth in the scientific realm. It took centuries to convince men of the truth that the earth was an ellipse, that it was round. Men have been slow to accept the truth of scientific discovery in the fields of medicine. In whatever field of learning or progress we may enter, we can see the force of prejudice as it stands opposed to truth. Now this mind set is true, both in obtaining truth and in using it after it is thoroughly proved. Prejudice often stands as a wall built against truth, trying to prevent its influence or use, no matter how advantageous or valuable it may be. In religious thinking, this attitude is true.

We would like to say today that in the religious world, in the world of religious study, there is no prejudice; but that statement simply is not the case. There is no field of thinking where prejudice is a greater enemy than in religion. There is no place where people yield more readily to the appeal of prejudice, to blind their eyes to truth, than in the realm of religion. Certainly, it should not be so, but we must face the reality. Religious prejudice blinds men to the plain and evident truths of the Bible. It hardens men against the conviction that comes from the study of all the evidence of the inspiration of God's great Book. It blinds men to the divinity of Jesus Christ, the Son of God.

Scarcely any force has exerted so destructive an influence among men than religious prejudice. It has caused the most bitter feelings and the most severe persecutions and sufferings to be found in the history of mankind. It is one of the gravest enemies of the church of our Lord today. Prejudice has separated, and has kept separated, the so-called Christian forces of our generation. If prejudice could be thrown aside and overcome, the barriers of sectarianism and denominationalism in our country would be broken. Unity and peace and love as the Bible teaches would be permitted to prevail among all professed believers in Jesus Christ. Is it not true that so often the prejudice of men is more precious in their religious thinking than all of the truth that can ever be preached?

But rather than lament the problem, we should be searching for the solution. What is the solution? I propose that truth alone can overcome prejudice. The truth of God's word is the only answer. Truth—God's truth as found in the Bible—is a solution to the prejudices that now plague the hearts of men. Jesus says, "Thy word is truth" (John 17:17). Again, Jesus says, "And ye shall know the truth, and the truth shall make you free" (John 8:32). God's truth is able to free us from doubt and from prejudice. Obedience to God's truth will free us from sin (Romans 6:17-18) and make us the children of God.

The truth of God's teaching will cause us to rise above the religious divisions of the world today. It would cause us to bring to pass the Lord's prayer for unity in John 17. It would give attention to Paul's exhortation in 1 Corinthians 1:10: "Now I beseech you, brethren, by the name of our Lord Jesus Christ, that ye all speak the same thing, and that there be no divisions among you; but that ye be perfectly joined together in the same mind and in the same judgment." Obedience to the truth of God, as found in the New Testament, will silence the sectarian cry, "I am of Paul; and I of Apollos; and I of Cephas; and I of Christ." The statement that follows the question, Is Christ divided? should not be forgotten (1 Corinthians 1:12-13).

Denominational prejudice can be overcome only through adherence to the truth of the gospel of Jesus Christ. Let us be like Nathaniel. Philip simply told him, "Come and see." Nathaniel went to the Lord to find out for himself. I would today that those of you who are listening would make up your mind to look in the Bible for yourself. Matters not what the preacher or the priest or whoever may say. Each of us needs to decide 'I am going to look in that book for myself.' Let us find out for ourselves what the Lord has taught us. There is nothing mysterious about Christ or the church that He established. The whole of Christianity is based upon the open and free understanding of the gospel of Christ and of the work and the worship of the church that He established.

Churches of Christ would echo the words of Philip: "Come and see." We would today that it could sound throughout this entire area and in fact throughout the world simply: "Come and see." The Bible is our only creed. Please come and see. The gospel of Jesus Christ is the power of God to save and that alone we believe. Please "Come and see." The obedience of the gospel in faith and repentance and a confession of faith and a burial in baptism for the remission of sins is the means by which we are added to the church of our Lord (Acts 2:47).

# *Ways to Obey*

Good morning, everyone. We are indeed grateful for this Lord's Day that allows us the privilege of preaching the gospel of Christ. We trust that you realize, as David said, this is the day "Which the Lord hath made. We will rejoice and be glad in it." We trust this day is finding you in preparation to attend the house of the Lord to worship and to serve Him according to the ancient pattern. The Bible does lay down the fact that this is the Lord's Day and upon this day His people ought to assemble to worship. Many times, we find, however, that many disobey the Lord because they do not worship on this day. This is an amazing thing when we stop to ponder what the Bible teaches because it teaches that man is the crowning work of God's creation.

> In the beginning God created the heaven and the earth" so the first verse of the Bible declares. Every part of the creation had been formed and then God said, "Let us make man in our image, after our likeness: and let them have dominion over the fish of the sea, and over the fowl of the air, and over the cattle, and over all the earth, and over every creeping thing that creepeth upon the earth. So God created man in his own image, in the image of God created he him; male and female created he them (Genesis 1:26-27).

He surrounded man with everything necessary for his happiness and well-being; yet man is the only part of God's creation to dishonor Him. Even "The heavens declare the glory of God; and the firmament sheweth his handywork" (Psalm 19:1). The Father has shown His concern in His care for the birds and the flowers, and He even notes the fall of the sparrow. And He has abundantly shown His love for man, but man has so frequently and flagrantly disobeyed Him. God always blessed the obedient.

> Jeremiah, the prophet, says, "We will obey the voice of the Lord our God, to whom we send thee; that it may be well with us, when we obey the voice of the Lord our God" (Jeremiah 42:6).

Samuel says, "Behold, to obey is better than sacrifice, and to harken than the fat of rams" (1 Samuel 15:22).

Solomon says, "Let us hear the conclusion of the whole matter: Fear God, and keep his commandments: for this is the whole duty of man. For God will bring every work into judgment, with every secret thing, whether it be good, or whether it be evil" (Ecclesiastes 12:13-14).

"Jesus Christ became the author of eternal salvation unto all them"—that do what?—"that obey him" (Hebrews 5:9).

Jesus says, "Whosoever heareth these sayings of mine, and doeth them, I will liken him unto a wise man" (Matthew 7:24).

The Holy Spirit directed John to write in Revelation 22:14, "Blessed are they that do his commandments, that they may have right to the tree of life, and may enter in through the gates into the city."

Jesus says, "Not every one that sayeth unto me, Lord, Lord, shall enter into the kingdom of heaven; but he that doeth the will my Father which is in heaven" (Matthew 7:21).

Just as mankind is faced with a beautiful promise that God will always bless the obedient, we find in the same book that He has always condemned the disobedient. The Apostle Paul in Colossians 3:6 says, "The wrath of God cometh on the children of disobedience." Paul speaks of Christ's second coming:

The Lord Jesus shall be revealed from heaven with his mighty angels, In flaming fire taking vengeance on them that know not God, and that obey not the gospel of our Lord Jesus Christ: Who shall be punished with everlasting destruction from the presence of the Lord, and from the glory of his power (2 Thessalonians 1:7-9).

Jesus says, "Every one that heareth these sayings of mine, and doeth them not, shall be likened unto a foolish man, which built his house upon the sand" (Matthew 7:26). It is evident that our eternal destiny— listen—our eternal destiny depends on our decision. Man is a free moral agent, and each of us must make our own decision about whether to obey or disobey God. But Judgment Day is coming: "For we must all appear before the judgment seat of Christ; that every one may receive the things done in his body, according to that he hath done, whether it be good or bad" (2 Corinthians 5:10). Each will be judged and each will be blessed or condemned for all eternity. You must decide for yourself. How are you living today? Are you obedient or are you disobedient to God? It is difficult to think of man, whom God has so loved and so abundantly blessed, as being disobedient to the One who created and preserved him. Yet more today—at this moment—are being disobedient than are being obedient by living and worshiping in ways not authorized in His word.

Satan caused the first disobedience on earth, and he is causing men to disregard God's law today. Whether we admit it or not, he is the cause of all kinds of disobedience to God. But let's raise this question: How can we disobey God? In what way is it possible? I would like to point out that it is possible for every command of God to be disobeyed in at least five different ways. Each one can be fatal to the soul if the sinner does not repent. And man does not have to practice all of them to be eternally lost because James tells us in chapter 2 verse 10, "For whosoever shall keep the whole law, and yet offend in one point, he is guilty of all." We need to exercise care that we stumble not into any of these ways of disobedience.

**First Way to Disobey**: Some stubbornly and willfully refuse to obey God. As bad as that may sound, that is an absolute fact. Jesus says, "You will not come to me, that you might have life" (John 5:40). He also says "O Jerusalem, Jerusalem, thou that killest the prophets, and stonest them which are sent unto thee, how often would I have gathered thy children together, even as a hen gathereth her chickens under her wings, and ye would not!" (Matthew 23:37). In Hebrews 10:26-27, "For if we sin willfully after that we have received the knowledge of the truth, there remaineth no more sacrifice for sins, But a certain fearful looking for of judgment and fiery indignation, which shall devour the adversaries." Men have refused to accept Christ today. They deliberately cast aside the word, the Bible. They will not believe in Him that they might have life. They will not repent. They will not be baptized as He teaches. They will not live as He directs or worship Him in spirit and in truth (John 4:24). They will not seek first the kingdom of God, and His righteousness (Matthew 6:33). Can such people hope to be saved? Theirs shall be judgment and fiery indignation of God, for they will not obey the gospel of Christ.

**Second Way to Disobey**: But there is another way in which we may be disobedient to the Lord. We may add to the commands that God has given, and so disobey Him. God says in Deuteronomy:

> Ye shall not add unto the word which I command you, neither shall you diminish ought from it, that you may keep the commandments of the Lord your God which I command you (Deuteronomy 4:2).

> Proverbs 30:6 says, "Add thou not unto to his words, lest he reprove thee, and thou be found a liar."

> Revelation 22:18 teaches, "If any man shall add unto these things, God shall add unto him the plagues that are written in this book."

This principle has always been the rule of God and so it is today. But many are not satisfied with what God has written, and they feel His word is not complete. They rely on other books and teachings and feel that additional prophecies and continuing revelations are necessary. The plan of salvation and items of worship and simplicity of Christian living that the Bible gives are simply not enough for some people. They think the church of our Lord is not sufficient in organization and the Lord's name is inadequate. So, denominational creeds, and churches, and names, and organizations have been brought into existence; with each addition has been a disregard for the will of God. Peter says, "According as his divine power hath given unto us all things that pertain unto life and godliness, through the knowledge of him that hath called us to glory and virtue" (2 Peter 1:3).

The word transgress—listen—the word, transgress means to go beyond the limits set by law. John says, "Whosoever committeth sin transgresseth also the law: for sin is the transgression of the law" (1 John 3:4). When a man adds to God's law, he sins. It is just that simple. Christ's way is enough. His law is the perfect law of liberty (James 1:25). What a marvelous thing it would be if all would lay aside all things that man's wisdom has devised and be content simply to obey the will of Christ as it is written in the New Testament. Do you realize, today, that if that were to occur, all the division and the strife of sectarianism could be forgotten? For people become members of denominations by doing things that are not found in the Bible. Men are divided today over the things that have been added to the law of God. The distinguishing doctrines of denominationalism are not found in the Bible. Their distinguishing names have all been added to what the Lord gave. The Lord directs Paul to write to the church in Colosse:

> And let the peace of God rule in your hearts, to the which also ye are called in one body; and be ye thankful. Let the word of Christ dwell in you richly in all wisdom; teaching and admonishing one another in psalms and hymns and spiritual songs, singing with grace in your hearts to the Lord. And whatsoever ye do in word or in deed—*now listen to this*—whatsoever ye do in word or deed, do all in the name of the Lord Jesus, giving thanks to God and the Father by him (Colossians 3:15-17).

Evidently, obedience in these matters would make us pleasing in God's sight and united in our work for Him in the one body, the Church of Christ (Romans 16:16).

**Third Way to Disobey**: Not only do we disobey the Lord by adding to His word, some disobey God by taking away from His commands. You recall that Israel was warned not to diminish from the commands of Jehovah (Deuteronomy 4:2). In Revelation 22:19 we read, "If any man"—please notice the all inclusive statement—"If any man take away from words of the book of this prophecy, God shall take away his part out of the book of life, and out of the holy city, and from the things that are written in this book." Now, why will these things occur? Our part shall be removed from the book of life, from the holy city, and from the things written in this book—if we do what?—if anyone takes away from the words of the book of this prophecy. Now this rule still holds true today. When men begin to tell you there is part of the Bible they do not believe, you may rest assured they are not pleasing in God's sight. It all stands or it all falls together.

The virgin birth of Christ, the miracles He performed and those of His apostles, are as much a part of God's plan as that Jesus loved us and died for us. When men say you do not have to be baptized to be saved or you can be saved and go to heaven without being a member of the Lord's church, they are simply taking away from God's commands and striving to get others to disobey God in the same way. Labeling commands as nonessential is the work of disobedience. Men must still remember the command on Pentecost, "Repent, and be baptized every one of you in the name of Jesus Christ for the remission of sins, and you shall receive the gift of the Holy Ghost" (Acts 2:38). The church is the body of Christ, and He is savior of the body (Ephesians 5:23). Notwithstanding, all the arguments of man to the contrary, the Book still states that the church is the body and that Jesus is the Savior of the body. The example of the Lord's Supper in the worship of God on the Lord's Day (Acts 20:7) still stands. 1 Corinthians 11 still remains upon the pages of Holy Writ, and it always will. The ages have not changed it. All the disobedience of man has not made it less binding on us today.

**Fourth Way to Disobey**: But another way in which we may disobey God is by substituting other things in place of what God has commanded. Now we can add to it, we can take away from it or we can substitute things for what God has plainly taught. King Saul and the people of Israel bring back from the battle with the Amelekites, the king and sheep and oxen, things that should have been utterly destroyed. He said he brought them to sacrifice unto the Lord in Gilgal. Samuel says, "Hath the Lord as great delight in burnt offerings and sacrifices, as in obeying the voice of the Lord? Behold, to obey is better than sacrifice." We need to remember that every day of our lives. Regardless of what we may do, no matter how great our sacrifice or how grandiose our service, no matter if we are willing to traverse land and sea to work for the Lord, <u>if we do not obey Him and do it as He said, it is not acceptable</u>. "Behold, to obey is better than sacrifice, and to harken than the fat of rams" (1 Samuel 15:21-22).

In the Apostle Paul's day in Galatia, they were inclined to the same sin, therefore he says, "Though we, or an angel from heaven, preach any other gospel to you than that which we have preached unto you, let him be accursed" (Galatians 1:8). Jesus speaks of such disobedient ones saying, "But in vain they do worship me, teaching for doctrines the commandments of men" (Matthew 15:9). Other things have been, from time to time, substituted for plain commands of God. Jesus says, "Except ye repent"—now this is the Lord speaking to us—"Except ye repent, ye shall all likewise perish" (Luke 13:3). But in spite of that statement, men have substituted works of penance of their own liking. Paul says, "We are buried with him by baptism into death" (Romans 6:4). But in spite of Paul's statement, men have placed instead, sprinkling or pouring, as forms of baptism. The Lord has ordered in worship, "singing and making melody in your heart to the Lord" (Ephesians 5:19). But instead, mechanical instruments of music and robed choirs have taken the place, to a large degree, of congregational singing where each makes melody in his own heart before the Lord. The Lord's organization of congregational autonomy for the church has been supplanted by powerful forms of organization and political machinery to govern professed followers of Christ. Man seems to be able to find some substitute for any command of God. I guarantee you that regardless of what the command may be in the great Book, you may find today, not only one, but many substitutes for whatever that command may be. But we must remember to obey is better than sacrifice, no matter how elaborate or great the form of the substitutionary sacrifice that we are putting in its place.

**Fifth Way to Disobey**: I will mention one other way we can disobey the Lord: by neglect. So many know the will of God and intend to obey some day, but they die in disobedience. Since you and I began this study this morning, thousands have passed into eternity, many unprepared to meet God—people who fully intended to obey the Lord but didn't do it. We know to do good; but when we know it and we do it not, James says in chapter 4 verse 17, that such is sin. Many, like the five foolish virgins, will not be ready when the bridegroom comes. Possibly more members of the Lord's church shall fail in this regard than in any other. The sinner says I believe in Christ and I intend to be baptized but never gets around to it. He says I know I should be a Christian and he is almost persuaded. It is still true as we sing "almost cannot avail, almost but lost"—what a terrible, terrible doom. I wonder if it is your intention but you are making no real—no real effort to carry out that intention. How many are saying today, "I intend to go to church, I intend to live better, I intend to help in the Lord's work?" My friend, tens of thousands have died before you in this carelessness and neglect and have gone on to a Christ-less eternity.

In Hebrews 2:3, the apostle raises the great question, "How shall we escape, if we neglect so great salvation?" The answer is apparent. Men rob themselves of the blessings of salvation, of the companionship of fellow Christians, of the beauty and the blessings of Christian worship, of the hope and comfort that can fill the hearts of God's children; and die without God and without hope, all through plain neglect. Many a place on the pews of the house of worship in the Lord's church will be vacant today because some now listening will neglect to attend the worship. Many an assembly will mark absent those who are sinning through neglect. Many a child—listen to me—many a child is growing up as a monument of neglect on the part of some parent to take his little hand and lead him to the church of the Lord! When that child's feet turn to the paths of sin and delinquency, many times it is because those of us who are older have neglected to do our duty. God's will must be obeyed. God will not overlook our sins of neglect. We need to repent of them and seek the Lord's forgiveness in obedience to His commands.

In conclusion this morning, every command of God may be disobeyed by a refusal to obey, by adding to what He has given, by subtracting from His commands, by substituting something else for what God has deemed best, or by neglecting to obey what we know is right and best. We need to guide our hearts and lives and examine our every act to be sure that we are not among the disobedient. Remember this word, "Blessed are they that do his commandments, that they may have right to the tree of life, and may enter in through the gates into the city" (Revelation 22:14).

# *Our Unbelief*

Faith is such a small word; yet it divides the world's population into two vast segments: believers and unbelievers; that is, those who truly believe in God and those who do not. Faith in Christ creates a further division among believers and differentiates between those who believe in God but also accept that God has a Son, Jesus Christ. It separates between those who believe in Jesus and those who do not. Jews and Muslims, by and large, believe in God but do not believe in Jesus Christ. In John 14:1, Jesus says to the Jews, "Ye believe in God, believe also in me."

There are countless millions today, who live and die as complete unbelievers. How sad to think about those dying in a faithless condition, without faith in Jesus Christ. Doubtless, many believers will be condemned on Judgment Day, but the Bible says the unbeliever is condemned already (John 3:18). Why? They are condemned already because they have not believed in the only begotten Son of God. When our Lord was here on earth, He referred to a faithless generation in His own time. There have been many such generations since; and, I suppose, there are many yet to come. Thus, it is important to spread the testimony about Jesus to as many as we can so that all may have the opportunity to have faith in Him.

How do we get faith? How do we have a greater faith? What does the Bible mean when it says, "Lord increase thou our faith, help thou our unbelief?" Certainly the Bible has an answer, and we want to let the Bible speak. Without the Bible's testimony, there can never be faith. There is no great theological mystery about faith as some would have us to believe nor is faith something bestowed miraculously on some while it passes others by. The Bible teaches that God is no respecter of persons. He does not give messages to some while withholding them from others. He does not come down and do things for some that He does not do for others. From time to time, we hear testimonies that describe blinding lights, visions at night, whispering in the ears; indeed, we will often hear about someone telling us that they received special messages from God.

In fact, the New Testament is quite clear about how faith comes. In Romans 10:17, Paul says, the Bible says, "Faith cometh by hearing, and hearing by the word of God." And he has just said in verse 14, "How then shall they call on him in whom they have not believed? and how shall they believe in him of whom they have not heard? and how shall they hear without a preacher?" Paul, inspired by the Holy Spirit, did not seem to know anything about flashing lights, visions, whisperings in the ears, etc. Faith in Christ came by testimony of God's witnesses, according to God's word. This is the same as the faith we exhibit in anything else. Faith is simply belief. That definition brings it down to its essence. Faith is belief, trust, and confidence; and it can apply to anything. We might have faith in a person. The Germans, at one time, had a strong misplaced faith in Hitler. We might have faith in a politician. We might have faith in our medical advisor. We might have faith in our teacher.

It is the object of our faith that makes the difference. The process of faith is not hard to understand. Faith is based upon credible testimony, and that testimony for spiritual things comes by the word of God. There have been some beautiful, wonderful things written about faith: about the measure of faith, the quality of faith, the power of faith, but in all of these things its validity depends on the source. We might believe equally as strong that Caesar was assassinated as we would believe that Jesus was crucified. But the effects upon us of those two events will differ greatly. The object of our faith also regulates the degree and quality of our faith. It takes less faith to believe that a ninety-five year-old man, recently very ill, has died than it takes to believe that another man has lived to the ripe old age of 140 years. The testimony has to be stronger in the latter case. The testimony about Jesus Christ is exhausting, it is flawless, it is comprehensive, and it is incontrovertible.

God confirmed the testimony with wonders, divers miracles, and signs. Supernatural events required supernatural confirmation. The Gospel of John contains much about faith. John ends his gospel in with this information:

> Many other signs truly did Jesus in the presence of his disciples, which are not written in this book: But these are written, that ye might believe that Jesus is the Christ, the Son of God; and that believing ye might have life through his name (John 20:30).

That is such an important passage. Not to believe those truths is to make God a liar, according to 1 John 5:10. Listen to the passage again, "Many other signs truly did Jesus in the presence of his disciples, which are not written in this book." We are assured, however, that we have everything in this book that pertains to life and godliness. He says, "these are written"—let the world hear this message, let the church hear this message—"these are written that you might believe that Jesus is the Christ, the Son of God; and that believing you might have life through his name." Faith is the starting point.

Faith, where it exists, stems from our first real encounter with the claims of the Lord Jesus Christ. Paul, in Chapter 11 of Hebrews reminds us in verse five, that Enoch did not die, but he was translated directly into heaven because he pleased God so much; and that without faith it is impossible to please God (Hebrews 11:6). So, if we desire to please God, we must have faith. Faith is not optional if we want to please God. The scripture says, "He that cometh to God must believe that he is, and that he is a rewarder of them that diligently seek him." Thus, if we come to God, it must be upon this solid basis: that we believe in God, that we believe in Christ, and that we have confidence in His promises. This, then, is faith. It is the starting place for any kind of fellowship with Jesus Christ.

The Apostle Peter exhorts that we should, with great diligence, add to our faith. Please notice that faith is the foundation of it all. Add to your faith, virtue, knowledge, temperance, patience, godliness, brotherly kindness, and love. But we have to start with what? We have to start with faith without which we cannot please the God. Once conscious of having faith in Christ, what do we do then? If our faith is real, if it is of the required intensity, it will prompt us to change our way of living. It will move us to repentance, and it will urge us to obey Christ in the new birth and baptism, being immersed for the remission of our sins and rising to walk in newness of life.

After all, this is what the Apostle Peter told them on the day of Pentecost (Acts 2), when they cried out "men and brethren, what shall we do?" having been convicted by the preaching of the gospel. This faith came because Peter taught them they had crucified the Son of God and put Him to an open shame. So they said, "what shall we do?" Peter responds, "Repent and be baptized every one of you in the name of Jesus Christ for the remission of sins, and ye shall receive the gift of the Holy Spirit" (Acts 2:38). In Acts 22:16, he says, "Arise, and be baptized and wash away thy sins, calling on the name of the Lord."

But, we are not going to do any of those things if we do not have the proper faith in the Jesus Christ. We have to know something about the scriptures before we are going to make changes in our lives. Maybe that's one of the reasons we see so few changes being made in this day and time. Another question is Once we have such a faith, can we lose it? Is it impossible for it to wane? Can it be increased? Can we measure its strength? Can we measure its weakness? These are all questions that ought to concern us; and keeping in mind that faith is the assurance of things hoped for; it is the proving or foundation of things not seen, according to Hebrews 11.

We can learn a lot about faith by looking at some of the remarks made on the subject by the Lord Himself and by His apostles. For example, Jesus referred to the disciples as "ye of little faith." Stephen was referred to as a man full of faith. Jesus reckoned the faith of a certain Roman centurion, a Gentile, was greater than anything He had encountered among the people of God, the Jews. Paul talks to Timothy about faith un-fained and talks about those who had cast off their first faith. He also mentions the case of Hymeneus and Philetus, whose false teaching would overthrow the faith of some. Paul also talks about some who were weak in the faith; and some who, although poor in material things, were rich in faith.

When Jesus cured the two blind men—listen—when He cured the two blind men, He touched their eyes saying, "According to your faith, be it unto you" (Matthew 9:29). Their eyes were opened. By contrast when Jesus' own disciples were frightened by the storm, He asked them, "Where is your faith?" Paul hoped for an increase in the faith of the Corinthians, and he prayed that he might be able to perfect that which was lacking in the faith of the Thessalonians; later in his second epistle to them, he thanked God that their faith had grown exceedingly and that their love abounded one toward another.

So it is evident from these passages that our faith can be little or it can be great. It can be overthrown or it can be increased if we are willing to work on it. It can grow or it can wither. Faith, it seems, varies according to the strength and quality of the person. It comes back to the human factor: it depends on us.

Certainly, we have to begin with God's word, and we have to stay with it; but it still will depend on us and how we study and accept it. One might well ask: What is the test of our personal faith? How do we know if our faith is some small thing, or if it is mighty? How can we tell? Several interesting passages will help us in exploring this matter of faith.

We are indebted to James for the answer, for he warns that our faith may not only be diminished but it may actually be dead. He says, "Faith without works is dead." It can be dead as a corpse. James 2:18 addresses those who may think that faith and works are two completely separate virtues. Of equal worth is that a person is at liberty to choose one or the other as he pleases. James shows that this idea constitutes a complete misunderstanding of the position and that the two—faith and works—are inseparably linked. It is not a question of you have faith and I have works, but it is I will show you my faith by my works. Thus, our works, or lack of them, becomes the measure of our faith. That is, no works, no faith.

Faith is not, of course, only a question of our believing certain facts, but it includes trust in the author of our faith, our Lord Jesus Christ. If that confidence is present, it will prompt us to carry out Jesus' will. After all, James says, "The devils also believe" (James 2:19). We believe in Jesus, we share the belief of many others. The thing that separates us is repentance; it is the fact that we will allow our faith to work by love.

Our faith for Christ induces us to allow our faith to have expression in deeds for Him; but James goes further and says that if our faith culminates not in good works, it is not true faith at all or it is deceased faith. Then He says, "But wilt thou know, O vain man, that faith without works is dead?" (verse 20). James then quotes the case of Abraham as a classic case of where the works of Abraham are proof of his tremendous faith. The trust in God that Abraham had extended even to his being prepared to slay his only son. Hebrews 11 refers to Abraham and many other worthies who allowed their faith to dictate their actions or their works.

Some have suggested that Paul and James were not in agreement on the subject of faith, but this surely is nonsense. Paul merely compliments James when he says, "faith without works or works without faith will not justify." Neither one alone is going to do. Faith is truly a New Testament thing, for the word hardly ever appears in the Old Testament, and it refers specifically to faith in the Lord Jesus Christ. Certainly, these are such important points to understand about this matter of faith. I think about the little portion in the old song that says, "Oh, for a faith that will not shrink, though pressed by many a foe, that will not tremble on the brink of poverty or woe."

# *Providence of God*

Occasionally, someone wants to know, if there is such a thing as God's providence and can we know that we are in the providence of God? I want us to look this morning in Romans 8:28. This passage has its setting in the teaching concerning the grace of God and the assurance of the Christian's hope, through the Holy Spirit. Let us mark how the apostle says these words: "And we know that all things work together for good to them that love God, to them who are the called according to his purpose." Now this is the word of God; this is His eternal truth as revealed by the Holy Spirit, through the Apostle Paul. We are reminded of John 3:16, where the Bible says, "For God so loved the world, that he gave his only begotten Son, that whosoever believeth in him should not perish, but have everlasting life." In Romans 5:8, we read, "But God commendeth his love toward us, in that, while we were yet sinners, Christ died for us." God so loved our souls that He sent His own Son, the sacrifice for our sins, to die upon Calvary for each and every one of us. The world has never known so great a love except in Jesus Christ our Lord. It has given all of us the privilege of sharing that love by becoming children of God.

When we consider how sinful we are, we think also of the great love of God in heaven who is long-suffering toward men. God desires that all repent of their sinful ways, whatever they are and, in obedience to the Lord's gospel, be baptized for the remission of their sins as we read in Acts 2:38. Thus, God's love has provided the means of escape from the wages of sin, which is death (Romans 6:23; Romans 6:3-4; Acts 2:38).

The Apostle Paul in 2 Corinthians 5:14 says, "The love of Christ constraineth us"; in other words the love of Christ in reality leaves us no choice—such love surely calls forth the best that we are able to give. But God's love is not only a great promise; it is far-reaching. God says in Galatians 3:26-27, "For ye are all the children of God by faith in Christ Jesus. For as many of you as have been baptized into Christ have put on Christ." Now think about what he is saying. He wants us to know that we should love Him enough to be obedient and to be born into His family. But God's love does not stop at this point. God's love provides for His children to be heirs of His eternal promises. "The Spirit itself beareth witness with our spirit, that we are the children of God: And if children, then heirs; heirs of God, and joint-heirs with Christ; if so be that we suffer with him, that we may be also glorified together" (Romans 8:16-17).

Certainly, the Bible teaches that God cares for His children, even though sometimes we hear people doubting that; and perhaps in times of duress and trouble we wonder if Jesus does care? Is He really concerned about us and what happens? He taught us to cast all our cares upon Him, the Bible says, "For he careth for you" (1 Peter 5:7). In Hebrews 13:5-6, we have His great promise, "I will never leave thee, nor forsake thee. So that we may boldly say, The Lord is my helper, and I will not fear what man shall do unto me." Every day of their lives, God's children can have the assurance of the providence of God. Jesus teaches that as He provided for the fowls of the air and the lilies of the field, so also He would care for His children. The Master teaches His disciples to pray saying, "Give us this day our daily bread" (Matthew 6:11). Jesus says that God notices the fall of every sparrow and numbers the hair on every head (Matthew 10:29-30). So God knows every need, and He is able to supply our needs for every day. He will supply those things that are good for His children.

We are reminded of the words of Luke, as he is giving us the parable of the midnight visitor in which explains that a man, because of his importunity, is able to get his friend to get up and give the things he needs. Luke 11:13 reads, "how much more shall your heavenly Father give the Holy Spirit to them that ask him?" God has not treated the world as one who winds up a clock or a watch and leaves it all alone to run down. He has not treated us as a parent who would desert the tiny baby to be exposed to the perils of life unaided. God has created us all, and His spiritual children are also created in Christ as newborn babes as we can read in Ephesians 2:10 and 1 Peter 2:2.

The tenderness of His affection, like that of the parent, comes to each one of those spiritual babes in Christ. Further, that spiritual child grows deeper in love for the Father. It is so true, as James says— listen—"draw nigh to God, and he will draw nigh to you" (James 4:8). The experience of life only deepens the appreciation of the Christian for the understanding heart of God. The closer he draws to God, the nearer he finds God is to him. Let us look at the text again:

"we know that all things work together for good." Now the text does not say, we think, or we hope, or we wish, or some of the best minds agree. The Holy Spirit chose for Paul the expression, we know, and left no room for doubts or fears or uncertainties. Therefore, because of all the evidence of faith in Paul's teaching and in his life, we accept his words. And notice how inclusive his words are. Every event of our life, not just a part of it, but the God of our salvation and the God of our eternal hope is able to have part in the everyday events of those who love Him and who are called according to His purpose. These are some amazing promises given to His people.

Furthermore, we read, we know that all things work together, for good. The events of life are in the hands of God. He can fit them together so that the ultimate end may be good. You remember the case of Joseph, as he spoke to his brothers who had so mistreated him, he says, "You meant evil against me; but God meant it for good" (Genesis 50:20) (RSV). So there is a double agenda of what we see happening here, but there is a God in heaven who is working for His children. We know that all things work together for good.

Some events in life, when taken separately are not necessarily to our immediate liking, but they can work to the end for good. I am sure all of us can think of some things that have occurred in our lives that we wonder how could it possibly—how could that possibly have been for our good. It may be pointed out that salt alone does not taste very good but blended into the food, gives flavor and zest to the food, does it not? So also, some of the trials of life may seem difficult; and to the unbelieving, they may taste bitter. But to the Christian, God's hand can blend those trials with such love as to lead to the good of his soul. Now we are not talking about Satan, we are not talking about sin, we are not talking about evil, but we are talking about all those things that are being discussed here in Romans 8; and he certainly is talking about trials and afflictions and troubles, all manner of things.

Paul mentions these things that happened in his life: trials, misfortunes, pain, loss, disappointments, all of those things. In fact, the apostle says, "The things that happened to me have fallen out rather unto the furtherance of the gospel" (Philippians 1:12). I am glad Paul said that. I am sure at the time, he could not possibly have seen how those things could be to his good, but later, as he looks upon them he says, "The things that happened to me have fallen out rather unto the furtherance of the gospel."

Maybe you are asking this morning, well what is good? He says that God is able to work all things together for our good. What is good? I suppose most people would answer that good is health or wealth or fame or something related to these. Good with God, is not necessarily material. Good with God is a spiritual value. God is good, and all that promotes the development of God within us is good, but anything that separates from God is not good, whatever it may be, whether fame or fortune or pleasure. Sometimes the greatest tragedy of life for a man's spiritual well being lies in his acquiring money or fame and some measure of worldly success. We have all known situations like that.

Stop to consider the young man who came running to Jesus and fell down before Him, saying, "Good Master, what shall I do that I may inherit eternal life?" (Mark 10:17). This young man must have been likable, for verse 21 says, "Then Jesus beholding him loved him." But the tragedy was that his possessions kept him from following Jesus. Many a person has failed to heed these words in Luke 12:15: "For a man's life consisteth not in the abundance of the things which he possesseth." Think about this passage, a man's life does not consist in the abundance of the things he possesses. In other words, the inventory of one's goods is not necessarily the inventory of one's soul. Poverty is sometimes better than riches. Poverty may have its inconveniences, but it may be the means of helping an individual to reach beyond himself; and that could in many instances mean his eternal happiness. Times of sickness, times of hospitalization have often been times for reflection in which the Christian has been made to see the hand of God. As someone has so well stated it, when you are lying on your back, the only way you can look is up.

The rain must fall—the rain must fall so that the flowers may bloom, or the fruit be formed and grow to maturity. The sunshine may be more beautiful to our liking than the clouds or the falling rain, but the fact is, the rain must also come if we would have a harvest. It goes without saying this morning God truly loves us enough to see us suffer for good. I am not sure that means a great deal in the times in which we live but think of this as a parent, God loves His children enough to see them suffer for their good. He may even chasten them or discipline them for their profit that they may be partakers of His holiness (Hebrews 12:10). The person, who is undisciplined, is immature and undeveloped. If we would share the love of God, we must also share the discipline of His grace. This is life. We understand this fact if we stop to really ponder what is being said. In

Hebrews 12, the Bible insists that if we are without chastisement, then we are illegitimate and not sons. The Bible plainly declares God chastens every son that He receives. So we know it is good for us.

We must learn to say with the Apostle Paul—listen—"I can do all things through Christ which strengtheneth me" (Philippians 4:13). Paul was given a thorn in the flesh. Three times he asked the Lord to remove that thorn. Certainly, Paul knew how to pray, none of us doubts that. And he knew you can do a lot of things with a thorn except ignore it. He asked the Lord to help him to remove this thorn, but the Lord did not remove it. It helped him know the sufficiency of the grace of God, and he learned to trust in God more than in himself.

Surely, we are people who realize that God is able to provide. A Christians's faith causes him to know that God can give the best for each day. He can remove from our hearts the cares and the worries of life that trouble so many. We can look up to God, and we can know He looks down on us. How many times have we seen the protecting and providing hand of God in the lives of His children? We have seen it in our own lives and how many times have we been moved to say that God's hand was in it. God is able to open the door of opportunity and He can close the door of temptation. He can provide a way of escape, according to 1 Corinthians 10:13. He can grant healing in sickness and give the balm of His love in time of sorrow. Those are some great truths that we all desperately need to remember.

It is wonderful to know His providence. It is wonderful to be a Christian in view of the judgment when the Lord, in righteousness, shall judge all men. According to Acts 17:31; the Bible definitely teaches there will be a judgment. God has committed all judgment to the Son, and He will judge all men. It is wonderful now when we lie down and when we rise up, when we are asleep and when we are awake, just to know that we are under the providential hand of God. I think of the statement one of the old-time preachers used to say, "The Lord has let me blow along in front of the winds of providence." I think that is beautiful, and I think that should be the desire and the prayer of every one of us, that God would allow us to be under His providential hand and to blow along in front of the winds of providence.

The child of God can know that whatever happens today all through life can be made for our good by the providence of God. By faith, if we are Christians, we can put our hand in the hand of God and our lives in His care. But this promise is not just for everyone—it is for "them that love God." Here is the thing that we must stop to ponder: What does it mean to love God? The Bible says in John 14:15 that, "If you love me, keep my commandments." This promise is for those who have responded to the Great Commission and who are in Christ. They are members of the body of Christ.

How do you become a member of the body of Christ? Jesus says, "Go ye into all the world, and preach the gospel to every creature. He that believeth and is baptized shall be saved" (Mark 16:15-16). The Bible states in Acts 2:47, that the Lord added the saved to the church. When we are willing to accept the gospel: we believe it, we are willing to repent of our sins, we are willing to confess that Christ is the Son of God, we are willing to be immersed for the remission of our sins according to Acts 2:38; then the Lord will add us to the church. When we have obeyed these commands, then we are a part of those who love God and have been called according to His purpose. This is what the word of God says; so we must know that we are not just talking about an indiscriminate situation. This teaching means we must obey Him.

Question this morning: Do you love God? Have you been called according to His purpose? The apostle tells us that we are called by the gospel (2 Thessalonians 2:14). That gospel would tell us what to do to be saved. The Lord says, "If you love me, keep my commandments" (John 14:15). Each one of us—listen—each one of us must believe in Christ, repent of his sins, confess his faith in Christ as the Son of God, and be baptized for the remission of sins. Each one of us must decide whether he loves God enough to obey His commands in becoming a Christian and in living a godly and Christ-like life. Each one of us must decide whether he would claim the precious promises of God's providence. The promise of God is available to all. It is open to anyone who would accept it and lay hold on the hand of God's providence in obedient love. Today, we pondered the question and now what is your answer? Do you have the faith to say, today, where He leads me I will follow, and then arise and take up your cross and follow Him?

# The 23$^{rd}$ Psalm

The 23rd Psalm is one of the most wonderful pieces of literature in the entire world. It has been read by more people than any other Psalm in the Bible. It is wonderful that in times like these we still have this grand piece from the word of God that we might meditate upon it and study briefly the message it contains.

> The Lord is my shepherd; I shall not want. He maketh me to lie down in green pastures: he leadeth me beside the still waters. He restoreth my soul: he leadeth me in the paths of righteousness for his name's sake. Yea, though I walk through the valley of the shadow of death, I will fear no evil: for thou art with me; thy rod and thy staff they comfort me. Thou preparest a table before me in the presence of mine enemies: thou annointest my head with oil; my cup runneth over. Surely goodness and mercy shall follow me all the days of my life: and I will dwell in the house of the Lord for ever.

It is evident that the man who wrote this psalm was not only a man of God, he was not only conversant with the life of the shepherd, but he had been a shepherd. There is a wonderful relationship that exists between a shepherd and his sheep. They live together day and night, and they share hardships and joys together. David did not say the Lord is YOUR shepherd. He says the Lord is MY shepherd. This statement shows the special relationship David had with the Lord. Since he understood the close relationship between the shepherd and his sheep, he had a special insight into the relationship that existed between the Lord as the Good Shepherd and His sheep. I had the privilege recently of reading an account of an individual interviewing a professional sheepherder from the old country. Since this great piece of literature from God's word is based primarily on this situation, I would like to share some ideas that I will be most beneficial to us.

The story goes like this: Out in the Nevadan desert Fernando D'Alfonso, the Basque, roams with his sheep. He is a herder who is employed by one of the big sheep outfits of the West, one that has more than thirty bands of one thousand ewes each on the open range under the charge of competent shepherds. D'Alfonso, now sixty years of age and weathered by the years of exposure to the sun and wind, came to this country from the mountains of northern Spain more than thirty years ago. He is rated as one of the best sheep rangers in the entire state; and he should be, for back of him is the definite history of twenty generations of Iberian shepherds; and there are legendary tales of direct ancestors who herded sheep in the Pyrenees sheepwalks even before the time of Christ. D'Alfonso is more than a sheepherder, however, for he is a patriarch of his guild, having knowledge of traditions and secrets that have been handed down from generation to generation, just as were those of the gold beaters, the copper workers, the Damascus steel temperers, and other trade guilds of the pre-medieval ages. Despite his long absence from the homeland, spending most of his time far from human habitation and unusual means of modern communications, he is still full of the legends, the mysteries, the religious fervor, and the believing symbolism of his native hills.

The writer states—as I sat with him one night under the clear, starry skies, his sheep bedded down beside a pool of sparkling water, he suddenly began a dissertation in a jargon of Greek and Basque. When he had finished, I asked him what it was he had just repeated. After much dreamy meditation, he began to quote in English the 23rd Psalm. "David and his ancestors," said D'Alfonso, "knew sheep and their ways and he had translated a sheep's musing into simple words. The daily repetition of the Psalm filled the sheepherder with a reverence for his calling. He can look into the eyes of his charges and see the love and affection that David saw. Our guild takes the lodestone of its calling from this poem. It is ours. It is our inspiration. It is our bulwark when the days are hot or stormy, when the nights are dark, and when wild animals surround our bands. Many of its lines are the statement of the simple requirements and actual duties of a holy land shepherd in the care of his flocks, whether he lives at the present day or followed the same calling 3,000 years ago. Phrase by phrase it has a well-understood meaning for us."

**"The Lord is my shepherd; I shall not want."** Sheep instinctively know that, though they have been folded for the night, the shepherd has planned their grazing trip for the morrow. He may take them back over the same range; it may be he will go to a new grazing ground. They do not worry. Since his guidance has been good in the past, they have faith in the future, knowing he has their well-being in view.

**"He maketh me to lie down in green pastures."** Sheep graze from around 3:30 in the morning until ten o'clock. Then they want to lie down for three or four hours and rest. When they are contentedly chewing their cuds, the shepherd knows they putting on fat. Consequently, the good shepherd starts his flock out in the early hours with the rougher herbage moving through the morning into the richer, sweeter grasses and finally to a shady place for its forenoon rest, into the best grazing of the day. Sheep, while resting in such happy surroundings, not only have had the benefit of the good late eating; but, also have the atmosphere of the fine green pastures around them, giving them natural incentive for contentment and growth.

**"He leadeth me beside the still waters."** Every sheepman knows that sheep will not drink gurgling water. There are many springs high in the hills of the holy land whose waters run down to the valleys, only to evaporate in the desert sun. Although the sheep greatly need the water, they will not drink from the tiny, fast flowing streams until the shepherd has found a place where rock or erosion has made a little pool or else has fashioned out with his hands a pocket sufficient to hold a bucketful.

**"He restoreth my soul: he leadeth me in the paths of righteousness for his name's sake."** Holy land sheep are led, rather than driven in their wanderings in search of food. They exceed in herding instinct the Spanish Marino or the French Rambouillet. Each one takes its place in the grazing line in the morning and keeps the same position throughout the day. Once, however, during the day each sheep leaves its place and goes to the shepherd. The sheep approaches with an expectant eye and a mild little baa, whereupon the shepherd stretches out his hand and the sheep runs to him. He rubs its nose and ears, scratches its chin, whispers words into its ears and fondles it affectionately. The sheep in the meantime rubs against the shepherd's leg. If the shepherd is sitting down, the sheep is at his ear and rubs its cheek against his face. After a few minutes, the sheep returns to its place in the feeding line refreshed and made content by its personal contact.

**"Yea though I walk through the valley of the shadow of death, I will fear no evil: for thou art with me."** There is an actual Valley of the Shadow of Death in Palestine, and every sheepherder from Spain to Dalmatia knows of it. It is south of the Jericho road, leading from Jerusalem to the Dead Sea and is a narrow defile through the mountain range. It is necessary to go through this valley to get from the old-time feeding grounds of David and his tribesmen to those of Abraham and his descendants. Its sidewalls are more than 1,500 feet high in places, and it is about four and a half miles long. Yet, it is only ten to twelve feet wide at the bottom. The grade of the valley slopes from about 2,700 feet above sea level at one end to nearly 400 feet below sea level at the other. The valley is made dangerous because its floor has been badly eroded by waters from cloudbursts. Actual footing on solid rock is so narrow that in many places a sheep cannot turn around. Mules have not been able to make the trip for centuries, but herders have maintained the passage for their stock. Gullies as much as seven and eight feet deep have been washed in many places. It is an unwritten law of the shepherds that flocks must go up the valley in the morning and down toward the evening time, else there would be endless confusion should flocks meet in the defile.

**"Thy rod and thy staff they comfort me."** About halfway through the valley, the walk crosses from one side to the other at a place where the two-and-one-half-foot-wide path is cut in two by a gully that is eight feet deep. One section of the walk is about eighteen inches higher than the other; so in their journey down the valley, the sheep have to jump upward and across. On the opposite trip, they jump downward. The shepherd stands at this break and urges, coaxes, pets, encourages, and sometimes forces the the sheep to make the leap. As a result of slippery walkways, poor footing, or tiredness, sheep occasionally miss the jump and land in the gully. The shepherd's rod is immediately brought into play. The old-style crook is encircled around a large sheep's neck or a small sheep's chest, and is lifted to safety. If the more modern narrow crook is used, the sheep is caught just above the hooves and lifted up to the walk. Many wild dogs lurk in the shadows of the valley, looking for prey; and when they are encountered, the shepherd's staff comes into active use. After a band has entered into the defile, the lead sheep may come upon a dog. Unable to retreat, the leaders baa a warning; upon hearing this sound, the shepherd, skilled in throwing the staff, hurls it at the dog, who may be 150 feet away. In all but very rare instances, he succeeds in knocking the dog down into the washed-out gully where it is easily killed. Climatic and grazing conditions make it necessary for the sheep to be moved to the Valley of the Shadow of Death for seasonal feeding each year. They have learned to fear no evil, for their master is there to aid and to guide them across and to protect them.

**"Thou preparest a table before me in the presence of mine enemies."** This statement seems to convey a boastful, rather pagan thought of gloating over the hunger of others while feasting in the favor of Jehovah; however, David's meaning is simple when one knows the conditions of the holy land sheep ranges. Poisonous plants abound, and they are fatal to grazing animals. The most noxious is a species of whorled milkweed. It sinks its roots deep down in the rocky soils, and its eradication during the centuries has been impossible. Each spring the shepherd must constantly be on guard as the plant is on some of the best feeding ground. When the shepherd finds the milkweed, he takes his awkward old mattock, goes ahead of the flock, and grubs out every stock and root that he can see. As he grubs out the stocks, he lays them on the little stone pyres, some that were built by shepherds in Old Testament days; and by the morrow they are dry enough to burn. In the meantime, the field having been freed from poisonous plants, the sheep are led into the newly prepared pastures; and in the presence of their deadly plant enemies, they eat in peace.

**"Thou anointest my head with oil; my cup runneth over."** This phrase has been interpreted many times as symbolic of fullness of reward for well-doing. Literally, it is a statement of a daily task of a professional sheepherder in a most time-honored calling. At every sheepfold, there is a big earthen bowl of olive oil and a large stone jar of water. As the sheep come in for the night, they are led along the side of the wall to the gate in one end. The shepherd lays aside his woolen robe and his staff, but rests his rod across the top of the gateway just higher than the backs of the sheep. As each passes him in a single file, he quickly examines it for briers in the ears, snags in the cheek, or weeping of the eyes from dust or scratches. When he finds such conditions, he drops the rod across the sheep's back and the sheep steps out of line until all the sheep have been examined. Out of his flock of 250 ewes, the shepherd may find one or a dozen needing attention. Each sheep's laceration is carefully cleaned. Then the shepherd dips his hand in the bowl of olive oil and anoints the injury gently, but thoroughly. He is never sparing with the oil. Along with the treatment, the shepherd's love words are poured into the sheep's ears in sympathy. Then he dips the cup into the large jar of water, kept cool by evaporation in the unglazed pottery, and is brought out, never half-full, but always overflowing. The sheep will sink his nose down into the water, clear to the eyes if fevered, and drink until fully refreshed. Then, the sheep enters the sheepfold, and the next injured sheep is treated. When all the sheep are at rest, the shepherd places his rod in the corner, lays his staff on the ground, wraps himself in his heavy woolen robe, and lies down across the gateway facing the sheep for his night's repose. After all this care, can a sheep be blamed for soliloquizing in the twilight, as translated by David?

**"Surely goodness and mercy shall follow me all the days of my life: and I will dwell in the house of the Lord forever."** It is with confidence that David closes this, one of the grestest pieces of literature ever to have been penned and one of the most comforting passages ever to come from human hand. David was probably an old man when he wrote this Psalm. He had witnessed the tragedies and disappointments of his own life; but, in the midst of all that, he had come to know God—he knew Him as the sheep know their shepherd and as children know their parents. They know them in the sense that they have complete trust that their real needs will be taken care of. Throughout the Psalm, notice David's positive attitude. When he uses the word "surely" in this conclusion, he is not using a wishful "surely." Rather, it is a confident "surely" because he had such complete faith in God and in His promises.

If we allow it to, this Psalm can inspire us to have a greater faith than we have ever had before. It can inspire us to depend on God more than ever before for our spiritual needs and to make the decision to come to God in obedience to His word. David could know that he would dwell in the house of God forever because he had given himself to God and, because of that decision, he had come to a place of peace with God. We, too, can find peace with God and have the kind of confidence David had when we make the firm decision to follow the instruction God has given us in His word. I want to read with you one more time the 23rd Psalm:

> The Lord is my shepherd; I shall not want. He maketh me to lie down in green pastures: he leadeth me beside the still waters. He restoreth my soul: he leadeth me in the paths of righteousness for his name's sake. Yea, though I walk through the valley of the shadow of death, I will fear no evil: for thou art with me; thy rod and thy staff they comfort me. Thou preparest a table before me in the presence of mine enemies: thou annointest my head with oil; my cup runneth over. Surely goodness and mercy shall follow me all the days of my life: and I will dwell in the house of the Lord for ever.

# Power to Become the Sons of God

Good morning, everyone. We invite your attention today to the study of "Power to Become the Sons of God." One of the most striking passages in the New Testament is found in the book of John. In speaking of the coming of Jesus Christ, the divine writer says:

> He came unto his own, and his own received him not. But as many as received him, to them gave he power to become the sons of God, even to them that believe on his name: Which were born, not of blood, nor of the will of the flesh, nor of the will of man, but of God (John 1:11-13).

Let us first observe the setting of this great text. John opened his gospel with this declaration, "In the beginning was the Word, and the Word was with God, and the Word was God. The same was in the beginning with God." These sublime lines are a match for those of Moses, in Genesis 1:1, where he says, "In the beginning God created the heavens and the earth." So, our Lord was declared to be of the same eternal and divine nature as God—One of the three in the beginning: God, Christ, and the Holy Spirit.

His greatness is emphasized: "All things were made by him; and without him was not any thing made that was made. In him was life; and the life was the light of men" (John 1:3-4). Christ is the true life, and it was to Him that John the Baptist bore witness. Then Jesus came to the earth, and the Bible declares, "And the Word," which was Jesus, the Son of God, "was made flesh, and dwelt among us" (verse 14). He was born of the virgin, and He took upon Him the form or fashion of the fleshly body of man (Philippians 2:7-8). In that body dwelt the Son of God, known as the Son of Man, during the more than thirty-three years of His life here on earth.

I would like you to notice this morning the various reactions to His coming. First, the world did not know Him. Verse 10 declares, "He was in the world, and the world was made by him, and the world knew him not." Even with all of His greatness and power, the world did not recognize Him or acknowledge Him. Number two, He came unto His own and His own received Him not. This statement evidently referred to His own people of Israel. They existed as a people protected and preserved by God for the coming of the promised one of Israel, Jesus Christ, of the seed and lineage of Abraham and of David. But when He came, they received Him not. Please notice it was said of them, they knew Him not, but simply and pathetically, they received Him not.

Their prophets had spoken of Him and foretold His coming. Their institutions and sacrifices all had foreshadowed His coming and His Messiahship and His sacrificial death. However, like the wicked husbandman of the Lord's parable recorded in Matthew 21, they did not receive the Son. Rather, they rejected Him and set out to destroy Him. The very people, who should have been ready most to receive Him, of them it was said, "He came unto his own and his own received him not."

Thirdly, some did receive Him, and of them John says, "But as many as received him, to them gave he power to become the sons of God, even to them that believe on his name" (verse 12). This passage is a picture of the whole life of our Lord. When He was born in Bethlehem, there was no room for Him in the inn, nor during the three years of His ministry. The people were divided over His work and His teaching. Appraisals of His message and this passage cannot be forgotten, "He came unto his own and his own received him not" (verse 11). But I would like to point out this morning, that those who received Him were the ones who believed on His name. It is said of them, "To them gave he power to become the sons of God, even to them that believe on his name." This scripture has often been misquoted and misunderstood. Outstanding men have stumbled upon this passage. In commenting on verse 12, John Wesley said, "the moment they believe, they are sons." But the scripture does not agree with Mr. Wesley's idea of how to become the sons of God. Many of the religious teachers of the twentieth century have failed to understand the meaning of this text.

The passage does not say—please notice—does not say that believing in Christ was the only thing required to become the sons of God. Further, it does not say, "They were made sons of God the moment they believed." We must not conclude that all believers were sons of God, for example in John 12:42-43, "Nevertheless among the chief rulers also many believed on him; but because of the Pharisees they did not confess him, lest they be put out of the synagogue: For they loved the praise of men more than the praise of God." Surely, no one would contend that these chief rulers were made sons of God and members of the family of God, the church of our Lord, when they had neither enough faith in Christ, nor enough love for God to confess Christ as the Son of God, even though it was said of them, "they believed on him."

Another example is found in James 2, where the writer says, "the devils also believe and tremble." If faith in Christ were all that was required to make sons of God, then the devils would be sons of God, for they, too, are said to believe. Let us read again the text. John 1:12 says, "But as many as received him, to them gave he power to become the sons of God, even to them that believe on his name." These believers were given power to become sons of God. The word power means right, privilege, or authority. It is found 102 times in the New Testament. W. E. Vine in his *Expository Dictionary of New Testament Words* says that it means the right to exercise power, the right to act. Christ has given not sonship itself, but the power to become the sons of God. Marvin Vincent, in his *Word Studies in the New Testament*, defines power as the right; and points out that it means liberty of action, and then he says the Greek word for power is not merely possibility or ability, but legitimate right derived from a competent source, the word. The conclusion may then be stated that believing in Christ within itself does not make a person a child of God, but the believer in Christ has the right—the power—to act or the liberty to take the action that will make him or her a child of God.

The believer may or may not exercise the privilege given him by the Lord to become a child of God. Many of them have rejected the liberty of action extended to them, and in so doing they have failed to become God's children. God does not force men to become children. Each believer must exercise his own right in obedience to God's truth if he wants to become God's child. Further, some have said that the power, which is the word "power" in the text, has reference to the Holy Spirit. They would have us believe that God sends His Spirit in some miraculous or baptismal fashion to make men the sons of God; however, in Galatians 4:6, the apostle says, "And because ye are sons, God has sent forth the Spirit of his Son in your hearts, crying, Abba, Father." The gift of the Holy Spirit was to those already sons of God, and not in order to make people the sons of God. To this agree the words of the Apostle Peter in Acts 2:38, "Repent, and be baptized every one of you in the name of Jesus Christ for the remission of sins, and you shall receive the gift of the Holy Ghost." The gift of the Spirit and the indwelling of the Holy Spirit are for the children of God.

Does it not seem logical that we search the scriptures to determine how believers can become the sons of God? Since the Lord has given them such a right or privilege, then surely the Lord will give them direction about how to do so. Question: How do men become the sons of God? Let the scripture speak. In Galatians 3:26-27, the apostle says, "For ye are all the children of God by faith in Christ Jesus. For as many of you as have been baptized into Christ have put on Christ." In verse 29 he declares, "And if you be Christ's, then are you Abraham's seed, and heirs according to the promise." The conclusion, then, is clear, the believer in Christ is to be baptized into Christ; and to be in Christ is to be a child of God and heir according to the promise of God in Christ.

Another scripture that is equally plain is John 3:5. Jesus says, "Except a man be born of water and of the Spirit, he cannot enter into the kingdom of God." The new birth by which one becomes a child of God has two parts, 1) the birth of water and, 2) the birth of the Spirit. Both of these are absolutely essential. The birth of the Spirit is brought about by the word of God. In 1 Peter 1:23, the apostle says, "Being born again, not of corruptible seed, but of incorruptible, by the word of God, which liveth and abideth forever." This teaching is made clear in James 1:18 where he says, "Of his own will"—that is the will of God—"begat he us with the word of truth." It is by this means, then, that men are made believers in Christ; and, as believers, they have the right or the power to obey the Lord's command to be born of water. The birth of water has reference to Jesus' command to be baptized. He says, "He that believeth and is baptized, shall be saved" (Mark 16:16). Baptism is a burial in water and then a resurrection to walk a new life, according to Romans 6:3-7.

Let us consider Colossians 2:12-13. The apostle says, "Buried with him in baptism, wherein also ye are risen with him through the faith of the operation of God, who hath raised him from the dead. And you, being dead in your sins and the uncircumcision of your flesh, hath he quickened together with him, having forgiven you all trespasses." Now, let us read the text again. "But as many as received him, to them gave he power to become sons of God, even to them that believe on

His name: Which were born, not of blood, nor of the will of the flesh, nor of the will of man, but of God" (John 1:12-13). May we observe: first: these believers had the privilege to become the sons of God. Second: they became the sons of God by being born into God's family. Third: that birth into God's family was a spiritual birth, a birth of God.

I want you to notice the negatives that are set forth in this passage. First: He said not of blood. That is, Israel trusted in their blood of descent—that they were physical descendants of Abraham. But this new birth into God's family is not brought about by descent. It is not a matter of pedigree or history or how illustrious one's ancestors were or are. It is not who your parents were or whether you are Jew or Gentile. It is a new birth brought about by God, regardless of parental background, by faith in Christ as the Son of God. Second: it is not in the will of the flesh that one is born into God's family. This is not a new birth of man's choosing or of man's planning. It is not the product of human purpose. So, we notice, not of blood, not of the will of the flesh. Third: the apostle suggests or teaches that this new birth, making one a child of God, is not of the will of man.

The source of the regeneration is stated: it is of God. Human reasoning is repudiated. The ways of man cannot avail. Men can tell men how to become members of some organization of man, whether they be fraternal orders or religious orders, but only God can exercise His will to tell men how to be born into His family. God will make men children of God. It is by His will that we are begotten by the word of truth (James 1:18). In 2 Thessalonians 2:14, Paul says, "He called you by our gospel." In 1 Peter 1:23, Peter says we are begotten or born again by the word of God. The word of God teaches us in Galatians 3:26-27 that the means of becoming the children of God is: one, faith in Christ; two, baptism into Christ by which we put on our Lord. God's family is the church. May we never forget this fact. It is not the old family of Israel. It is the church of the living God, the pillar and the ground of the truth (1 Timothy 3:15). God's family as the body of Christ, over which Christ is the head and of which He is the Savior (Ephesians 1:23, 5:23). In speaking of Christ in Ephesians 3:15, we are told the whole family in heaven and earth is named. Therefore, God's family is to bear and to wear the name of Christ. This is God's plan for our salvation today.

In conclusion this morning, let us say this: That every child of God should live just such a life as will yield honor and glory to our Father in heaven and to our Lord Jesus Christ. As children of God, it is our privilege to worship, to serve God in His spiritual house, the church. We should never conduct ourselves in such a way as to bring reproach upon the God of our salvation. We should consider the great honor of being the children of God—please listen to me—it is a tremendous honor, one of the highest compliments that has ever been paid to us; that is, that we can be the children of God.

In 1 John 3:1-2, John says, "Behold, what manner of love the Father hath bestowed upon us, that we should be called the sons of God: therefore the world knoweth us not, because it knew him not. Beloved, now are we the sons of God, and it doth not yet appear what we shall be: but we know that, when he shall appear, we shall be like him; for we shall see him as he is."

Our Lord says, "In my Father's house are many mansions. ... I go to prepare a place for you" (John 14:2). May we so use the right or privilege that God has given us to both become the children of God and to be prepared when our Lord shall come again, that we can by the grace of God enter into that heavenly home that has been prepared for all the faithful children of God. Certainly, today, it is our prayer that you will obey the Lord. Today, if you believe in His will, you have the right to become His son in full, by completing your obedience to the gospel of Jesus Christ.

# *Not Far from the Kingdom*

It is during a conversation with a scribe that Jesus reveals there are people in this world who are not far from the kingdom of God. A scribe has come to Jesus and has asked a question hoping to trap and discredit Jesus, but he was so impressed with Jesus' reply that he was quick to admit he had been won over by the obvious wisdom of the Lord's answer. Jesus warms to the integrity of the man and says "Thou art not far from the kingdom of God" (Mark 12:34). How interesting that the scribe had been perceptive enough to recognize the truth when he saw it and that he is honorable enough to admit it. There is hope for all such people in this world; there is hope of their entering the kingdom of God. This remark by Jesus that the man is not far from the kingdom indicates, of course, that the man is not in the kingdom. He is not far from it but was not in it. This idea brings up an interesting thought. This passage suggests there is a demarcation line—that is—there is a line that is set that must be crossed before we can enter the kingdom of God. Jesus could have just as easily have said, glad to see you are in the kingdom; but He did not. Clearly, the scribe had an attitude of mind that is necessary to enter the kingdom, but he has not yet crossed the boundary line.

Paul says to the Christians of Colossae that they have been delivered from the power of darkness and have been translated into the kingdom of God's dear Son (Colossians 1:13). Now think about that statement. These people had obeyed the Lord in that they were delivered from the power of darkness, they had been translated, they had been transferred, and they had been transported into the kingdom of God's dear Son. They had crossed the line from the camp of Satan into the kingdom of Christ.

How far away was the scribe? We do not really know. We cannot tell; but Jesus says, "He was not far." This statement brings up an interesting thought. There must be countless thousands of fine men and women who live and die in a state similar to that of the scribe, not far but not in the kingdom of God. There must be countless thousands of good people who with a little encouragement and knowledge would readily enter the kingdom, but the problem seems to be in reaching them. Where are these people, and how do we reach them?

It surely must be a profitable exercise for us to identify and contemplate the reasons that men and women would shy away from actually crossing the threshold. Some, I suppose, feel they are quite as good as, and in some cases better than, the average church goer. They must feel, therefore, they are in effect already in the kingdom. Some feel, no doubt, that they are living the Christian life. Others believe that living the Christian life would be much too difficult, and they hope to throw themselves on God's mercy on Judgment Day. We have those who feel they are too good and those who feel they are too bad to be a part of the kingdom. Apart from these, there are those who, who through foolish pride, fear what family and friends might say, if they were to cross the line from the kingdom of Satan into the kingdom of God. There are those who are bewildered by the many discordant voices of the religious world; consequently, since they do not know what to believe, they end up suspicious of all different churches and sects and denominations. There are also those who are completely turned off by religious division and those who are completely indifferent to any suggestion that they ought to change their present lifestyle. There may also be many who think that a decent life is equal to being in God's kingdom, and those who would enter but do not know how.

It is my hope that this message may be heard by some who have been described above, that is, they are not far from the kingdom. I want to offer what I pray will be some helpful remarks this morning. I want us to study on the means of crossing the boundary line into the kingdom of God. First of all, before we are ever going to cross—whatever our moral status may be—before we ever cross the line from the kingdom of Satan into the kingdom of God, there must be a strong desire to do so. This point may seem self-evident: if such a desire is not present, all that follows is going to be flawed. The attitude of the penitent must be: speak Lord, for thy servant heareth; and we must regard God as the potter and we the clay. We must also be prepared to enter the kingdom on God's terms and not to seek to enter on our own terms or conditions. May I say to you that these terms are set in concrete in the New Testament, and they are non-negotiable; and they have been for 2,000 years. Jesus is the appointed lawgiver, and we must acknowledge Him in all things—not only acknowledge Him but do so with humility and great deference.

He who wishes to stipulate his own conditions of entry into the kingdom will never enter but will manifest an attitude quite unlike the scribe's and distance himself from the possibility of ever gaining admittance. So, the desire has to be there, the desire must be genuine, and it must be motivated by an eagerness to become a servant of Jesus Christ. It is not unknown for some to join the church just to please their parents, to appear respectable to an employer, or to reach some member of the opposite sex in the congregation. It also is not unknown for some parents to threaten to drop beneficiaries from their last will and testament unless such beneficiaries become members of their church.

There is another big factor about entering the kingdom and determining whether we are there or we are not there; and it is the word, faith. There must be desire, but there also must be faith in God. The rich of this world usually have access to all of the best things in this life, but we can thank God that in this question, those who are terribly poor, have just as ready access to the kingdom as any others; and how grateful we are for that. In fact, in our text from the book of Mark, it is said the common people heard Him gladly. What is required is a true and a very strong belief in God, "he that cometh to God must believe that he is, and that he is a rewarder of them that diligently seek him" (Hebrews 11:6). Without such faith, it is impossible to please God.

When you ponder this teaching, we are reminded of the poor victims of the slave trade who were subjected to great poverty and cruelty in the ships and in the fields; and yet God's praise was so often on their lips, and their faith in God has been an inspiration to us all. Many of the Jews believed in God, but that was not enough. Jesus says, "You believe in God, believe also in me." We must not only believe in the only true and living God, but we must also confess that Christ is His only Son and our Savior. John 3:16 is probably one of the best-known passages in the Bible and rightfully so. Remember, "For God so loved the world, that he gave his only begotten Son, that whosoever believeth in him should not perish, but have everlasting life." God so loved the world that He did what? He gave His only begotten Son, that whosoever believes in Him should not perish. Jesus says, "You believe in God, believe also in me." We must not only believe in the only true and living God, but we must confess that Christ is His only Son, and He is our only Savior.

The verse that follows John 3:16 reveals some important things—listen to it:

> For God sent not his Son into the world to condemn the world; but that the world through him might be saved. He that believeth on him is not condemned: but he that believeth not is condemned already, because he hath not believed in the name of the only begotten Son of God (verses 17-18).

From this affirmation of God's love, it surely follows that atheists and all skeptics who remain in that condition have no prospect of entering the kingdom of God. Active faith in the Lord Jesus Christ is an absolute prerequisite; we cannot cross the line from the kingdom of Satan into the kingdom of God without it. Indeed, it makes a great deal of sense. This truth is so vital that it causes the Lord Jesus Himself to say that those who do not believe on the Son are condemned already—condemned even now before the judgment. Jesus says, "You believe in God, believe also in me."

There is another factor in this crossing the line from the kingdom of Satan into the kingdom of God's dear Son. The crossing requires not only desire and faith; but it also requires repentance for us to cross the borderline between the realm of Satan and the kingdom of Christ. It requires, quite obviously, that we leave our past behind and that we mend our ways. We cannot expect to behave in the kingdom of God as we did in the service of the devil. We cannot—Jesus says—we cannot serve God and mammon. In short, we must drop our former lifestyle and repent of our previous mode of conduct. Surely this is not some mystery. This is the plainest of common sense, it would seem to me. There has been much written about repentance, but perhaps the best and shortest definition of the term was given in Christ's instructions to that woman who was taken in adultery when He says to her, "go and sin no more." How much plainer can it be? How much plainer can repentance be made? It means, go and sin no more.

John the Baptist, you remember, administered baptism of repentance. Those who thronged to receive his baptism were required to confess their sins and to show some evidence of contrition. They were required to bring forth fruit, he says, "meet for repentance." He did not defer to the multitudes who were not far from the kingdom, and they evidently came in thousands. Indeed, those in the city of

Jerusalem came out there. The people from Judah, the entire region round about Jordan, and their consuming desire was to enter the kingdom—they were more than happy to hike those many miles to get to where John was and then to search for him in the wilderness, as well. I think this example points out something we need to note. It illustrates the intensity of their desire to enter the kingdom. It is significant that these people inquired of John as to what form their repentance should take, because they already believed in God, and as to what would constitute the evidence of such repentance.

John suggested that the person who had two coats should give one to him who had none and likewise he who had surplus of bread should give to those who had none. The publicans received the charge that they should exact only the correct amount of taxation from the people. The soldiers were instructed to do violence to no man; neither make any false charges against any (Luke 3:10-14). Think about it, those intent upon entering the kingdom had to change from being selfish and self-centered to being liberal with belongings and sharing their bread and their possessions—and those like the publicans, whose stock in trade was deceit and falsehood, had to stop it. They had to revert to honesty and to fair trading; and those like the soldiers who were men of violence had to espouse gentleness and fairness in all their dealings. There must be few, indeed, who could not see the common sense in repentance. The kingdom of God was no place for violence; it was no place for cruelty or robbery or villainy of any kind. All these things had to be left behind in the kingdom of Satan or the kingdom of darkness; and Peter reminds us that we must not return to these things (2 Peter 2:22). In the most graphic of words he says, "The dog is turned to his own vomit again; and the sow that was washed to her wallowing in the mire."

But now entry into the kingdom would not be accomplished yet. A person may have the desire, he may have faith, he may be determined, and he may repent of his sins; but entry into the kingdom is marked by a conscious act. Now think about it and what we are saying: Entering into the kingdom is marked by a conscious act, which declares to the world that we have crossed the boundary line; and that is our immersion in the waters of baptism. It is not only necessary that the future lifestyle must improve but also that the sins of the former mode of life be dealt with and erased. Up to this point, we have blotted our lives with all kind of problems, and we must start afresh with a new page. We are going wipe the slate clean and start over.

Christ came not to call the righteous but sinners to repentance. Thank God for that. The blood of Christ can cleanse all types and forms of sin, and a man cannot be too deeply dyed in sin to have his sins washed away so that he can enter the kingdom. The dregs of humanity entered, and still enter, the kingdom; and this group includes robbers and murderers, thieves, prostitutes, homosexuals, liars and the like. All had to be washed clean to start life afresh, as guiltless as newborn babies. How can such a marvelous change be accomplished? Do you really believe that it can? Is it possible? It not only can be accomplished but it is accomplished by the power of God, the blood of Christ, and the baptism of the penitent sinner in the watery grave.

Even Paul himself, as he agonized over the enormity of his past sins, especially against Christians, was instructed by Ananias, to "arise, and be baptized, and wash away thy sins, calling on the name of the Lord" (Acts 22:16). The Apostle Peter called upon those who had murdered the Christ, "to repent, and be baptized every one of you in the name of Jesus Christ for the remission of sins, and ye shall receive the gift of the Holy Ghost" (Acts 2:38). These things wait for us upon our willing submission to the holy ordinance of baptism. This is the new birth spoken of by Jesus when He says, "except a man be born of water and of the Spirit, he cannot enter the kingdom of God" (John 3:5). We must all—listen—we must all be reborn in a spiritual birth, of the water and of the Spirit.

Paul reminds the Christians at Corinth that evil men will not inherit the kingdom of heaven. He names off some of the blackest sins that you can imagine, and he says those are not going to inherit the kingdom of heaven. But he goes on to say, "and such were some of you."—looking at the members of the church in Corinth—"And such were some of you: but ye are washed, but ye are sanctified, but ye are justified in the name of the Lord Jesus" (1 Corinthians 6:9-11). So, by the grace and power of God it is possible to wash away our sins, by baptism, no matter how degenerative and evil we might have become.

Few could be as wicked as the Christians at Corinth had been, and yet Paul says they had been washed clean and thereby had been sanctified and justified. So, what is the message? The message is, before we can enter the kingdom of God, we must have a bath, not for the cleansing of the physical body but for the soul. Very few of the thousands who were baptized in the Jordan, came out of the water with clean bodies. That river was muddy and dirty, but their souls had been cleansed whiter than white, whiter than snow, clean and bright, they came forth as innocent as the newly born.

You remember that Paul calls baptism, the bath of regeneration and he says that in Titus 3:5—look at it carefully. In Titus 3:5, "Not by works of righteousness which we have done, but according to his mercy he saved us, by the washing of regeneration, and renewing of the Holy Ghost." Let us take a look at that. The word washing is from the Greek word LOUTRON, and they tell me that this word occurs only twice in the New Testament, and it means a laver or a bath. Regeneration also occurs only twice, here and in Matthew 19:28; and it is from the Greek word PALIGGE, which means a re-creation, a rebirth, regeneration and thus the washing of regeneration literally means the bath of rebirth. How interesting, that the Lord has provided and applies all this teaching to baptism.

So, in order to enter the kingdom of God, we must stop all our unrighteousness of the past, and we must wash away our sins in the waters of holy baptism. We must be immersed in the bath of regeneration. We must be born again, of what? Jesus says of water and of the Spirit. We must emerge from that watery grave to walk in newness of life. You remember that Paul discusses this beautifully at length. He says, "Know ye not, that so many of us as were baptized into Jesus Christ were baptized into his death? Therefore we are buried with him"—listen—"buried with him by baptism into death: that like as Christ was raised up from the dead by the glory of the Father, even so we also should walk in newness of life" (Romans 6:3-4). Paul is saying that we do not walk in newness of life until we emerge from that watery grave.

Sadly, this wonderful and priceless offer, from a benevolent and gracious God, goes largely unheeded and thousands upon thousands are dying in their sins. Go back and look at Mark when you have the time. He commends the attitude of the scribe and says he was not far from the kingdom. I do not know how far away he was, but he was not far. We do not hear any more about this man, and we do not know whether he entered the kingdom or not. It may well be that he died in the state of being not far from the kingdom, or the church. I fear there are many today who are in similar conditions—not far from but not in the kingdom—and they die in that condition. Paul was preaching the gospel to King Agrippa and he said "almost thou persuaded me to be a Christian" (Acts 26:28). Almost is not enough, almost avails nothing. Those who are almost Christians will be almost saved and will almost go to heaven. May the Lord help us be almost and altogether as Paul was. Thank you for listening. It has been our pleasure to study with you the Holy Scripture this day.

# *Predestination*

Good morning everyone. Once again, we have the privilege of studying with you the Lord's word. We are thankful to have in our listening audience those of you who have expressed that you are pleased to hear the gospel. We are grateful to know that we have people who want to know the things the Lord has to say. Today, we will discuss with you one of the doctrines that is being taught in our world that we believe is in opposition to the truth of God; and in turn, we will set forth what we believe the Bible teaches.

It is interesting to think about doctrine in our twentieth century. It is interesting to note that the typical view today is that doctrine really does not matter. Recently, an individual was heard to remark, "I have better things to do than to worry about someone else's doctrine." How typical is this attitude of the average denominational view of doctrine. To them, doctrine refers to the denominational tenant that separates them from another denomination; and since they believe that no denomination is essential to go to heaven, why worry about any doctrine? This idea about the unimportance of doctrine is a far cry from what the Bible teaches. The Apostle Paul says:

> For the time will come when they will not endure sound doctrine; but after their own lusts shall they heap to themselves teachers, having itching ears; And they shall turn away their ears from the truth, and shall be turned unto fables. But watch thou in all things, endure afflictions, do the work of an evangelist, make full proof of thy ministry (2 Timothy 4:3-5).

It is evident, even from a cursory reading of the passage, that sound doctrine is the truth, the word of God. Doctrine is that which is taught. Also, we note that doctrine is always pictured as singular when it comes from God but plural when speaking of men or devils; so we are concerned today with the sound doctrine, or the truth of God.

May the Lord help us to realize that when we speak disparagingly of doctrine we are showing a willful ignorance of the word of God; in fact, we speak against the very works of our God. We cannot separate deity from doctrine. It is an amazing thing that in the world in which we live we have so many doctors who are opposed to doctrine; actually, the basis of the word doctor suggests doctrine. It would be hard to think of a doctor who does not have doctrine (teaching) as respects his own field. But there are those in the realm of religion who claim to be doctors who have no doctrine. The Bible teaches the apostles possessed the doctrine of Jesus Christ. Today, we invite your attention to a special question, and it does involve the doctrine of God's word and some doctrines outside His word.

The question today is this: Did God before the foundation of the world, unconditionally elect, predestinate and foreordain that some should be saved and others lost? Now in importance, this question is not one whit behind any other question we might discuss. It may sound like a dry and uninteresting subject, but please rest assured that the souls of untold thousands and thousands of people rest on the answer to this question. Many have an interest in this subject, and they want to know the truth about it. I am thankful that we can teach just what God has said in His word about this great question. If the Bible teaches the doctrine of foreordination, predestination, and election, I am ready to accept it and begin preaching it. But we learn from our study that God's teachings are contradictory to this theory; thus, I cannot afford to believe and teach it. Rather I must teach just what the Bible says. I believe every listener with the same mind listening to this broadcast will admit that this is the right approach. If the Bible teaches it, we want it; if the Bible does not teach it, we do not want it, regardless of who may espouse it.

For fear that some might not understand just what is meant by the doctrine of foreordination, election, and predestination, I am going to quote from the writings of the ones who believe in it. I am quoting this passage not to prove or disprove the doctrine, but I am quoting it to define the doctrine:

> By the decree of God, for the manifestation of his glory, some men and angels are predestined unto everlasting life and others foreordained unto everlasting death. These angels and men thus predestinated and foreordained are particularly and unchangeably designed; and their number is so certain and definite that it cannot be either increased or diminished. Those of mankind that are predestined unto life, God, before the

foundation of the world was laid, according to his eternal and immutable purpose and the secret counsel and good pleasure of his will, had chosen in Christ unto everlasting glory out of his mere free grace and love without any foresight of faith or good works or perseverance in either of them, or in any other thing, in the creation or conditions or musings moving thereunto.

That, my friends, is the theory. And it is taught by the same ones who say: "God from all eternity did by the most wise and holy counsel of his own will, freely and unchangeably ordain whatever comes to pass." Again, it is said: "God's decrees are the wise, free and holy acts and the counsel of his will. Whereby, from all eternity he hath for his own glory unchangeably foreordained whatever comes to pass, especially concerning angels and men." If we take a good at this doctrine, we can see it is out of harmony with the Bible and all good reasoning; therefore, it simply is not true.

First, if the doctrine here set forth is true, it is impossible for man to err. For if everything that comes to pass is ordained of God, it cannot be wrong. If a man lies, God not only ordained that he should, but he unchangeably foreordained he should before the world began. If he kills, commits adultery, steals, or commits any other crime, it all comes about by God's unchangeable foreordination. Thus, according to this idea, God is the author of every sin that has ever been, is, or ever will be committed. If God foreordains every sin, Jesus misses it in John 8:44, when He says to sinners, "Ye are of your father the devil, and the lusts of your father ye will do." He should have said, if this is true, "ye are of your father, God, and the lusts of your father, ye will do." Is not this sufficient to prove beyond any possible doubt that God has not unchangeably ordained everything that comes to pass?

If one continues to contend that God has ordained everything that has, does, and will come to pass, many complications that cannot be ignored will arise. In the beginning, God gave Adam the command that of the tree of knowledge of good and evil, "Thou shall not eat of it: for in the day that thou eatest thereof thou shall surely die" (Genesis 2:17). But Adam ate the fruit of that tree. If God had unchangeably foreordained everything that comes to pass, He had thus ordained that Adam would disobey His command even before He gave it to him. Can anybody conceive of the God of heaven doing such? He gave Adam the command not to eat, but He could have said to him "now I have already from the foundation of the world unchangeably ordained that you will break this command and then thou shall surely die." How could a just God do such a thing? The fact is He could not and He did not. If this idea were true, it would place God in a ridiculous position in giving the Ten Commandments to the Israelites on Sinai. There He told them not to worship other gods, to remember the sabbath day, to honor father and mother; not to kill, commit adultery, steal, bear false witness nor covet. Yet according to the doctrine, He had unchangeably foreordained from the foundation of the world, hundreds of years before the Decalogue was given, that they should disobey these very commands. Then, after they broke them, He punished them for doing so. Now, I ask, is there any kind of sense or any kind of justice in that? You know there cannot be.

No wonder the land has so many infidels and skeptics in it. The doctrines, commandments, and opinions of men have misrepresented God. Whereas He is holy, just, righteous, and good, He is represented by the doctrines of predestination, as being unholy, unjust, unrighteous, and evil. If I thought that God—listen to me—if I thought God was the kind of character this theory represents Him to be, I would not work to build up His cause, but with every bit of energy in my body and soul I would fight it—and, I believe I would be right. But I know God is not that kind of character. Therefore, in every way I can, I want to build up His cause among men, and with the Psalmist, I say, "Thy word is a lamp unto my feet, and a light unto my path" (Psalm 119:105). "The entrance of thy words giveth light; it giveth understanding unto the simple" (Psalm 119:130). Again, "My lips shall utter praise, when thou hast taught me thy statutes. My tongue shall speak of thy word: for all thy commandments are righteousness" (Psalm 119:171-172).

Many places in the Bible declare that God is righteous. Listen to some of them: "The righteous God trieth the hearts and reins" (Psalm 7:9). "For God is in the generation of the righteous" (Psalm 14:5). "The judgments of the Lord are true and righteous altogether" (Psalm 19:9). How different these words are from the idea of predestination that says God commands people not to do certain things, yet He has already foreordained they will break His commands and be punished as a result. If He did that, how could His judgment be true and righteous? Psalm 145:17 reads, "The Lord is righteous in all his ways, and holy in all his works." We—Christians or sinners—need to realize that every doctrine in God's word, every passage, every word is in harmony with this one great truth. How could such be said of the Lord if He does as some think He does?

But let us look at the other side of this theory. The other side of this theory teaches that God, before the foundation of the world, elected, predestined, and foreordained that some men should be saved and others lost regardless of their faith, good works, or perseverance. The question for us to settle this morning is: Is that doctrine true? It is a doctrine, but is it a doctrine from God, or is it one from men? No doubt, thousands of listeners are bothered about this teaching, and they want to know what the Bible says. Jesus says in John 17:17, the "word of God is truth" and that truth can set us free.

If God selects one man to be saved and another to be lost without any conditions on their part, how and why does He make the selection? I know there are many points in some of God's commands that I do not understand (Deuteronomy 29:29). For example, I cannot understand how that dipping seven times in the waters of Jordan had anything to do with the cleansing of Naaman's leprosy, other than his faith in God and obedience to His command (2 Kings 5). The same is true with the Israelites, looking at the brazen serpent and being healed (Numbers 21). But the doctrine of foreordination and predestination tells us that no faith or obedience is involved in God's selecting one to be saved and the other lost. If that be true, I still question how God makes the selection. If God were to unchangeably foreordain—listen—if He were to unchangeably foreordain and predestinate that I should be saved and another should be lost without any conditions on my part, He would without a doubt be a respecter of persons. The Bible plainly says He is not.

Peter says in Acts 10:34-35: "Of a truth I perceive that God is no respecter of persons: But in every nation he that feareth him, and worketh righteousness, is accepted with him." Does that sound as if God is a respecter of persons or that He will save unconditionally? It rather sounds like the very opposite. It promises salvation to one who fears Him and works righteousness. Paul gives more teaching that upsets the foreordination and predestination theory: "Tribulation and anguish, upon every soul of man that doeth evil, of the Jew first, and also of the Gentile; But glory, honor, and peace, to every man that worketh good, to the Jew first, and also to the Gentile: For there is no respect of persons with God" (Romans 2:9-11). If the Bible is true, and it is, the theory we have explained this morning is not true.

Paul, through inspiration, tells us that the one who commits sin will be punished from the presence of the Lord and the one who does righteousness will be blessed. The apostle also says about the subject:

> And whatever you do, do it heartily, as to the Lord, and not unto men; knowing that of the Lord ye shall receive the reward of the inheritance: for ye serve the Lord Christ. But he that doeth wrong shall receive for the wrong which he hath done: and there is no respect of persons (Colossians 3:23-25).

This teaching is clear as it is in Ephesians: "And, ye masters, do the same things unto them, forbearing threatening: knowing that your Master also is in heaven, neither is there respect of persons with him" (Ephesians 6:9). So, we know the Lord is no respecter of person. If in the Lord's word, there is a single condition laid down for the salvation, the doctrine of predestination is entirely upset. Are there any conditions for salvation? Indeed there are. Jesus says in Luke 13:3, "Except you repent, ye shall all likewise perish." Again, Jesus says in Mark 16:16, "He that believeth and is baptized shall be saved; but he that believeth not shall be damned." Thus, faith and baptism are conditions upon which salvation is based.

Again, in John 3:16, Jesus says, "For God so loved the world, that he gave his only begotten Son, that whosoever believeth in him should not perish, but have everlasting life." Here the Lord makes belief a condition for salvation. He does not mention foreordaination by God from before the foundation of the world. Jesus says, "That whosoever believeth and is baptized shall have eternal life." The Lord again lays down a condition. In Philippians 2:12, Paul says, "Work out your own salvation with fear and trembling." How could they work out their own salvation if God worked it out before the world began? Or, how could they work out their own salvation if God unchangeably has foreordained that they should be condemned? They could not. In 2 Corinthians 5:9, the apostle says, "Wherefore we labor, that, whether present or absent, we may be accepted of him."

Much more might be about this subject. But I hope the things said this morning are sufficient to cause you to take a close look at the doctrine of predestination. The Bible simply does not teach this doctrine. We invite your questions or your comments if you would like for us to pursue a greater study of this subject.

# *The Lord's Day*

Today is the Lord's Day. It is an important day to every Christian. It was on the first day of the week that our Lord Jesus Christ came forth from the tomb. In Mark 16:9, we read, "Now when Jesus was risen early the first day of the week." It was very early in the morning, the first day of the week that the women went out to the tomb of Jesus. They found a young man clothed in a long white garment who says, "Ye seek Jesus of Nazareth, which was crucified: he is risen; he is not here: behold the place where they laid him" (Mark 16:6). From that morning until this day, the message of the resurrection of our Lord has been the joy of the hearts of all the Christians in every century. The first day of the week has been a day to bring to the minds of Christians the fact of that resurrection.

The Apostle John speaks of the Lord's Day in Revelation 1:10, where he says, "I was in the Spirit on the Lord's day." This term, the Lord's Day, occurs only in this passage in the New Testament. According to Mr. Vincent in his *Word Studies of the New Testament,* this reference is to the first day of the week, the festival of the Lord's resurrection. Mr. Albert Barnes writes, "The term was used generally by the early Christians to denote the first day of the week. Most all Bible students recognize that this is true." The early writers of the first and second century referred to the first day of the week as the Lord's Day. Twice, we find in one of the early writers, the writings of Ignatius, about A.D. 101, where he refers to the Lord's Day as the first day of the week. Pliny, a Roman scholar, who lived in the last of the first century, A.D. 62 to 113, points out the Christian recognition of this day of worship.

Justin Martyr, who wrote in the first part of the second century, describes the Christian assemblies on the first day of the week as times of worship and prayer and a time when the Lord's Supper was eaten and alms were collected. He gives us this reason for this particular day: Christ arose on the first day of the week. Irenaeus lived in the last of the second century. He writes of the Christian worship saying, "The Lord's resurrection may not be celebrated on any other day than the Lord's Day and on this alone can we observe the breaking off of the pascal feast." In the fourth century a well-known writer said, that it was called the Lord's Day because the Lord rose from the dead on that day. It was the emperor Constantine, who in 321 A.D., declared the first day of the week as the Lord's Day and that it could be considered as a holiday in his entire realm. In so doing, Constantine did not establish the day of worship, but he made each Lord's Day a holiday so that the subjects of his empire might have the privilege of observing the day the Christians had been using as the day of worship for almost three centuries.

Let us observe several facts in regard to the Lord's Day:

1. Christ's resurrection was on the first day of the week, as we pointed out in Mark 16:1-9.
2. Christ appeared with His disciples after His resurrection on the first day of the week, according to John 20:19. The time of his appearance was so designated, even as those appearances on the day of His resurrection had been on the first day of the week.
3. The church was established on the first day of the week. It was the day of Pentecost according to Acts 2. Pentecost was on the day after the Jewish sabbath (Leviticus 23:15-16), thus making it the first day of the week or the Lord's Day.
4. The church met for worship on this day. In Acts 20:7, we are told, "And upon the first day of the week, when the disciples came together to break bread, Paul preached unto them." In 1 Corinthians 16:2, Paul instructs the Christians saying, "Upon the first day of the week, let every one of you lay by him in store as God has prospered him." These two parts of Christian worship, the Lord's Supper and the collection of money, were designated items in the church of the Lord upon the first day of the week. May we say, also, that the early Christians observed not only these items on that day in the church but also they sang psalms and hymns and spiritual songs (Ephesians 5:19). They prayed together (Acts 2:42). Their assemblies were times of exultation and of edification. In 1 Corinthians 14:26, Paul says, "Let all things be done onto edifying." These facts point out the day of worship as the first day of the week and the items they did during their worship

when Christians came together to worship God. It was a regular, weekly observance; and they were to exhort one another not to forsake such an assembly of the saints (Hebrews 10:25).

I would hasten today to add that we must not confuse this day with the Jewish sabbath. The sabbath was on the seventh day of the week. When God gave the sabbath to the Jews, He said, "Remember the sabbath day, to keep it holy. Six days shalt thou labour, and do all thy work: But the seventh day is the sabbath of the Lord thy God" (Exodus 20:8-10). The sabbath was given to the children of Israel after they were delivered from Egyptian bondage. The Bible, in no place, mentions that man ever kept the sabbath prior to this time. In Deuteronomy 5:15, the connection between the deliverance and the sabbath is specifically pointed out. Nehemiah 9:13-14 says it was at Mount Sinai that the sabbath was made known to the children of Israel. The sabbath was a part of the law of Moses, which was given only to the children of Israel. Christ and His disciples observed the sabbath because they were the children of Israel and because they lived under the period of the law of Moses and continued to do so until that law was fulfilled or taken away.

In Ephesians 2:15 we are told how Christ, in His death, abolished in his flesh the enmity, even the law of commandments contained in the ordinances. Colossians 2:14 declares how Christ took the law out of the way, nailing it to His cross. Therefore verses 16 and 17 say, "Let no man judge you in meat, or in drink, or in respect of an holyday, or of the new moon, or of the sabbath days: Which are a shadow of things to come; but the body is of Christ." These things were of the law of Moses, a law that ended when Christ died on Calvary. No longer were they to be judged by that law. It had been abolished; and the gospel of Christ, the perfect law of liberty, had been given to take its place.

The Lord's Day is not the Christian's sabbath. So many times we hear someone using this expression. The sabbath was not commanded for the Christian, but it was given to the Jews. The Christians were taught to keep as their day of worship the first day of the week and not the seventh day. This expression, the Christian sabbath, was formed by those who did not fully understand the fact that the old law commanded the sabbath observance but that the new law in Christ, the law for Christians, the New Testament, commanded the first day of the week as the day of worship. This Bible truth should be impressed upon every student of the Bible, and we should never be allowed to forget it. The Lord's Day came when the church began. That was after the Lord's death, burial, resurrection, and ascension to heaven. Many people seem to remain so confused upon this particular point, that I think it is so necessary for us to study it. I trust that this lesson may be some help for those who may have difficulty with this particular question.

We might raise some other questions about other special days. In the New Testament, the simplicity of the Christian worship was outlined and the Lord's Day was taught as the time when Christians met to worship God. But men soon drifted away. Special times of worship other than the Lord's Day began to be emphasized. The form of their worship was patterned more after their heathen neighbors than after the New Testament. The Lord's plan was laid aside, or at least it was supplemented by special festivals that the Lord had not given.

One of these festivals that was given was called Easter. The observance of Easter was a point of controversy as far back as the beginning of the fourth century. The Council of Nicaea in 325 A.D. attempted to regulate the observance of this day and establish the means of determining the day of the year on which it would be kept by those who observed it. The New Testament does not teach that Easter is a day of worship. The word Easter occurs in the King James Version of the Bible in (Acts 12:4). But in the American Standard Version and the more recent Revised Standard Version, this error has been corrected. The passage has reference to the Passover and not to the festival of Easter, as men know it today. Every Bible student should be aware of this fact, and every Christian must be teaching such things. Christians are to have a greater recognition and appreciation of the importance of the Lord's death and resurrection, than just an annual festival or to ever consider such in the light of the modern-day customs and practices of most religions of our day.

The word Easter is from the Anglo-Saxon Eostre and the German Ostara, the name of the heathen goddess of spring and life. The name was applied to the festival and celebrating the coming of the spring and then was adopted by many as the name of the so-called Christian festival, with the specific purpose of celebrating once each year the resurrection of Jesus. Christians were—I remind you—were taught to worship God each Lord's Day, the first day of every week. Each week, they were to remember the death of Christ and proclaim their faith in the resurrection of the Lord. But each first day of the week was to be a resurrection day to them and not just once a year.

I want you to think with me today about what all Christ's resurrection means. It is the very center and heart of the Christian faith, and upon this truth rests all the other facts of the gospel of Christ. As Paul says, "And if Christ be not risen, then is our preaching vain, and your faith is also vain" (1 Corinthians 15:14). The reality of our salvation depends upon the resurrection. If Christ be not risen, then He is not the divine Son of God and not able to deliver us from sin. If Christ is not risen, there will be no resurrection of the dead at all. The teaching of a life after death and the hope of heaven will all be a myth and all to no avail. But the proof is abundant concerning the resurrection of Christ. The Bible teaches that Christ appeared many times to His disciples after His resurrection. Paul declares to the Corinthians:

> And that he was seen of Cephas, then of the twelve: After that, he was seen of above five hundred brethren at once; of whom the greater part remain unto this present, but some are fallen asleep. After that, he was seen of James; and of all the apostles. And last of all he was seen of me also, as of one born out of due time (1 Corinthians 15:5-8).

The disciples saw Christ ascend to heaven (Acts 1). Their receiving the Holy Spirit on Pentecost is further testimony and proof of the resurrection (Acts 2:33). There was no doubt with them. There should be no doubt in our minds today. Jesus says, "I am the resurrection, and the life: he that believeth in me, though he were dead, yet shall he live" (John 11:25). God has given us the victory through our Lord over death and hell and the grave. When the Lord comes again, He will raise all of the dead (John 5:28-29). All men shall stand before Him in judgment (2 Corinthians 5:10). In the judgment, the Lord will separate the good from the bad, the obedient from the disobedient, and the righteous shall enter into life eternal; but the wicked shall be sent away to everlasting punishment (Matthew 25:31-46).

May we plead with you today, that we might all remember His resurrection every Lord's Day, first by becoming Christians in obedience to the gospel of Christ through faith and repentance and confession of the lovely the name of Jesus and being baptized in Jesus' precious name for the remission of our sins. Then, as Christians and faithfully living as the followers of Jesus, we can prepare ourselves to worship God in spirit and in truth upon each Lord's Day and thus proclaim our unending faith in the Lord's resurrection. We can then point men to the fact: the Lord is coming again. In so doing, we will prepare ourselves for the time when the Lord shall return to receive home His saints. Let us make up our minds that we shall use this day for Him, to be present today for the worship of God at the appointed time, to use this day to worship and to serve God—to use this day to meditate upon God's goodness, to count your many blessings. Serve the Lord, today, upon the Lord's Day. May we close with the prayer and the plea that we may all be ready when the Lord comes? That He will receive us home to heaven in that last great day!

# *Misconceptions about the Church*

Ladies and gentlemen, one more time we are privileged to come to you with the word of God. Today, we would like to study with you the subject, "Misconceptions Concerning the Church of the Lord Jesus." It is a sad thing to be misunderstood. One labors under a tremendous handicap when he is not understood properly. Yet it seems that in every relationship in life many people will be more likely to misunderstand than to understand the truth on any issue, but the most misunderstood institution in the world is the church of Jesus Christ and what it teaches. So, I am choosing today to speak to you on the theme of misconceptions about His church.

Many misunderstand the mission, the nature, and the destiny of the New Testament church—sometimes because of ignorance—for they have have failed to investigate it properly. They are unlike the ancient Bereans who "searched the scriptures daily whether those things were so" (Acts 17). Sometimes misconceptions about the church are because of prejudice. They are like the Pharisees to whom Jesus says:

> For this people's heart is waxed gross, and their ears are dull of hearing, and their eyes they have closed; lest at any time they should see with their eyes, and hear with their ears, and should understand with their heart, and should be converted, and I should heal them (Matthew 13:15).

They have their own preconceived ideas, received by tradition from their fathers.

Let us examine some of these misconceptions. First, many sincere people misunderstand the position of those in the church about the Old Testament. Many accuse us of not believing in the Old Testament scriptures. They charge us with saying they have no place in Christianity since they are superseded by the New Testament. Permit me to make very clear my attitude toward the Old Testament by reading two passages, one from the New Testament and another from the Old: "All scripture is given by inspiration of God" (2 Timothy

3:16). But were the Old Testament scriptures inspired of God? David, the Psalmist of Israel, says, "The Spirit of the Lord spake by me, and his word was in my tongue" (2 Samuel 23:2). It is no wonder the Apostle Peter says, "For the prophecy came not in old time by the will of man: but holy men of God spake as they were moved by the Holy Ghost" (2 Peter 1:21).

Without question, the Old Testament is as true today as it ever was, but Christians are not to regard it as their source of authority in Christian work and worship today. The Hebrew writer says, "God, who at sundry times and in divers manners spake in time past unto fathers by the prophets, Hath in these last days spoken to us by his Son" (Hebrews 1:1-2). In days gone by, God spoke to His people by history, poetry, proverbs, and prophecy by Moses, Elijah, Jeremiah, Isaiah and many others; but today He speaks to us only through Jesus Christ, who is an authority superior to all who preceded Him.

John says, "The law was given by Moses, but grace and truth came by Jesus Christ" (John 1:17). Thus, Paul declares, "We are not under the law, but under grace" (Romans 6:15). Why then was the law of Moses given? Paul both asked and answered that question in these words:

> Wherefore then serveth the law? It was added because of transgressions, till the seed should come to whom the promise was made. ... But before faith came, we were kept under the law, shut up unto the faith which should afterwards be revealed. Wherefore the law was our schoolmaster to bring us unto Christ, that we might be justified by faith. But after that faith is come, we are no longer under a schoolmaster (Galatians 3:19, 23-25).

The Old Testament is a part of God's word; yet it contains the law given to the Israelites and does not—does not apply to us today. It gives many types and shadows that point to Jesus and should be studied diligently by Christians today. It is impossible for one to understand clearly many things in the New Testament without a knowledge of the Old. The Old Testament should be regarded as the greatest of all records because it contains the oldest and only true account of the creation of the world and the origin and development of man. It testifies of Christ and should be used as evidence of the divinity of our Savior. "Search the scriptures; for in them ye think ye have eternal life: and they are they which testify of me" (John 5:39).

The writings of the holy men of old warn us of disobedience. About the Israelites, Paul says, "Now these things were our examples, to the intent that we should not lust after evil things, as they also lusted. ... And they are written for our admonition, upon whom the ends of the world are come" (1 Corinthians 10:6, 11). They sustain our hope: "For whatsoever things were written aforetime were written for our learning, that we through patience and comfort of the scriptures might have hope" (Romans 15:4). Therefore, let no one misrepresent us about the value we place on the Old Testament scriptures. They are a part of God's inspired revelation to man; and, as such, all who desire to please Him must recognize them. It is nothing less than tragic that anyone would feel the Old Testament, the book that played a significant role in preparing the way for the coming of Christ, should be relegated to a state of uselessness—especially since there is no intimation from God that such was His will.

But secondly, many honest but misinformed people misunderstand the church concerning the personality, the nature, and the work of the Holy Spirit. When we preach on the power of the word of God in the conviction of the conversion of the sinner, they accuse us of not believing in the Holy Spirit at all. But this conception is not only due to a misunderstanding of us but it is because they err, not knowing the scripture. No sinner has ever been converted to Christ without the Holy Spirit having some part in that conversion, but the question is—what part? In the parable of the sower, Jesus declares concerning the seed that fell to the wayside: "Those by the way side are they that hear; then cometh the devil, and taketh away the word out of their hearts, lest they should believe and be saved" (Luke 8:12). Notice the expression, "lest they should believe and be saved." The word is Spirit filled, for Jesus says "The words that I speak unto you, they are spirit, and they are life" (John 6:63). When Jesus promises the Holy Spirit to the apostles, He says, "And when he is come, he will reprove the world of sin, and of righteousness, and of judgment" (John 16:8).

On the first Pentecost after the resurrection of Jesus, Peter, being filled with the Holy Spirit, preached the sermon that brought such conviction that they were pricked in their hearts and said to Peter and the rest of the apostles, "Men and brethren, what shall we do?" (Acts 2:37). What brought such conviction? Please read the first part of this verse: "Now when they heard this, they were pricked in their heart." Peter was the preacher, but the Holy Spirit was speaking through him. It was the Holy Spirit that guided the apostles to pen the New

Testament scriptures, and our preaching today is Holy Spirit filled only as it is in harmony with the New Testament. The New Testament teaches that the Holy Spirit operates in the conversion of sinners through the word of God, not independently of the word. In Ephesians 6:17, Paul says, "The sword of the Spirit, which is the word of God." The only sword the Spirit uses in conversion is the word of God.

Where sinners have never heard the gospel, they do not receive the Holy Spirit. Why? Because the Holy Spirit uses the word of God as His instrument of operation. But we must never misunderstand or underestimate the marvelous power of the Holy Spirit through the word. This sword is sharper than any two-edged sword and is living and active and powerful. The Bible teaches it is the power of God to salvation (Hebrews 4:12; Romans 1:16). There is nothing in conversion that the Holy Spirit does that he does not use the word of God to do. That is the reason we are commanded to preach the word. When we preach the word, we are preaching what the Spirit has commanded; thus, by hearing, believing, and obeying the gospel, we are obeying the commands of the Holy Spirit. Therefore, we most assuredly believe that the Holy Spirit operates in the conversion of sinners today. We are misrepresented when it is said, "They do not believe in the work of the Holy Spirit in converting men."

Thirdly, some accuse the church of Jesus Christ of not believing in salvation by grace, charging we believe we can earn our salvation by works. Without exception, members of the body of Christ believe salvation is by the amazing grace of God. Without His grace, unmerited by man's work, man would be without hope and without God. Along with this accusation goes another one: that we do not believe in salvation by faith. The reason for this misconception is that we will not preach salvation by faith only—this teaching is in direct opposition to God's word, for the Bible plainly declares that we are justified, not by faith only (James 2:24). Like salvation by grace, salvation by faith is only possible when man exercises faith and obedience to the commands of the Lord. Paul says, "For by grace are you saved through faith, and that not of yourselves: it is the gift of God: Not of works, lest any man should boast" (Ephesians 2:8-9). Here the writer says salvation is both by grace and by faith. God and man enter into a contract: we are saved by grace, which is God's part. We are also saved by faith, which is man's part. God will not—will not—impose His grace upon anybody. Man must exercise his faith by obeying God's commands to receive God's grace.

Paul declares that "faith cometh by hearing, and hearing by the word of God" (Romans 10:17). Here faith is not God-given. It is exercised on the part of the believer. God will not believe for man. Therefore, we are saved by grace and through faith. Paul says, "And that not of yourselves" (Ephesians 2:8). Certainly, man does not merit or attain salvation without God's merciful and immeasurable grace. We would be without redemption; hence, it is the gift of God. For what is the gift of God? Not grace, for that prompted God to offer the gift. Not faith, for that enables us to receive the gift. How you are saved is the subject under discussion in the passage. So, salvation is the antecedent of it. It is salvation that is the gift of God and not of works lest any man should boast. Man does not earn it. God in His mercy provides it. For everybody?—oh no—but only for those who will receive it through what? Through the obedience of faith.

Fourthly today, some charge those of us in the church of Jesus Christ, as believing in the church more than in Christ. Sometimes, it is expressed: you folks preach too much "churchanity" and not enough Christianity. But, actually, you cannot separate Christ from the church over which He rules as the supreme head. Paul says, "And he is the head of the body, the church" (Colossians 1:18). Hence, Paul further says, "Unto him be glory in the church by Christ Jesus throughout all ages, world without end. Amen" (Ephesians 3:21). The church is the bride of Christ (2 Corthinians 11:2). One cannot speak evil of a wife, without speaking evil of the husband. Neither can one exalt the husband without the wife sharing that honor. In the model family, they rise or fall together. "What therefore God hath joined together, let not man put asunder" (Matthew 19:6). So, it is with reference to Christ and His church that they are inseparably joined.

I would like to suggest also that misconceptions sometimes are offered in this realm—an accusation, I should call it, is offered that we of the church of Jesus Christ do not believe in a religion that is heartfelt—that our religion is the kind that has no effect upon the heart. In contrast, we believe, because the Bible so teaches, that the religion of Jesus Christ is truly a heartfelt religion. My brethren in Christ believe the gospel of Christ must be understood with the heart, believed with the heart, obeyed from the heart, producing a change of heart, a purity of heart, and a holiness of life, all which are surely to be enjoyed in the heart. What is a heartfelt religion actually? With some, a heartfelt religion is a change of heart, with some it is regeneration, with others it is conversion, and still with others it is the direct operation of the Holy Spirit on the heart. But the whole subject of heartfelt religion is made plain in the scriptures when they explain what the heart really is, in a biblical sense. Think with me for a few minutes. What is the spiritual heart? From a biblical point of view, it is not the fleshly lobe, the part within our left breast that pumps blood to the body. David says, "Your heart shall live for ever" (Psalm 22:26). But certainly, then, David was not speaking with reference to the physical heart, for it will die and go back to the dust of the earth with the rest of the natural man. So, it remains that David was speaking about the spiritual entity of man that death cannot disturb.

In exhorting His disciples to lay up treasures, not on earth but in heaven, Jesus says, "For where your treasure is, there will your heart be also" (Matthew 6:21). In the same connection, the Apostle Paul says, "Set your affection on things above, not on things on the earth" (Colossians 3:2). Thus, in one sense the heart of man is his affection as is made clear in 2 Samuel 15:6: "So Absalom stole the hearts of the men of Israel." He stole what? He stole their affections. After His resurrection, Jesus asks His disciples, "Why do thoughts arise in your hearts?" (Luke 24:38). To Simon the sorcerer, Peter says "Repent therefore of this thy wickedness, and pray God, if perhaps the thought of thine heart may be forgiven thee" (Acts 8:22). From these passages, we conclude that the heart of man is his mind, for the heart thinks and a thought is a mental act, and a mental act is the operation of mind. Hence, the heart is the mind as well as man's affection.

We can discuss many matters about the heart: exercise of the heart, nature the heart, character of the heart, change of heart, purification of the heart. But today we have seen that a sinner must understand the gospel of Christ with his heart—that he must believe it with all his heart, obey it from the heart which produces, of course, a change of heart, a purity of heart and such as enjoyed with all the heart. Can you get any more of a man's heart than this into religion? A religion that embraces this much of the heart is definitely a heartfelt religion. This is the religion you can afford to die by; it will enable the saint of God to sing the song of victory in the hour of death. It will cheer our poor weary hearts, as we travel amid the sorrows and joys of this world, looking toward a happy home in the sweet by and by.

In conclusion, we plead with you to take the Bible and examine these statements. If you would like to be associated with Bible-believing people, we invite you to study the word of God with us.

# *The Death of the Righteous*

Good morning, everyone. One more time we enter into a study of God's word. Today I invite your attention to one of the most unforgettable characters in the Old Testament. That individual is a man by the name of Balaam. He is introduced in Numbers 22 as a prophet of God, and his reputation at that time is good. His name is known to Balak, the king of Moab, who says of Balaam: "I wot that he whom thou blessest is blessed, and he whom thou curseth is cursed" (Numbers 22:6). Balak recognized the truthfulness of Balaam's words in the past and wanted him to come and pronounce a curse upon his enemies, for he says, "They are too mighty for me" (Numbers 22:6). But Balak's enemies just happened to be the children of God, the children of Israel. God had blessed them and had brought them up out of Egypt. How could Balaam curse the people whom God had blessed?

You recall that Balak sent the elders of Moab and the elders of Midian with gifts in their hands to ask Balaam to come and curse Israel. Thus, Balaam had to make the decision as to whether or not he would go. Take a good look at the conflict. Balak, the king of Moab, wanted him to curse the people; but God says, "Thou shalt not go with them; thou shalt not curse the people: for they are blessed" (Numbers 22:12). Balaam's first answer to the messengers of Balak was, "Get you into your land: for the Lord refuseth to give me leave to go with you" (verse 13). Balaam was put to the test and how simple it would have been for him to have answered with a positive "No." The Lord had spoken. Balaam knew what was right, but he let his inclination be seen by saying, "The Lord refuseth to give me leave to go with you."

It is a serious thing to tamper with conscience. Balaam understood what he should do, but the temptation was so strong. Balak sent more princes, yet more honorable than before, and Balak says "For I will promote thee unto very great honor, I will do whatsoever thou sayest unto me" (verse 17). When the first temptation was not answered firmly, the second had a stronger appeal; so Balaam became confused in his time of conflict. Please notice that Balaam had some desire to do the right thing—some of his words are worth remembering. His answer to Balak's servant was, "If Balak would give me his house full of silver and gold, I cannot go beyond the word of the Lord my God, to do less or more" (verse 18). As a prophet, he recognized his limitations. He was to speak the word of the Lord, only. He was not to do more or less. This is a lesson many, many people have never learned, but Balaam's attitude emphasizes this great truth.

When he presented his parables, he spoke, not curses but blessings upon those people. Each of the three parables became more forceful and stronger in the statements of God's blessing upon His people. Then he says, "How shall I curse, whom God has not cursed? or how shall I defy, whom the Lord has not defied?" (Numbers 23:8). Balaam spoke those words, "Let me die the death of the righteous, and let my last end be like his!" (Numbers 23:10). Surely, then, he had some desire to do the right thing because he asked that he might die the death of the righteous; however, the tragic result is Balaam failed. He spoke the word of the Lord, but his heart had been swayed to the temptations of Balak. When the temptation was permitted to have its way, even his desire to die the death of the righteous was swept aside.

In Numbers 31:16, we are told it was through the counsel of Balaam that Balak caused Israel to sin, and there was a plague among the congregation of the Lord. The sin of Balaam is mentioned in Jude 11, where we read, "Woe unto them! For they have gone in the way of Cain, and ran greedily after the error of Balaam for reward, and perished in the gainsaying of Core." This reference places a woe upon those who, like Balaam, seek reward for teaching sin. Peter rebukes evil workers in 2 Peter 2:15-16: "Which have forsaken the right way, and are gone astray, following the way of Balaam the son of Bosor, who loved the wages of unrighteousness; But was rebuked for his iniquity: the dumb ass speaking with man's voice forbade the madness of the prophet."

In Revelation 2:14, when the angel writes to the church at Pergamos, he condemns the false teachers among them saying, "Because thou hast there them that hold the doctrine of Balaam, who taught Balac to cast a stumblingblock before the children of Israel, to eat things sacrificed unto idols, and to commit fornication." Balaam—how tragic this is—Balaam died among the enemies of the Lord. He was killed with the sword, as we read in Numbers 31:8. His death was in keeping with the life he lived. He was a prophet for profit, and that was wrong in God's sight. The noble desires he may have once had had been choked out by the evil desire for the reward of evil. Instead of the death of the righteous, Balaam died the death of the wicked.

All we can conclude today is simply this: Balaam reaped what he sowed! He had an opportunity to do right, but temptation was there to bid him to do the wrong. He could have chosen the reward of the righteous, but his choice was the reward of evil. God's law has always been, "For whatsoever a man soweth, that shall he also reap. For he that soweth to his flesh shall of the flesh reap corruption; but he that soweth to the Spirit shall of the Spirit reap life everlasting" (Galatians 6:7-8). Man should never be deceived; please remember, God is not mocked. Our reward shall be in keeping with the life we live. In the Day of Judgment, we shall all shall stand before God. All men shall be judged "according to their works" (Revelation 20:12).

Every one of us, today, must choose whether we want to die the death of the righteous and receive a righteous man's reward; or live the life of the wicked, die the death of the wicked, and receive a wicked man's wages of eternal destruction. If we live the life of the wicked, like Balaam, then we shall perish with the wicked. So often the ways of unrighteousness are so appealing as it was in the days of Balaam. The sands of life appear so inviting and so alluring—a person may have a strong desire for the reward of the righteous but the appeal of sin is too strong for him to overcome. So, he yields to the wrong, hoping that somehow he will receive the reward of the righteous.

Most people want to go to heaven. I believe you really want to go to heaven. And, the vast majority of people think they are going there. Various religious polls have indicated that from ninety to ninety-eight percent of the people questioned were of the opinion that they are going to heaven when they die. There is a desire in the hearts of most for a better place, and heaven is the answer to that desire. Therefore, most people feel they will go there someday.

But I would like for us to stop and think and raise this question: what is the basis for this hope of so many, many people? Is it enough just to want to go to heaven? Is that all there is to it? Is it simply a matter of wishing that some way, somehow, God will take us to heaven? Evidently, the ordinary person never stops to consider this question with any great degree of seriousness. Yet this ought to be the most serious of all matters that ever crosses the mind of man. Let the Lord Jesus Christ answer the question. In Matthew, Jesus says:

> Not every one that saith unto me, Lord, Lord, shall enter into the kingdom of heaven; but he that doeth the will of my Father which is in heaven (Matthew 7:21)

Please notice then, that our entrance into heaven is dependent upon our obedience to God. John, the revelator, says:

> Blessed are they that do his commandments, that they may have right to the tree of life, and may enter in through the gates into the city (Revelation 22:14).

If we would enter heaven, we must do His commandments, today. The Lord's commands are righteous. In Psalm 119:172, David says: "All thy commandments are righteousness." When we obey the righteous commands of God, we become righteous. Jesus says of His own obedience "Thus it becometh us to fulfill all righteousness" (Matthew 3:15). If we would be righteous, we also must obey the teaching of our Lord and thus be righteous before Him. This righteousness is included in the gospel of Christ. Paul teaches this fact in his letter to the Roman church: "For therein is the righteousness of God revealed from faith to faith: as it is written, The just shall live by faith" (Romans 1:17).

The gospel of Christ teaches us to become Christians. Jesus teaches, "He that believeth and is baptized shall be saved" (Mark 16:16). The Apostle Peter preaches Christ on Pentecost and tells his listeners, "Repent, and be baptized every one of you in the name of Jesus Christ" (Acts 2:38). At the house of Cornelius, please remember, that the Apostle Peter says, "Of a truth I perceive that God is no respecter of persons: But in every nation he that feareth him, and worketh righteousness, is accepted with him" (Acts 10:34-35). Jesus teaches, "Blessed are they which do hunger and thirst after righteousness: for they shall be filled" (Matthew 5:6). There must be a strong desire to be righteous, and we can be.

To be righteous means to obey the Lord's commands and to live for Him. In so doing, the Lord becomes our righteousness. Paul expresses his desire in Philippians 3:9, "Not having my own righteousness, which is of the law, but that which is through the faith of Christ, the righteousness which is of God by faith."

I would like, last today, to talk with you about the death of the righteous who live for Christ. Let us express it with the words of Revelation 14:13, "Blessed are the dead which die in the Lord from henceforth: Yea, saith the Spirit, that they may rest from their labors; and their works do follow them."

To die the death of the righteous in the Lord, again we remind you, means to live the life of the righteous. There is no other way, and there is no other real hope; and I will be less than your friend today if I did not point this out and amplify it. Not all who desire the reward of the righteous are righteous. Even as Jesus says:

> Many will say to me in that day, Lord, Lord, have we not prophesied in thy name? and in thy name of cast out devils? and in thy name done many wonderful works? And then will I profess unto them, I never knew you: depart from me, ye that work iniquity (Matthew 7:22-23).

Many profess to be righteous but do not obey the Heavenly Father; therefore, the Lord shall say to them, "Depart from me, ye that work iniquity."

Probably one of the most pertinent questions today would be:

> How much do you want to die the death of the righteous?

> Do you want it enough to live the righteous life that Christ has taught us in the New Testament?

> Do you want to die the death of the righteous enough to hunger and thirst after righteousness?

I find that many say they want such a hope, but they never find the time to become a Christian or to study the Bible or to pray. They do not have time to go to church or to worship God. To live for Christ seems too difficult a task in our modern society; but they think somehow, someway, they will go to heaven. May our hope of heaven be genuine, may it be based upon the righteous commands of our Lord, and the precious promises of His eternal truth. I hope our desire will be so expressed in our being true and faithful followers of Christ and members of the Lord's church so that people can know that we want to die the death of the righteous.

May God help us to be warned by the example of Balaam. Please do not tamper with your conscience, learn to say no to temptation, and make up your mind to do the Lord's will, now. In so doing, we will find salvation and peace and hope and the reward of the righteous. God's promises will never fail. Our Lord is the same yesterday, today and forever. He shall bless the righteous in death and raise them to eternal life with Him in that city called heaven.

# *Contending for the Faith*

Good morning, everyone. We invite your attention this morning to the words of Jude. We invite your attention to the very beginning part of his letter, and he begins it thusly:

> Jude, a servant of Jesus Christ, and brother of James, to them that are called, beloved in God the Father, and kept for Jesus Christ: Mercy unto you and peace and love be multiplied. Beloved, while I was giving all diligence to write unto you of our common salvation, I was constrained to write unto you exhorting you to contend earnestly for the faith which was once for all delivered unto the saints. For there are certain men crept in privily, even they who were of old written of beforehand unto this condemnation, ungodly men, turning the grace of our God into lasciviousness, and denying our only Master and Lord, Jesus Christ (This is Jude 1-4 ASV).

Jude was the brother of James, the writer of the book of James, one who was prominent in the church in Jerusalem, according to Acts 15:13; Galatians 1:19; and Galatians 2:9. He identifies himself as the servant of Jesus Christ. The word servant here means a willing slave, one who has chosen completely to serve his Lord. We may say further that he was a fleshly brother of Jesus, though Jude himself does not mention this fact. In Matthew 13:55, he is listed as one of the sons of Joseph and Mary. Along with the rest of his brethren, he did not believe in the deity of Jesus during His personal ministry as he should have, according to John 7:3-8. But after the crucifixion and resurrection, Acts 1:14 says they were with Mary in the upper room in Jerusalem together with other disciples of the Lord, and I quote, "These all continued with one accord in prayer and supplication."

Jude was an ardent believer in the Lord Jesus as the son of God. He now considered his relationship as that of His servant. He is guided by the Holy Spirit; and he writes concerning the salvation they all share in Christ. Please notice that Jude writes concerning the Faith. He calls it "the faith once for all delivered unto the saints." The definite article "the" is used in designating one faith, and so it was. The expression "the faith" is used many times in the New Testament. In Acts 6:7, we are told of the great company of the priests who were obedient to the faith. Paul in Galatians 1:23 speaks about the churches in Judea who knew him as "he which persecuted us in times past now preacheth the faith which he destroyed." In 1 Timothy 4:1, he warns that in the latter times some shall depart from the faith. Again in 1 Timothy 5:8 he says, "But if any provide not for his own, and especially for those of his own house, he has denied the faith, and is worse than an infidel." In 1 Timothy 1:19, he writes of some who made shipwreck of the faith. When he comes to the end of his life, Paul writes, "I have kept the faith" (2 Timothy 4:7).

The expression "the faith" means the whole plan of the gospel of Christ. Directed by the Holy Spirit, Paul speaks in Galatians 1:8-9 of the curse of God that rests upon any man would preach any other gospel. In verse 23, he says he preached the faith that he once destroyed. He says this gospel was given him by revelation (Galatians 1:11-12), "But I certify you, brethren, that the gospel which was preached of me is not after man. For I neither received it of man, neither was I taught it, but by the revelation of Jesus Christ." This statement makes it plain that the faith and the gospel are different expressions with the same meaning, referring to God's great plan of salvation through Jesus Christ. All of God's great plan is based upon faith. As we read in Hebrews 11:6, "But without faith it is impossible to please him: for he that cometh to God must believe that he is, and that he is a rewarder of them that diligently seek him."

The gospel is a system of salvation by a working, active faith. The gospel tells us of a Savior—listen now—it tells us of a loving Savior, who through His death atoned for man's sins and by His righteousness we are healed spiritually. Man must accept the sacrifice by faith. The Jews had a law to keep that meant salvation on human merit. Heathen religions have given to the world different systems of ethics to regulate their lives; but they present no atoning sacrifice, no grace or mercy, and no Savior whose blood can wash away sins. Yet all these blessing are given in God's divine plan of faith in the Lord Jesus Christ. In Christ, we can be the children of God by faith (Galatians 3:26-27). We can be justified by faith (Romans 5:1). Our hearts can be purified by faith (Acts 15:9). The just shall live by faith (Galatians 3:11). For we walk by faith, not by sight (2 Corinthians 5:7). Christ dwells in our hearts by faith (Ephesians 3:17). Hebrews 4 tells us of the eternal rest that remains for those who have faith and who fail not through unbelief.

But we raise the question this morning: Does faith exclude obedience? Obedience is rather the expression of faith; in fact, it is a part of faith itself. James writes:

> What doth it profit, my brethren, though a man say he hath faith, and have not works? can faith save him? If a brother or sister be naked, and destitute of daily food, And one of you say unto them, Depart in peace, be ye warmed and filled; notwithstanding ye give them not those things which are needful to the body; what doth it profit? Even so faith, if it hath not works, is dead, being alone. Yea, a man may say, Thou hast faith, and I have works: shew me thy faith without thy works, and I will shew thee my faith by my works (James 2:14-18).

Then James warns of the devils who also believe and tremble. By the example of Abraham, he teaches how faith is made perfect by works and says, "Ye see then how that by works a man is justified, and not by faith only" (James 2:24). He concludes by saying, "For as the body without the spirit is dead, so faith without works is dead also" (verse 26).

Men repent because of faith in Christ, who says, "Except ye repent, ye shall all likewise perish" (Luke 13:3). Men confess their faith in Christ before other men because they believe in their hearts that God raised Him from the dead. "For with the heart man believeth unto righteousness; and with the mouth confession is made unto salvation" (Romans 10:10). Those who really believe—listen—those who really believe in Christ are baptized because he says, "He that believeth and is baptized will be saved" (Mark 16:16). They are buried in baptism, even as Christ was buried, and raised by the glory of God, the Father (Romans 6:1-6). So also as the children of God, they worship God and live and serve and die in faith in Christ as the only begotten Son of God. Every act of obedience is but the manifestation of the great faith in Christ and in His gospel plan of salvation.

I want you to notice in our lesson that Jude says that this faith was "once for all" delivered unto the saints. Jude disclaims any purpose to write something new. He was writing concerning their common salvation, something that they all shared together. It was the faith shared by the saints. The saints were the children of God then living, not canonized men as some would have people believe today. The New Testament used the term saints in reference to the members of the Lord's church then living on earth. Paul writes to the church at Rome, saying, "To all that be in Rome, beloved of God, called to be saints" (Romans 1:7). To Corinth, he writes:

> Unto the church of God which is at Corinth, unto them that are sanctified in Christ Jesus, called to be saints, with all that in every place that call upon the name of Jesus Christ, our Lord, both theirs and ours: Grace be unto you, and peace, from God our Father, and from the Lord Jesus Christ (1 Corinthians 1:2-3).

The New Testament teaches that all Christians are saints. These early Christians were followers of Christ by faith, that faith which had been delivered to them.

Notice too, that the faith once for all delivered unto the saints was a final deposit. The Lord did not give His revelation in installments as the centuries passed. It was once for all delivered or handed down unto the saints. This is one of the greatest and most absolute condemnations of those who claim the revelations or new visions or dreams or prophecies. It refutes the claim of the Roman church, which claims to be a living voice, continuing to speak through living representatives. It is an absolute refutation of pretended revelators such as Joseph Smith. Pretended revelators like Mrs. L. N. G. White or another pretended revelator Mary Baker Eddy or any other person today. Any person today who claims to speak by inspiration or revelation—any faith that is different from that revealed in the New Testament—is condemned and refuted. Jude's statement is clear: It is the faith that was once for all delivered unto the saints. It was delivered once for all time, for all generations, for every century, from that time until time shall be no more.

Paul writes, "Though we, or an angel from heaven, preach any other gospel unto you than that which we have preached unto you, let him be accursed. As we said before, so say I now again, if any man preach any other gospel unto you than that ye have received, let him be accursed" (Galatians 1:8-9). The faith Paul preached was the same as that of Jude. It is the faith of the gospel of Christ. Peter affirms the completeness of God's revelation as he tells us, "According as his divine power hath given unto us all things that pertain unto life and godliness, through the knowledge of him that hath called us to glory and virtue" (2 Peter 1:3). Please notice that Peter is stating in the first century, that God hath—not will—but God hath given unto us all things that pertain unto life and godliness. So, this scripture teaches us that God's word is complete. His revelation is sufficient. It was once for all delivered unto the saints and was written under the direction of the Holy Spirit sent from God. Men should not—must not—attempt to add to or take from that which has been written. It is ours to obey that we might enjoy salvation that can be ours by faith. We must conclude with Paul, "So then faith cometh by hearing, and hearing by the word of God" (Romans 10:17).

Christians are to earnestly contend for the faith. The word contend, as used by Jude, means to strive for, to expend extreme effort, to fight vigorously for the faith against its foes. Yet, it is not a physical combat. Jesus says, "My kingdom is not of this world: if my kingdom were of this world, then would my servants fight, that I should not be delivered to the Jews: but now is my kingdom not from hence" (John 18:36). Christ's kingdom is a spiritual kingdom. It is not defended or contended for with swords or military forces in mortal combat. The contending—please listen—the contending is to be done by moral persuasion and through teachings of the word of God. The Bible, as the sword of the Spirit, is the emblem of warfare. As firm believers in the word of God, Christian men can press the Bible against all false teachers and against all the enemies of the faith. There is nothing to fear in the battle against error: "this is the victory that overcometh the world, even our faith" (1 John 5:4).

Further Jude says that we are to contend "earnestly for the faith," a contending with the whole heart—with full heart—completely given to the task at hand. There is no doubt, and there is no relenting. The battle is to be pressed, wholeheartedly and continuously, and with all the vigor of our being. But why is it necessary—one may ask—why is it necessary to contend earnestly for the faith? Jude does not leave us in doubt. He tells us that false teachers had crept in privily. They had corrupted the grace of God, turning the people unto lasciviousness or lustful thinking. Possibly, they were like the Nicolaitans at Ephesus or Pergamos, which John condemned in Revelation chapter 2. These were individuals who spread disregard for God and for the purity of life that Jesus taught. These false teachers were like the modernists of our own time, who profess superior knowledge, who spread teachings of disregard for God's word, in the name of religion, and would absolutely uproot the divine institutions of his home and the church.

The world today is pressing their selfish ideas. Others are contending for the traditions and corrupt doctrines. Still there are others who would deny the virgin birth of our Lord and Savior. Some deny the vicarious death of Christ and would make the cross of Calvary repulsive in the minds of man. We do have today some very definite enemies of the cross. They are individuals who are turning the grace of God into lasciviousness. There are corrupt men with corrupt practices on every hand. Therefore, as Christians, we must contend earnestly for the faith once for all delivered to the saints. In fact—let me put it this way—our eternal destiny depends upon contending earnestly for the faith. Every member of the Lord's church ought to rise to meet the challenge—would you please hear me—the welfare of the Church of Christ is at stake. The salvation of dying souls of men and women hang in the balance.

Perhaps the greatest question that we can possibly raise this morning is: Can the Lord depend on you? Are you a Christian? Have you embraced the faith taught in the New Testament? Has your faith led you to obey the gospel of Christ? Has your faith let you to repentance and to a confession of your faith among men—to a burial in baptism for the remission of your sins? Are you living as you should? Are you following the example of the Savior? Are you worshiping and serving God as He directs you? Are you standing firmly for the truth of God and for the faith in Christ Jesus our Lord, never swayed by the forces of evil? Are you really pressing the battle in Jesus name? God would have you to quit yourselves like men. He says be strong. Contend earnestly for the faith, and God will give you the victory through our Lord Jesus Christ. He calls for men and women—he calls for strong people—men of courage and conviction that will hold high the banner of Prince Emanuel. May God help each Christian listening today to have a courage to contend for the faith. May you, my friend, if you are not a Christian, become one before this day is over. This is our fervent prayer in Christ's Holy name.

# *Drawing Back*

Ladies and gentlemen, we invite your attention this morning to the subject "Drawing Back unto Perdition." The Bible has given us many incentives to encourage us to live for Christ. We should always have these incentives before us. This morning we would like to encourage you to think how much God loved us and how He sent His Son to die for us on the cross of Calvary. We would like you to consider His provisions for our salvation and the gospel of Christ—provisions for simple forgiveness of our sins through the acceptance of His grace and our obedience to His teachings.

Let us remember the abundant spiritual blessings that are provided for those who live in Christ. Some of these are the comfort and strength of the Lord in our time of need, the continuous blessings of His presence in the forgiveness of our sins, the privilege of prayer, the opportunities of worship, the glorifying of the name of our Lord in serving others. Indeed, all spiritual blessings in heavenly places are offered to those who are in Christ (Ephesians 1:3). The Christian has the hope of eternal life. It was for this purpose that Jesus came; in fact, He says, "I am come that they might have life, and that they might have it more abundantly" (John 10:10). To His disciples, He says, "I am the way, the truth, and the life: no man cometh unto the Father, but by me" (John 14:6). In verse 19, our Lord says, "Because I live, ye shall live also." What a tremendous promise that really is: "Because I live, you shall live also." Therefore, "the gift of God is eternal life through Jesus Christ our Lord" (Romans 6:23). Because of these great provisions of God's love and of God's mercy, we are encouraged to become Christians, to live for Christ each day of our lives, and to be faithful and true to Christ even unto death (Revelation 2:10).

I want to think of the exhortations that we have in the Holy Scriptures, especially in Hebrews 10. The entire book of Hebrews was written to encourage faithfulness to Christ in times of great trial. In Hebrews 10:19-25, Hebrew Christians were exhorted to avail themselves of the privileges of the new and living way, through Christ as their sin offering and their great High Priest. Beginning with verse 22, the writer says:

> Let us draw near with a true heart in full assurance of faith, having our hearts sprinkled from an evil conscience, and our bodies washed with pure water. Let us hold fast the profession of our faith without wavering; (for he is faithful that promised;) And let us consider one another to provoke unto love and to good works: Not forsaking the assembling of ourselves together, as the manner of some is; but exhorting one another: and so much the more, as you see the day approaching (Hebrews 10:22-25).

Now a good question would be this: Why were these exhortations to faithfulness given? It was because—first of all—it was because many were falling away from their first faith in Christ. Some were going back to their old way of life and rejecting the sacrifice of Jesus. In their willful or deliberate sin of turning away from Christ, they exposed themselves to the fearful looking for of judgment and fiery indignation, the vengeance of the Lord. They were reminded by the apostle that it is a fearful thing to fall into the hands of the living God. Some of them had endured a great fight of afflictions and some had shown compassion upon Paul in his bonds as a prisoner and took joyfully the loss of their goods, knowing they had the promise of a better and enduring reward in heaven. And, therefore, they were taught, "Cast not away your confidence, which hath great recompense of reward" (verse 35). They needed the faith to continue.

The words of the prophet were, "The just shall live by faith" (verse 38). Thus, the examples of faith are given in the following chapter to cause them to continue to be faithful unto the Lord; but inspite of all of this, some were drawing back. They were shrinking back from the faith that one time they professed. As Isaiah the prophet expresses concerning the people in his day, "They are gone away backward," (Isaiah 1:4). The warning is given in Hebrews 10:38, "But if any man draw back, my soul shall have no pleasure in him." In Luke 9:62, it is recorded how Jesus says, "No man, having put his hand to the plough, and looking back, is fit for the kingdom of God." Those people who drew back from serving the Lord were what we would call "backsliders." They started out to serve the Lord, they slipped back into sin, and they fell away from their faith in Christ. This is a tremendous danger. It was a danger in that day, and it is a serious danger today. In fact, it is one of the chief matters of concern in our country right now. More than sixty-three percent of the people in America make some profession of faith in matters of religion, but so many of them have drifted back into disregard for the things of God. A larger percentage of our population than ever before profess religion, but the proportion of those who are faithful to their profession is often relatively small. One Texas editor of a religious journal estimated that the losses are often as high as seventy-five percent and among college and university students even reaches eighty to eighty-five percent. Now this influence that is occurring in the world is often felt in the Lord's church. Often, we learn of those who once became Christians but who have turned back into sin. I am confident that in this listening audience this morning, we have some who are in this condition. We want you to know today, my brother or my sister—we want to know that we are concerned about your salvation. We would warn you in the words of the scripture, "It is a fearful thing to fall into the hands of the living God" (verse 31).

But why will people draw back from serving God? There are several reasons that are given in the scriptures, and we invite you to consider them with us. First of all, some have remembered their former ways. Even though they once believed in the Lord as their Savior and realized they needed to repent and be baptized for the remission of their sins, they did not forget those sins from which they once turned. They are like Israel in the days of Moses. God delivered Israel from Egyptian bondage, but some of them remembered their former ways and desired to return to Egypt. Secondly, some forget that the Lord's blessings have been great and have been abundant, and they fail to consider the precious promises of God's word. It was so in the time of Isaiah. Isaiah says that "Israel doth not know, my people doth not consider" (Isaiah 1:3). Men today frequently fail to consider the blessings the Lord has provided for them, and thus they turn back into sin.

But another reason is this: Some people love the world, and thus they forsake the Lord. It is said of Demas in 2 Timothy 4:10. Paul says, "Demas hath forsaken me, having loved this present world." The world offers many appealing temptations. That is true, and man is basically the same and the nature of the temptation is still the same; but the opportunities to engage in worldly and sensual sins have multiplied. On every hand, there are temptations that cause men and women to forsake the Lord. There are temptations to cause our young people to turn aside from living for the Lord. Fourthly, the condition of our society today is filled with the attitude of compromise with sin. We no longer are shocked by sin. Moral standards have so often been forgotten. The biblical principles of honesty and purity and virtue have been cast aside by so many. The practices of wrong have been given the appearance of acceptance and have been condoned in high places.

The homes of America have been breaking up because of the prevalence of divorce in disregard of God's law. More than eighty percent of American families have one or more in that family who use alcoholic beverages. Gambling and vice and crime have reached an all time high in this country. The attitude has developed more and more that others are doing certain things. Why not us? But there can be no compromise of right and wrong, regardless of what may appear to be. Regardless of what we may do and if the whole world should turn that direction, there can be no compromise of right and wrong. Right is always right, and wrong is always wrong. There can be no compromise between the two. Just because others are doing something does not make it right, even though the majority of people might be engaging in it. God said a long time ago, "Thou shalt not follow a multitude to do evil" (Exodus 23:2).

Now, I propose to you that that same principle still stands today and is taught in the New Testament. But the draw to the multitude has caused many a person to draw back from serving God. The desire to be accepted or the desire to be popular or the desire for some business advancement at the cost of sacrificing Christian principles, all of these have had their influence in drawing back people from God's service.

But there are others who simply have grown weary in well doing. Dare I say, as I preach to you this morning, that in this audience somewhere there is one or more of you who has not turned to sensuality, you have not forsaken the Lord so far as disbelief in God. You still believe in the church. Some of you simply have grown weary in well doing. You remember the admonition of the Apostle Paul in (Galatians 6:9). He says, "Let us not be weary in well doing: for in due season we shall reap, if—if we faint not." The cost of being faithful to the Lord is sometimes very great, and that I do not deny. The work of the Lord calls for continuous effort. Every day brings new opportunities and new responsibilities. Some people easily get tired and weary of continued effort, so they slide back into the ways of sin and neglect. They forget the greatest rewards that heaven will offer for those who are faithful to the very end of life. Such drawing back—my friend—such drawing back is evidence of a lack of faith. The Lord is not slack concerning his promise, but men let their faith fail. The Lord told Peter, "I have prayed for thee, that thy faith fail not" (Luke 22:32). But Peter did not heed the Lord's warning at that time. He denied the Lord when among his enemies. Many a person has failed to maintain his faith by continued study and by communion with God; and so in the hour of trial his faith has failed.

Next let us notice this important statement in the text of Hebrews 10. The writer says, "We are not of them who draw back unto perdition; but of them that believe to the saving of the soul" (verse 39). I dare say that this ought to be the aim of every Christian. We should, above everything else, desire to be of those who believe to the saving of the soul. But those who draw back—please remember friend—those who draw back, draw back unto perdition. This is the horrible end of the backslider. The end is perdition. This word perdition means loss or destruction. It occurs eight times in the New Testament. Judas was called the son of perdition (John 17:12). The man of sin, Satan's servant, who would be revealed, was called the son of perdition in 2 Thessalonians 2:3. He will exalt himself above all that is called God, or that is worshiped; so that he sitting in the Temple of God would claim to be called God. By his signs and lying wonders in deceivableness of unrighteousness, he would deceive men. Such a force is at work in the world today in the cloak of religion, but the man of sin shall be destroyed and all those who are deceived thereby. In 1 Timothy 6:9, the love of riches is said to drown men in destruction and perdition. In 2 Peter 3:7, he speaks of the perdition of ungodly men. In Revelation 17:8 and 11, the evil beast is spoken of as going in to perdition. In Philippians 1:28, the adversaries of the gospel, who sought to terrify the faithful, are said to have an evident token—listen to this—an evident token of perdition and that is the proof of their own destruction. To draw back to perdition, therefore, means to draw back to eternal destruction. The backslider who does not repent has before him only one end, that of eternal destruction or perdition.

Let us remember, "It had been better for them not to have known the way of righteousness, than, after they have known it, to turn from the holy commandment delivered unto them" (2 Peter 2:21). Shall we forget this solemn warning? May we call upon you today to return to the Lord? I do not know where you are today. I do not know what your plans are, but may we plead with you today? The Lord's plan to the erring or backsliding Christian is: number one He wants you to repent, and He wants you to pray God that perhaps the thoughts and intents of your heart may be forgiven (Acts 8:22). James 5:16 says, "Confess your faults one to another, and pray one for another, that you may be healed." God loves you today. He loves a backslider and wants you to repent. God loves all men and wants all of us to repent. He wants us all to become Christians and to be faithful to Him every day that we live. The Lord's promise is "Be thou faithful unto death and I will give thee a crown of life" (Revelation 2:10).

In conclusion, our prayer is that God's love and mercy may constrain you, my friend, to live for Christ. If you are not a Christian, we would pray that you may become a Christian without delay. Please call upon those who will sponsor this program or who will make the announcements; please call upon these people to assist you in your obedience to the Lord. We would like to do so. Time is rapidly passing. So, may we remind you to serve the Lord, NOW! Tomorrow maybe too late.

# *Love*

The reading of the Holy Scripture is from 1 Corinthians 13, beginning with verse one:

> Though I speak with the tongues of men and of angels, and have not charity, I am become as sounding brass, or a tinkling cymbal. And though I have the gift of prophecy, and understand all mysteries, and all knowledge; and though I have all faith, so that I could remove mountains, and have not charity, I am nothing. And though I bestow all my goods to feed the poor, and though I give my body to be burned, and have not charity, it profiteth me nothing. Charity suffereth long, and is kind; charity envieth not; charity vaunteth not itself, is not puffed up, Doth not behave itself unseemly, seeketh not her own, is not easily provoked, thinketh no evil; Rejoiceth not in iniquity, but rejoiceth in the truth; Beareth all things, believeth all things, hopeth all things, endureth all things. Charity never faileth: but whether there be prophecies, they shall fail; whether there be tongues, they shall cease; whether there be knowledge, it shall vanish away. For we know in part, and we prophesy in part. But when that which is perfect is come, then that which is in part shall be done away. When I was a child, I spake as a child, I understood as a child, I thought as a child: but when I became a man, I put away childish things. For now we see through a glass, darkly; but then face to face: now I know in part; but then shall I know even as also I am known. And now abideth faith, hope, charity, these three; but the greatest of these is charity.

That which I just read to you is one of the greatest works known to man. It is the answer to so many questions in our lives. Why did God come in the flesh and die vicariously for the sins of mankind? How shall I respond to the death of Christ on Calvary? What can I do to become like Jesus? How can I live at peace with my fellow men on earth? How can I come to know God, so as to have the hope of eternal life with Him? How can I live so at to prove that I am a Christian?

These questions may seem unrelated; but if it seems so, it is only because you have not realized that one word is necessary to answer them all and that one word is "love." "But God commendeth his love toward us, in that, while we were yet sinners, Christ died for us" (Romans 5:8). "If ye love me, keep my commandments" (John 14:15). "A new commandment I give unto you, That ye love one another; as I have loved you, that ye also love one another. By this shall all men know that you are my disciples, if you have love one to another" (John 13:34-35). "Beloved, let us love one another: for love is of God; and every one that loveth is born of God, and knoweth God. He that loveth not knoweth not God; for God is love" (1 John 4:7-8).

Carnal romance and eroticism had been in the world before Jesus came. As well, obedience to commandments had been in the world prior to His sojourn among men. But by virtue of his life and teaching, we have a biblical doctrine of love that was not in the world before Jesus came. Understanding the true concept of love is necessary to to our living and to our salvation. The world and even some within the church have lost sight of the true biblical doctrine of love. People in the world commonly regard love as a statement or a feeling for someone. While emotion may be involved in love, it is not necessarily so and certainly must not be equated with love. Some think of love only as a sensual type of passion. A popular philosophy of our time, situation ethics or the new morality, sets love over against authority and rules for behavior and uses it as an excuse for the selfish pursuit of pleasure.

To many religious people, for instance in the Jesus movement, love is a "spiritual high" that serves to unite all men as brothers in Christ, regardless of doctrine, manner of worship, or name that may be worn. This spirit is even being seen in some quarters among our brethren. To those people, Christianity is a kind of gooey love that accepts falsehood and evil. They accept it equally with truth and righteousness. These views represent tragic failures of understanding and can be effectively combated only after we have learned the correct biblical doctrine of love.

The Bible nowhere, so far as I know, gives a formal definition for the word love. It emphasizes the importance of the values of love (1 John 4:11-12). It enumerates certain characteristics of love, such as we have just read (1 Corinthians 13:4-7). It warns that without love, no man can legitimately claim to belong to Christ (1 John 4:8). By careful study of what the word of God teaches about love, we can formulate a correct definition. Negatively, the love spoken of in the New Testament is no mysterious visitation that comes and goes unexpectedly and is beyond the control of our will. As we shall notice shortly, loving or not loving an object or a person is altogether a matter of one's choice. Love does not necessarily involve liking and may, in fact, be directed toward someone we do not like at all. Love can even be commanded (John 13:34). Love can be taught (Titus 2:4).

All of these concepts are totally foreign to the notion of love that is in the minds of most people. What then is love? It is the willingness to seek another's pleasure or well-being at the sacrifice, if necessary, of one's own. I think it is important that we understand that definition. I want you to notice how this definition fits the word love as is used in the scriptures. First, God so loved the world (John 3:16). Now was God drawn to man by a warm feeling of emotional affection? Did He like man as a rebellious sinner? I am persuaded we cannot answer that question in the affirmative, but He did love man. He was willing to seek our well-being at great sacrifice to Himself; thus He gave His only begotten Son for our salvation. Second, we are commanded; love your enemies (Matthew 5:44). Does this command mean that we are obligated to feel affection for one who hates us or attempts to do us harm? Does it mean that we must like him and appreciate what he is doing? I think that is absurd. But we must love him in that we refuse to return evil for evil. We desire to see him turn from his evil to a better way of life and to do what is within our power to bring about such a change in him. Thus, it is that love, while it frequently involves emotion, does not always include warm affection for its object. We love God, our faithful brethren, and our families with great affection. We love them with personal appreciation for who they are and what they have done for us. We love sinful men and certain willful erring brethren, in spite of the absence of such affection and personal appreciation.

The Bible speaks to us about degrees of love. These considerations lead us to weigh this matter, and it is an important matter. Surely, there must be degrees of love. There are certainly degrees of the love of God. All men are made in the image of God, but not all men stand before God in the same status. Some men, made in his image, are in arrogant rebellion against God. Others have seen the rebellion against Him and have accepted divine grace in their salvation. God's love is not equal toward these two classes of men. As a proof that this is indeed the case, notice that God loves the entire world, even sinners in rebellion against Him. As well, there is a special sense in which Jesus promises the Father will love those who keep His word, that is, those who are Christians. "If a man love me, he will keep my words: and my Father will love him, and we will come unto him, and make our abode with him" (John 14:23). No father loves the children outside his family as much as he loves his own children. How special is the love of God toward those who have been born anew into His spiritual family. He establishes an abode with these children by making them members of the body of Christ (Galatians 3:26-27). He abides with them by means of His indwelling Spirit (1 Corinthians 6:9-20). He accepts their worship, hears their prayers, and continually cleanses them with the blood of Jesus. He is in constant fellowship with His own as they walk in the light (1 John 1:7).

There are also degrees of love that Christians manifest toward others. Just as sinners and saints are objects of God's love in different degrees, so are these two categories of men loved to different degrees by God's children. We ought to love people in the world, that is sinners, as our neighbors (Matthew 22:39). We must do good to them and seek their salvation. But our love to our fellow Christians in the church is a special love that involves spiritual fellowship in Christ, a fellowship we cannot extend to those outside of Christ. Notice how the scriptures bear out this idea. Well after He had given the commandment to love our neighbors as ourselves, Jesus tells His disciples, "A new commandment"—notice the words—"a new commandment I give unto you, That you love one another; even as I have loved you, that you also love one another" (John 13:34). The love for men as neighbors is a universal command, but this new commandment is considerably narrower in its scope. It imposes the responsibility of distinguishing between true Christians and mere pretenders of the name. Love has been extended to its ultimate degree—its ultimate degree that is possible actually—among humans within the spirit of truth and Christian fellowship. Consider for example Paul's exultation to the Galatians, "as we have therefore opportunity, let us do good unto all men, especially unto them who are of the household of faith" (Galatians 6:10; 1 Thessalonians 3:12).

One of the great errors of our day is the attempt to make love the basis of spiritual fellowship; and its failure to distinguish between true Christians and those who are still outside the faith. Love is not the basis of fellowship. We need to speak that precept from the highest hills. Love is not the basis of fellowship. It is the result of fellowship. Truth is the basis of fellowship (1 John 1:7; Romans 16:17). A new commandment to love one another as Christ has loved us applies to those who stand within the sphere of the true faith. Now, does this mean that if a man is an unbeliever or merely wearing the label Christian without having actually obeyed the truth, does this mean we are justified in pushing him aside and refusing to show him any love? Of course not, he is still covered by our responsibility to love our neighbors as ourselves.

Now let's notice how this type of love demonstrates itself. The first commandment is "Thou shall love the Lord thy God with all thy heart, and with all thy soul, and with all thy mind" (Matthew 22:37). If one truly believes the personal infinite God of the Bible exists and that He has proved His love for man by providing Jesus as the sinner's substitute, surely he will be compelled to love God in return. Certainly, we do not love God because He needs our love but because we need Him and we need His love. Thus, compelled to love Him, we will love Him completely with our heart, soul, mind, and strength. The outward expression and proof of such love will be obedience to God's commands. "For this"—listen to this passage—"For this is the love of God, that that we keep his commandments" (1 John 5:3). Notice that we can know our love for God is real only if we obey Him. Love is not, then, as certain liberals and situationists argue, antagonistic to instruction and commandment but actually depends upon them.

Do you love God? Don't answer—now think about it with me—don't answer by telling me that you have an indescribable feeling in your heart. Now that feeling may or may not relate to real love for God. Rather, answer me by telling whether or not you have obeyed the commandments of God that are relative to your salvation from sin. That is the way you determine whether you love God or whether you do not.

Now, the second commandment is, "Thou shall love thy neighbor as thyself" (Matthew 22:39). We know the Samaritan loved the man who was wounded by the road by what he did for him (Luke 10:29-37). What did he do? He gave of himself, time, effort, money on another's behalf. We must learn to love our neighbors, not in word only, which is all too common, but in deed, also. We must see our neighbors as persons made in the image of God and be anxious to seek their physical and spiritual good (Matthew 7:12). Especially must we seek to lead our neighbors to Christ and salvation in Him.

The third or new commandment is, that those who are in Christ must love one another as Christ has loved us (John 13:34). We must avoid differences with our brethren whenever possible. We must pray for one another and bear one another's burdens (Galatians 6:2). When offenses among brethren do arise, we must move in with all possible haste to heal the breach (Matthew 5:23-24). We must be willing to admit when we are at fault and eager to forgive others when they are at fault (Ephesians 4:32). This love must be conscious and visible among Christians. It must exhibit itself in the unity of believers so the world can know that we are truly God's people and that Jesus was sent from God (John 17:21).

The conclusion of this whole matter is that we have received God's love and salvation and, thus, we exhibit love for our neighbors and our brethren daily. We, then, must come to share the greatest of all of God's gifts: salvation. It is through this means that God's purpose is accomplished. Love is greater than tongues. Love is greater than healing. Love is greater than any spiritual gift. Read Paul's words in 1 Corinthians 12:31 and his words in chapter 13:1-3 and verse 13. While these miraculous gifts are not within the reach of men living in our generation, love is in the reach of all. We are so concerned, sometimes, about this gift and that gift and whether this teaching applies or does not apply that we forget that love is within the reach of everyone. If you feel the warmth of God's love and you are willing to return His love by obedience to His commands, then He will save you from your sins. Then in your new state of salvation, you will be enabled by God to demonstrate what real love is to those who are around you. Living the Christian life, which is controlled and characterized by divine love, you will lead others to the Savior, who stands ready to receive all men who will but come!

# The Church at Corinth

In the eighteenth chapter of Acts of the Apostles, verses 1 through 11 is the story of the preaching of the gospel at Corinth. As we studied about the gospel being preached in Jerusalem and Samaria to the eunuch, to Cornelius and to his house, and to the jailer at Philippi, we would like now for you to open your Bibles and let us read together about ancient Corinth. Beginning with verse 1 of chapter 18 we read:

> After these things Paul departed from Athens, and came to Corinth; And found a certain Jew named Aquila, born in Pontus, lately come from Italy, with his wife Priscilla; (because that Claudius had commanded all Jews to depart from Rome:) and came unto them. And because he was of the same craft, he abode with them, and wrought: for by their occupation they were tentmakers. And he reasoned in the synagogue every sabbath, and persuaded the Jews and the Greeks. And when Silas and Timotheus were come from Macedonia, Paul was pressed in the spirit, and testified to the Jews that Jesus was Christ. And when they opposed themselves, and blasphemed, he shook his rainment, and said unto them, Your blood be upon your own heads; I am clean: from henceforth I will go unto the Gentiles. And he departed thence, and entered into a certain man's house, named Justus, one that worshiped God, whose house joined hard to the synagogue. And Crispus, the chief ruler of the synagogue, believed on the Lord with all his house; and many of the Corinthians hearing believed, and were baptized (Acts 18:1-8).

Thus, the gospel was preached for the first time in Corinth and many obeyed the gospel.

The city of Corinth in the Apostle Paul's day was located in Achaia to the south of Macedonia where Paul had been preaching. Old Corinth was burned by the Romans in 146 BC and the city was rebuilt by Julius Caesar about 100 years later. It was colonized by Roman free men. It claims Zenus as its patron goddess and to her was dedicated a large temple where 1,000 priestesses served in harlotry before the people. The morals of the city were low, and sin was on every hand. There was much vice and little regard for God. Paul had come to this wicked city to preach about Christ. But God told him, "Be not afraid but speak, and hold not thy peace: For I am with thee, and no man shall set on thee to hurt thee: for I have much people in this city. And he continued there a year and six months, preaching the word of God among them" (Acts 18:9-11).

Next, let us notice Paul's preaching at Corinth. "He reasoned in the synagogue every Sabbath, and persuaded the Jews and the Greeks" (verse 4). He "testified to the Jews that Jesus was Christ" (verse 5). His message to them is the same message that he has preached everywhere he has gone before. He preaches Christ to them. Some years later when Paul writes the first of his letters to these believers at Corinth, he reminds them, saying:

> And I, brethren, when I came to you, came not with excellency of speech or of wisdom, declaring to you the testimony of God. For I determined not to know anything among you, save Jesus Christ, and him crucified. And I was with you in weakness, and in fear, and in much trembling. And my speech and my preaching was not with enticing words of man's wisdom, but in demonstration of the Spirit and of power. That your faith should not stand in the wisdom of men, but in the power of God (1 Corinthians 2:1-5).

Notice what the results of his preaching were. In verse 6 we read that some "opposed themselves and blasphemed." Verse 12 declares, "the Jews made insurrection with one accord against Paul and brought him to the judgment seat." But Gallio, the deputy of the city cared not for these things. Therefore, Paul turned to preach to the Gentiles. In verse 8, he says "many of the Corinthians hearing believed, and were baptized."

In 1 Corinthians 1:14-16, Paul names Crispus and Gaius and the household of Stephanus as among the many who hearing, believed and were baptized. The Corinthians did the same thing as others when the gospel of Christ was preached before. One, they heard the gospel. Two, they believed in Christ. "So then faith cometh by hearing, and hearing by the word of God" (Romans 10:17). Three, they were baptized. These are the same steps that that man must take today in receiving salvation from Christ. For Christ Himself says, "He that believeth and is baptized shall be saved" (Mark 16:16).

Next, we could raise this question: Into what were they baptized? Now Paul goes into the city of Corinth, he preaches, they hear, they believe, they are baptized, but I want to know into what are they baptized? In 1 Corinthians 12:12-13, Paul speaks of the church as the body of Christ. "For as the body is one, and hath many members, and all the members of that one body, being many, are one body: so also is Christ. For by one Spirit are we all baptized into one body, whether we be Jews or Gentiles, whether we be bond or free." In Romans 6:3, "Know you not, that so many of us as were baptized into Jesus Christ were baptized into his death?" In Galatians 3:27, he writes, "For ye are all the children of God by faith in Christ Jesus. For as many of you have been baptized into Christ have put on Christ." Thus, those at Corinth, like the Christians at Rome and in Galatia, have been baptized into the body of Christ. Christ is the head of the body, the church. The church is His body (Ephesians 1:22-23). To be baptized into Christ is to be baptized into the body of Christ. The body of Christ is the church of Christ. The Corinthians and all who obey the words of Jesus are baptized for the remission of sins, being buried with Him in baptism (Romans 6:3; Colossians 2:12). They are added to the church that Christ had established on Pentecost, in Jerusalem, according to the second chapter of Acts. In Acts 2:47, we are told "the Lord added to the church daily such as should be saved." Men obey the gospel of Christ to be saved, and the Lord adds them to the church. They are baptized into the church. This rule holds for all, from Pentecost until this day. Those who obey the Lord in Jerusalem become the church in Jerusalem. The Corinthians who hearing, believe, are baptized, and became the church at Corinth. The church at Corinth was like the church in Jerusalem. As Christians, they are members of the Lord's church, added to the church by our Lord. They are all members of the same church. There is no difference.

When Paul writes to the church at Rome, he is in Corinth and sends greetings from the churches, saying, "The churches of Christ salute you" (Romans 16:16). When Paul addresses his letters to these Christians at Corinth, he says, "Unto the church of God which is at Corinth" (1 Corinthians 1:2; 2 Corinthians 1:1). Paul uses the term "church of Christ" and "church of God." These are certainly scriptural names and names that can be applied to the church today. They are used in connection with the same church, not different denominations.

This thought leads us to the discussion of the next division of our lesson about calling.

The church of Jesus Christ at Corinth was not denominational. Denominations as they exist today were unheard of at the time the church existed in ancient Corinth. The first modern denomination came into existence hundreds of years later. The New Testament does not teach denominationalism or denominational division. The Bible sets forth Christ and His church. Remember the words of Paul to the Corinthians, "Is Christ divided?" (1 Corinthians 1:13). Christ taught and prayed for unity, not division (John 17). He wanted the people at Corinth to be united, not divided. Therefore, He directs Paul to write, "Now I beseech you, brethren, by the name of our Lord Jesus Christ, that ye all speak the same thing, and that there be no divisions among you; but that ye be perfectly joined together in the same mind and in the same judgment" (1 Corinthians 1:10). Now notice that this was Christ's will then and is Christ's will today. He wanted them to be united, and He wants us to be united. His will has not changed. The church at Corinth was to be one, united in their faith, united in their work, and united in their hope. We are taught in Ephesians 4:3-6, we are to "endeavor to keep the unity of the Spirit in the bond of peace. There is one body, and one Spirit, even as you are called in one hope of your calling; One Lord, one faith, one baptism, One God and Father of all, who is above all, and through all, and in you all."

Consider with me the theme of denominationalism. Now these can be seen as we observe what happened at Corinth. Paul had laid one foundation. He says in 1 Corinthians 3:11, "For other foundation can no man lay than that is laid, which is Jesus Christ." As the Lord says, "Upon this rock, I will build my church" (Matthew 16:18). Now Paul has built the church at Corinth upon that solid foundation, the Lord Jesus Christ. But there soon arose contentions among them. Paul condemned these contentions, saying, "Now this I say, that every one of you saith, I am of Paul; and I of Apollos; and I of Cephas; and I of Christ. Is Christ divided? Was Paul crucified for you? Were you baptized in the name of Paul?" (1 Corinthians 1:12-13). Following after men instead of Christ caused their division. That same idea in every generation has created and maintained denominationalism. Men can be united in Christ. But the following of man and the teachings of man will bring only division and strife. Paul condemned it then, and it stands condemned today.

If men would preach only Christ—listen—if they would preach only Christ and Him crucified, if they would use only the Bible as their guide and chastise man and their teachings and their creeds, denominationalism would vanish from among men. Men would become united in Christ. To this end, we should dedicate our faith and our work to obey God rather than men, to be united and not divided. Let us please our Lord and go to heaven. Our honest and humble prayer, in the name of our Christ, is that we may point men to the Lord's truth on this vital point. But some may ask, can people be united today? Is it really possible? I want to answer again, yes, yes, unity is God's plan. It is the Lord's plan. It is the New Testament's plan. Man cannot only be united but should be united in the Lord's work today just as they were nineteen centuries ago. The churches at Jerusalem, at Philippi, at Rome, at Corinth, and at all other New Testament churches should become our example.

With the New Testament teaching to guide us and direct us, we can be Christians only today. As Christians, we can be united in serving the Lord and the church of our Lord. This plan is not narrow or selfish. It is the Lord's plan. In order to accomplish this unity, each one of us must do our part. The Lord has made our responsibilities individual. As individuals, we must obey Him, and then we can all be united as fellow Christians in the Lord's church.

Let us notice some ten steps for each of us to follow in order to obtain this unity in Christ. Please listen. (1) Each person must hear the gospel of Christ. (2) He must believe in the Lord Jesus Christ as the Son of God. (3) He must repent of his sins, for except you repent you shall all likewise perish. (4) He must confess his faith in Christ (Romans 10:10). (5) Each one must be baptized of the one baptism, a burial in water in obedience to Christ for the remission of sins (Acts 2:38). (6) Then the Lord will add each to the church (Acts 2:47). Thus, man will be separated from all denominationalism and sectarian ties and become a member of the one body, the church of our Lord Jesus Christ, which has been purchased by the blood of Christ. Even as Paul says, "For by one Spirit are we all baptized into one body." (7) To each Christian, Christ will be an example in manner of life and in obedience to the Father. Each life will be filled with those Christ-like qualities that will radiate a Christian in bloom. (8) As Christians together, Christ's plan of worship will be our plan as we unite to worship the Lord in spirit and in truth (John 4:24). As the Corinthians prayed and sang (1 Corinthians 14:15) and observed the Lord's

Supper (1 Corinthians 11:23-29), and taught and were commanded upon the first day of the week, "but let every one of you lay by him in store as God has prospered him" (1 Corinthians 16:2), so will we do today. (9) Christ's name will be ours to wear, individually and collectively; we will be called the church of Christ or the church of God (Romans 16:16; 1 Corinthians 1:1-2). As His followers, we will be called Christians (Acts 11:26; I Peter 4:16). We must remember that "neither is there salvation in any other: for there is none other name under heaven given among men, whereby we must be saved" (Acts 4:12). Lastly, heaven will be our hope (Ephesians 4:4). If we are true to our Lord, heaven shall not only be our hope, heaven shall be our home.

In conclusion, may I remind you that we must realize as Paul writes in 2 Corinthians 5:10, "We must all appear before the judgment seat of Christ; that everyone may receive the things done in his body, according to that he hath done, whether it be good or bad." Let us follow the Lord's plan for the church at Corinth. God help us to be Christians and Christians only!

# *God's Plan for Religious Unity*

Good morning, everyone. Once again we have the privilege of studying the word of God, and we appreciate having you in our listening audience. This morning we invite your attention to the subject: "God's Plan for Religious Unity."

There have been several articles in the newspapers in recent weeks about various movements toward religious unity. Possibly you have read some of them. This discussion has been going on for many, many years in the different protestant churches. Different plans have been proposed, and some religious groups have formed recognized unions for their activities. Most of these movements and plans, however, have the idea of union rather than unity as their objective. The word union suggests a rather loose relation as compared to unity. Unity in matters of religion would suggest a real, vital and living close relationship for Christian believers.

I want you to think for a few moments with me what religious unity could mean in this world. Think how wonderful it would be if all professed Christians were united in true Christian fellowship. Consider the happiness that could be realized if sectarian barriers were destroyed and all religious bitterness was forgotten. Think how many families who are now divided over religion could be brought together in better understanding and peace. Emphasis could be placed on nearness to God and the truth in Christ rather than on the divided allegiances to divergent creeds and to denominational doctrines.

True religious unity could be a mighty uniting force in communities and towns and cities in our country. Missionaries in foreign fields could have far greater influence in trying to convert heathen nations to the true God. It is not infrequent that we hear of idolatrous people suggesting to missionaries to go back home and unite and then return and tell them about God. Surely, we can see the reason for such a request. As it is, so often missionaries must explain the theological problems they have among themselves instead of teaching the gospel of Christ. So called Christendom, as we often refer to it, is a paradox.

Its forces seem united while in reality they are so divided. Different religious groups have many similar points in their professions of faith in Christ and in God; however, the barriers of sectarian names and sectarian doctrines prevent the exercise of real Christian fellowship.

These barriers are a tremendous hinderance to the advancement of true Christianity, both in our own communities and throughout the world. The minds of many people are disturbed over these matters, and many good people are deeply concerned about them; and it is with these facts before us that we present this lesson today. We begin the lesson by raising this question: Is religious unity actually possible? All of your life you have heard people preaching about religious unity. You have heard people read and quote the prayer of Jesus in John 17 that all might be one, but many people have come to believe that such unity really is not possible. According to the word of God, it IS possible. His plan in the New Testament is one that can unite men, not divide them. The Lord Jesus Christ has not commanded something that is impossible. The teachings of Christ are reasonable and practical, and they can be followed by men today. Jesus established one church. He taught His disciples saying, "Upon this rock I will build my church" (Matthew 16:18). In the second chapter of the book of Acts, we are told of the beginning of that church or kingdom. God raised up Christ from the grave and the Bible teaches that He ascended to heaven.

God made Him both Lord and Christ. Jesus had fulfilled the prophecies of the Old Testament. He had been crucified for the sins of men, and it was His purpose to reconcile both Jew and Gentile unto God in one body by the cross (Ephesians 2:16). It is evident, then, that the Lord wanted all men to be united in one body, the church. The Apostle Peter taught men what to do to be saved. He says, "Repent, and be baptized every one of you in the name of Jesus Christ for the remission of sins, and ye shall receive the gift of the Holy Ghost. For the promise is unto you, and to your children, and to all that are afar off, even as many as the Lord our God shall call" (Acts 2:38-39). Verse 41 says, "Then they that gladly received his word were baptized: and the same day there were added unto them about three thousand souls." So the church continued to grow. In verse 47, he declares, "The Lord added to the church daily such as should be saved." Thus, in Acts the second chapter, we see the beginning of the church of our Lord. It was made up of the saved whom the Lord added to His church. It was a united and happy church.

Our Lord prayed for the unity of His disciples. His prayer is recorded in John 17:20-21. He prayed, saying, "Neither pray I for these alone, but for them also which shall believe on me through their word; That they all may be one; as thou, Father, art in me, and I in thee, that they also may be one in us: that the world may believe that thou has sent me." The Lord's prayer was for the unity of all who believed on Him. It was for the same divine unity that He had with the Father, He wanted this unity to be theirs, also. Notice He stated the desired end for that unity—"That the world may believe that thou hast sent me." As believers in Jesus Christ today, this prayer of our Lord should mean to us "doing all that we can do to accomplish this unity for which our Lord prayed." Also, it is evident that the present divisions of professed believers are not in keeping with the Lord's prayer. Rather they stand in open defiance and disobedience to His prayer.

Not only did Jesus pray for the unity of His disciples, the Bible teaches that the apostles taught Chrisitan unity. They were directed in their teaching, of course, by the Holy Spirit. They taught as the Holy Spirit revealed the truth unto them (John 16:13). Even the words of their teaching were given by the Holy Spirit. Therefore, their teachings were inspired of God, and they were one in what they taught (1 Corinthians 2:13). Paul says in 1 Corinthians 1:10, "Now I beseech you, brethren, by the name of our Lord Jesus Christ, that ye all speak the same thing, and that there be no divisions among you; but that ye be perfectly joined together in the same mind and in the same judgment." The Lord wanted the Christians at Corinth to be united as the children of God. Paul rebuked them for the division that existed among them. Paul says, "Now this I say, that every one of you saith, I am of Paul; and I of Apollos; and I of Cephas; and I of Christ. Is Christ divided? was Paul crucified for you? or were ye baptized in the name of Paul?" (1 Corinthians 1:12-13). It is evident from Paul's wording that CHRIST is not divided and THEY were not to be divided. The Lord's church should be united as one body, both in the local congregation, as at Corinth, and in the church as a whole. God is a God of unity, not of confusion nor of division. In 1 Corinthians 14:33, we read, "For God is not the author of confusion, but of peace, as in all"— listen—"ALL churches of the saints."

I would like to put it plainly. Division is wrong. Division is sinful. The Lord hates the man who sows discord among brethren (Proverbs 6:19). Paul teaches Christians in Romans 16:17, "mark them which cause divisions and offences contrary to the doctrine which you have learned; and avoid them." Division within a congregation is wrong; and division should not exist between different congregations. As well, division between Christian brethren is always wrong.

When men are divided, at least one of them has violated the teachings of our Lord; and unless the wrong doer repents and is reconciled with his brother, the judgment of the Lord will be against him. It was Satan who separated men from God in the beginning. His work has continued through the years, and I will assure you the devil wants division because it is harmful to the work of God. But God wants UNITY. The question resolves itself into the following: Shall we follow Satan or shall we follow God's plan for unity? Each person listening today must answer for himself and in answering let us hold before us that division violates God's will—division is sinful. Unity is possible, and it is right among the children of God.

Perhaps then, the best question would be: How can unity be obtained? First of all, Christ is the answer. Jesus came to save men (Luke 19:10). He invites all men to come to Him (Matthew 11:28-30). He is the One of whom God spoke saying, "This is my beloved Son in whom I am well pleased; hear ye him" (Matthew 17:5). Jesus says, "I am THE way, THE truth, and THE life: no man cometh unto the Father, but by me" (John 14:6).

Secondly, not only is Christ the answer, but the Bible is the basis for unity in Christ. The Bible is the inspired word of God. It contains "all things that pertain unto life and godliness, through the knowledge of him that hath called us to glory and virtue" (2 Peter 1:3). It is not to be changed or perverted (Galatians 1:8-9).

Men are not to add to its teaching nor take away from that which God has written (Revelation 22:18-19). The principles of God's truth, when they are believed and obeyed, will make us right with God; and they will unite all true believers with one another. Faith in God's word, the Bible, will unite men. God's word should be our only guide in all matters of religion, and this is the only common ground upon which we can stand and be united so that we can be pleasing in God's sight. It is particularly worth noting that when we accomplish this goal, we have what is called the unity of the Spirit, not a unity of opinions or a unity of friends or a unity of ideas, but a unity of the Spirit; and we would thus be one in Christ.

So, Christ is the answer when we raise the question, How can unity be obtained? CHRIST is the answer! The Bible is the basis for unity in Christ. I want to tell you one more thing: we must learn to love one another even as Christ has loved us. Jesus gave the commandment, "That ye love one another; as I have loved you, that you also love one another. By this shall all men know that ye are my disciples, IF ye have love one to another" (John 13:34-35). Love is the tie that should bind all Christians to each other, even as to God. True, genuine Christian love is fundamental to Christian unity. We cannot have unity without this genuine love. In order to obtain this kind of unity, we must be willing to add to certain things to our lives and it is also true that to have this kind of unity we must be willing to lay aside some things. First of all, we must be willing to lay aside our own opinions. When Bible truths are mixed with the opinions of men, division will be the result. Therefore, we plead with you, let us speak where the Bible speaks; let us be silent where the Bible is silent. Let us do Bible things in Bible ways and call Bible things by Bible names; in so doing, we shall accomplish the unity for which Jesus prayed.

Another thing we must be willing to lay aside is our sectarianism and our denominationalism. Some things are not taught in the scripture. There are many things that are being taught in our day that simply are not in the Bible. It may sometimes come as a shock to us that some of these things we have heard all of our lives just simply are not in the word of God. There are things that came into existence hundreds of years after God had given the Bible to men. The doctrines and practices and names and creeds of denominationalism, which divide men today, are not found in the Bible. In order to attain unity, all of these must be laid aside. Men cannot be united in some sectarian body. But we can obtain unity in the body of Christ, which is the church revealed in the New Testament. I would like to point out this too, that the Roman Catholic church is not the way of unity. The various ecumenical councils and movements of the Roman church have as one of its aims the unity of men under its dominion. I remember something I read many years ago. It was carried in an associated press dispatch under the heading that the Pope expects church unity under the Vatican and the dateline was Vatican City. The first paragraph reads that the particular Pope in power has called for Christian unity but asserted that a unified Christianity is possible only under the Roman Catholic church. The traditions and laws and teachings of the Roman church are not in keeping with the Bible's teaching. Therefore, we may plainly say Christian unity cannot be obtained under the Roman Catholic church. The Religio-political organization of this particular church stands opposed to the free exercise of Christian fellowship of believers in Christ under the direction of Christ as the only head of the church that He established.

This is only one example. There are many so called ecumenical movements that would propose unity of all men under its particular organization. I propose to you today that unity in this world shall not be accomplished in any of these organizations but only when we return to the simplicity of the Lord's plan. In Ephesians 4:3-6, we are taught to "keep the unity of the Spirit in the bond of peace. There is one body, and one Spirit, even as ye are called in one hope of your calling; One Lord, one faith, one baptism, One God and Father of all, who is above all, and through all, and in you all." These seven ones express God's plan for us now. They state the perfect pattern for the unity that is pleasing to God. But maybe you are saying: "What can I do?" I would like to say, you can do your part. You can believe in Christ as the Son of God, you can become a Christian as the gospel of Christ directs you to and be nothing more or nothing less. Through faith—and it is possible for you to believe in the Lord. Through repentance—and you can repent. Through confession—and you can confess your faith in the Lord. Through baptism—you can be immersed in His name for the remission of your sins. By so doing, you can become a Christian; nothing more, nothing less—not a generic Christian belonging to some movement but just simply a Christian. Let the Lord add you to the church as one saved by the grace of God and become an heir of heaven. Be faithful in living a pure and holy life in your worship of God by the assembling with the saints. You can love your fellow Christian, your neighbors, and even your enemies. You can follow Christ, and you can go to heaven when this life is over.

I hope we can realize that God DOES have a plan for religious unity. Our Lord has never taught us to be ONE and then left us without a plan. We would not ask men to come to us, but the churches of Christ are pleading for men to be united in CHRIST, according to the teachings of the New Testament. We earnestly and humbly pray that this lesson may help someone to understand better and to obey the Lord and surrender his life in service to Him.

# *Memorials*

Good morning, everyone. Once again, we have the privilege of being in the land of the living and studying together the word of God. No greater privileges could we possibly have than these two. The Bible teaches that if we plan to do anything, we ought to say, "If the Lord will, we shall live, and do this, or that" (James 4:15). The Lord has been gracious to us in that He has allowed us to live and, indeed, we believe it is His will that we study His word. In fact, the Bible assures us that it pleases God by the foolishness of preaching to save those who believe. We are grateful for your interest in this broadcast and for those of you who faithfully listen. We trust that you will not be disappointed as we continue to study time after time. Anytime we can hear from you, we would be happy to do so. This, of course, assures us that you are there, that you are listening, that you are searching the scriptures with us and this, of course, is the joy in doing this study— knowing there are those who are in some way being helped and encouraged along the way by this time together.

Our study this morning is simply Christian Memorials. In Luke 22:19, we have a simple statement and yet one that is quite profound. The Lord Jesus says, as He was instituting His Supper, "This do in remembrance of me." These words were spoken by our Lord to His disciples in that upper room in Jerusalem as He gave to them the institution of the Lord's Supper, the sacred memorial through which His disciples for all time would remember His death and suffering on the cross. Yet in addition to this memorial, there are others of great significance, and I think we are aware, even with a casual reading of the Holy Scripture, that on various occasions the Lord would say, "This do in remembrance." Or He would set up something that would cause the people to say "What meaneth this service?"

We believe, today, that memorials are both natural and universal. They are not peculiar to any particular class of people. Everywhere I have ever been or even of those people of whom I have read, I find memorials—among the savage and the civilized, the rich and the poor, the ignorant and the learned, the old and the young. All have relics and memorials. Passing through this great land of ours, we often see monuments that have been built to call our attention to a particular battle or some hero; and all these things are there lest we forget. The world has built great monuments to its leaders, but the name of Jesus Christ shall be kept above all others until the end of time by three great monuments: Baptism, the Lord's Supper, and the Lord's Day.

Christian baptism is a picture of Christ's burial and resurrection. The Lord's Supper relates to His death and His second coming. The Lord's Day celebrates His rising again from the dead upon the first day of the week. Let us consider for a few moments these three imperishable monuments as they relate to Jesus Christ, noticing first of all, baptism.

Most people probably realize there are monuments and memorials, but I think we fail sometimes to realize that baptism is, within itself, a monument that the Lord has left for us. The Bible teaches that Jesus was baptized for this purpose; in fact, in His own words He says, "Suffer it to be so now ... to fulfill all righteousness" (Matthew 3:15). Jesus submitted to the baptism of John because it was God's commandment. God had an ordinance called baptism that He preached to the people through John, and it was understood to be the baptism of repentance for the remission of sins (Mark 1:4). Yet in spite of the fact that Christ was sinless and needed no remission of sins, He submitted to baptism because it was God's command. In His own words, He would "fulfill all righteousness" or He would fulfill God's ordinances. Even though John's baptism has been superceded by Christian baptism (Acts 19:1-5), the Lord commands today that the penitent believer be immersed. In Acts chapter two, we find on Pentecost in answer to the inquiry of the multitude, "What shall we do?" Peter says unto them, "Repent, and be baptized every one of you in the name of Jesus Christ for the remission of sins, and ye shall receive the gift of the Holy Ghost" (Acts 2:38). Those who will not submit to Christian baptism, stay out of the church because they are not loyal to Christ and they refuse to do what He did and what He commanded. How can anyone live the Christian life whose faith is not equal to the test of baptism in the very beginning?

Baptism has a spiritual significance. We are all aware that baptism is for the remission of sins. We are aware that it is a part of the new birth. We are aware that it is that which puts us into Christ, but I wonder if we are aware of its spiritual significance so far as being a monument. We are persuaded that it is more than just an arbitrary command. If baptism were no more than a mere form, then a person could be baptized in his sleep. But baptism has a deeper meaning than merely immersion in water or obedience to a command of Christ. In Christian baptism, we have fellowship with Jesus in His death, His burial, and His resurrection. Paul says, "Know ye not, that so many of us as were baptized into Jesus Christ were baptized into his death? Therefore, we are buried with him by baptism into death: that like as Christ was raised up from the dead by the glory of the Father, even so we also should walk in newness of life" (Romans 6:3-4).

Why can we not see the beautiful picture that baptism is? We are baptized into His death where He shed His blood, which blood cleanses us from all sin; and we are raised in the likeness of His resurrection to live a new life in Him and with Him. I trust we can clearly see that only immersion, only a burial in the watery grave and a resurrection therefrom, can properly symbolize the death, the burial, and the resurrection of Christ. The sprinkling or pouring of a few drops of water upon the believer cannot scripturally signify the true meaning of Christian baptism. Therefore, Paul affirms there is "one baptism" (Ephesians 4:5). The baptized believer becomes a new creature in Christ, for Paul declared that we are "baptized into Christ" (Galatians 3:27). Also, he says, "Therefore if any man be in Christ, he is a new creature: old things are passed away; behold, all things are become new" (2 Corinthians 5:17).

In order to grow in this new life, the new born babe in Christ must be reminded of His Lord consistently and continually. Jesus knew the tendency of the human heart to wrap itself up in the present and forget the past. Therefore, He instituted the Lord's Supper to keep before us His suffering and His death. We are careful to erect a monument over the grave of our loved ones; and each time we visit the tombs, we are reminded of their sacrifice and their love for us. Paul says, "For as often as ye eat this bread, and drink this cup, ye do shew forth the Lord's death till he come" (1 Corinthians 11:26).

But how often should we eat the bread and drink the cup? The apostolic church assembled each first day of the week to observe this sacred institution. Concerning the church at Troas, Luke says, "And upon the first day of the week, when the disciples came together to break bread, Paul preached unto them, ready to depart on the morrow; and continued his speech until midnight" (Acts 20:7). This memorial feast is a lasting monument, and it still stands. Each Lord's Day, Christians meet for the observance of the Lord's Supper, the most appropriate and the most precious monument that has ever been viewed by humankind.

We come now to a discussion of the third Christian memorial, the Lord's Day. The sabbath and the Lord's Day must be properly distinguished, one from the other, because one is of the Old Testament given to the Jews under the law while the other is of the New Testament to be observed by Christians only. The law of Moses has been fulfilled—it has been done away. In the Gospel of John, we find this plain declaration, "For the law was given by Moses, but grace and truth came by Jesus Christ" (John 1:17). Paul clearly teaches that in the death of Christ upon the cross, He abolished the law entirely. Hear the inspired apostle, "Blotting out the handwriting of ordinances that was against us, which was contrary to us, and took it out of the way, nailing it to his cross" (Colossians 2:14).

The command unto the Jews to "Remember the sabbath day, to keep it holy" (Exodus 20:8) was part of the law of Moses that has been done away in Christ. Nine of the ten commandments are to be found in the New Testament so far as the spirit and the teaching of those commandments; however, they are given to us with a deeper significance. But the fourth command regarding the sabbath is not to be found in the New Testament. Nowhere—nowhere in the New Testament are Christians commanded to keep the sabbath day holy. Jesus observed the sabbath because He lived and died under the law of Moses. The apostles often preached on the sabbath day in the synagogues because the Jews to whom they were then preaching still worshiped on that day, being observers of the law of Moses, not having learned that Christ had abolished the law.

Christians have another day, the first day of the week. Since the early Christians assembled to break bread (Acts 20:7) on the first day of the week, Paul says to the church at Corinth, "Upon the first day of the week let every one of you lay by him in store, as God hath prospered him, that there be no gatherings when I come" (1 Corinthians 16:2). Exiled on the Isle of Patmos, John the beloved disciple was in the Spirit on the Lord's Day (Revelation 1:10). The sabbath was a memorial institution, but what did it memorialize? Moses said to the nation of Israel, "And remember that thou wast a servant in the land of Egypt, and that the Lord thy God brought thee out thence through a mighty hand and by a stretched out arm: therefore the Lord thy God commanded thee to keep the sabbath day" (Deuteronomy 5:15). The Israelites had their special days, special ordinances to memorialize certain events of their national history. The Passover feast reminded the Jews of the deliverance of their fathers from the death angel while they were still in Egypt. Pentecost reminded the Jews of the giving of the law on Mount Sinai fifty days after the deliverance of their fathers from bondage, while the sabbath reminded them of the opening of the Red Sea and the deliverance of the people from Egyptian servitude.

We, in the United States, cannot observe July 4th without remembering what happened on July 4th—well, I guess we could, and I suppose that some do—but one would suppose that upon this day, he would recall certain things that occurred in this world on July 4, 1776. The Jews could not observe the sabbath, surely, without remembering the opening of a passageway through the Red Sea. To Americans, July the 4th is full of meaning, but it means nothing to the people of other nations. It would be useless for them to observe it. Likewise, it would be useless, not living under the law, the Old Testament, to observe the sabbath which was a holy day, holy unto Judaism, memorializing a fact of Israelite history.

Christianity has these three great facts: The death, the burial, and the resurrection of our Lord. The gospel rests upon these three great pillars. Read 1 Corinthians 15:1-4 when you have the opportunity. What in Christianity memorializes these facts? Now, if the facts of the gospel are the death, the burial, and the resurrection of Christ, then there should be something that would recall these three great events of all time. Is there a memorial of the death of Christ? Yes. It is the Lord's Supper (1 Corinthians 11:26). In fact, the apostle declares that so often as we observe it we commemorate—and we do preach, we do proclaim, we do tell forth—the death of Christ until our Lord shall come again. Is there a monument of the burial of Christ? Yes. It is Christian baptism. In Romans 6:3-4, Paul says, "Know ye not, that so many of us as were baptized into Jesus Christ were baptized into his death? Therefore we are buried with him by baptism into death: that like as Christ was raised up from the dead by the glory of the Father, even so we also should walk in newness of life." Is there a monument of the resurrection of Christ? What is that monument? It is the Lord's Day or the first day of the week or Sunday. It is this very day on which we are studying this passage together. This, indeed, is the day the Lord has made. This is the Lord's Day. Christ arose from the grave on the first day of the week, and we today celebrate and commemorate that great event. This fact explains why the early Christians met on the first day of the week for the breaking of bread, and it should explain why we are meeting upon the first day of the week and that shortly from the time we close this lesson, we will, both here in this city and throughout this country and other countries, be observing the Lord's Day.

In our study, I trust you have been able to appreciate again these three great monuments: the Lord's Supper, Christian Baptism and the Lord's Day. So appropriately do they memorialize the three great facts of the death, the burial, and the resurrection of our Lord upon which rests the great superstructure of Christianity. Let us be faithful to observe them properly and scripturally. Think about yourself today. Are you planning to observe these things today? Are you planning to be in the house of the Lord or to assemble with the house of the Lord today to worship and to serve Him and to let the world know that you will keep these great memorials to the Lord?

We are grateful for your listening today as we studied together. We would be happy to hear from you in response to this lesson. If there are any particular subjects that you would like to hear discussed, we would be very happy to hear from you and we would be more than happy to present these subjects in future studies.

# *Past, Present and Future*

Ladies and Gentlemen, we invite your attention once more to the word of God. We invite your attention to this particular question, "What will you do with today?"

All of man's relation to time seems to fall into three parts—the past, the present, and the future. Each one of these plays an important part in the thinking, the actions, the planning, and the successes of an individual's life. Which is the most important to you? As I sat down to ponder this question, I found it most interesting. What really is most important to us? ... yesterday ... today ... or tomorrow? About which of these do you think the most? Which is the most dangerous for you? ... yesterday ... today ... or tomorrow? Let us consider the value and the place of each one: ... the past ... the present ... and the future. Let us weigh each one carefully so that we place the emphasis in the proper place.

First of all, think about the past. Each day we live soon slips from us and becomes a part of that great eternity of the past. As we look back over the past, we see all of the days of our lives from the day of our birth until this moment. Each moment has escaped totally beyond our recall. The deeds and the words of yesterday—good or bad—have taken their place there. If we wasted the opportunities of yesterday, they are gone forever. Do you remember this quotation that is taken from an old reader that we had in school when we were small? "Lost—yesterday. somewhere between sunrise and sunset; two golden hours, each set with sixty diamond minutes. No reward is offered, for they are gone forever."

The past may teach us many lessons. History, I have found, can be a good instructor. We may profit by our mistakes if we really try. Our failures can be used to strengthen us and to prepare us for success when we properly evaluate them. Many a player has recovered a fumble to lead him to a touchdown. Yet, some mistakes have led men to disaster. God has recorded the faults of men as well as the good qualities of character within His word. He wants us to be forewarned that we might be forearmed and that we thus do not stumble into the same pitfalls. Those things were written for our learning and our admonition. They were written for our examples and also, as Paul would say, our "ensamples." Some people live too much in the past. They may be boasting or reveling in the achievements of the past and thus neglect the task of today.

Or, on the other hand, they may so burden themselves with regrets or the failures and mistakes of yesterday that they cannot carry the load of labor for the present. We should be thankful for the good and repent of the bad. But do not linger too long in the past, lest you forget the value of the present.

Paul the Apostle, looking backward, wrote:

> This one thing I do, forgetting those things which are behind, and reaching forth unto those things which are before, I press toward the mark for the prize of the high calling of God in Christ Jesus (Philippians 3:13-14).

There are many times when we, too, must forget those things that are behind if we would press forward. Do not let the memories of yesterday rob you of all the beauties of today. Do not let the success or failure of yesterday keep you from the duties of today.

Next, let us consider the future. There, in the future, are all the tomorrows that we hope to have if by, the grace of God, we live and if it is His will. Each one of them will quickly recede before us as they one by one become what we call today. Tomorrow always holds an enchantment to most of us—that golden tomorrow when certain things we trust will be.

To every Christian, tomorrow is a day of hope, a time to reap the harvest and the rewards of the work of today. Eagerly we look forward to what each today will bring. In the great future, in the golden future, lies the eternity of blissful reward in the heavenly home of our Saviour and our God. The future, to the faithful children of God, holds rest from our labors (Revelations 14:13). It holds peace and joy and eternal reunion. So, with Paul, as Christians, we "press toward the mark for the prize of the high calling of God in Christ Jesus." Indeed, we must "seek those things which are above, where Christ sitteth on the right hand of God" (Colossians 3:1). And we are surrounded by what Paul calls "a great cloud of witnesses," that is, the witnesses of God's faithful. We must:

> Lay aside every weight, and the sin which doth so easily beset us, and let us run with patience the race that is set before us, Looking unto Jesus the author and finisher of our faith; who for the joy that was set before him endured the cross, despising the shame, and is set down at the right hand of the throne of God (Hebrews 12:1-2).

Tomorrow may be a golden thing in your mind, but let me please remind you—tomorrow can be a dangerous thing. Some worry about tomorrow—what will it bring? Will it be good or ill? What kind of burden will they have to bear ... tomorrow? What trouble will they face ... tomorrow? How can they provide the things necessary ... tomorrow? They forget that the Lord is able to provide the things that are best for each day when it comes. You remember that Jesus taught His disciples "Take therefore no thought for the morrow: for the morrow shall take thought for the things of itself. Sufficient unto the day is the evil thereof" (Matthew 6:34). In our own words, we can express His meaning by saying—do not worry, do not worry or be anxious about tomorrow. Let each succeeding day provide for itself. Each day has enough cares or troubles of its own. We must live each day as it comes.

You remember, the Lord taught us to pray, "Give us this day our daily bread." The Lord never taught us to pray, "Give us this day our daily bread and, Lord, while you are at it, please give me tomorrow's, too, because you see, Lord, you never know what may happen tomorrow." He did not teach us to pray thusly. He taught us to pray, "Give us THIS DAY our daily bread" (Matthew 6:11). With each coming day, He will give the blessings for that day. The Christian is to look up to God, "casting all your care upon him; for he careth for you" (1 Peter 5:7). In our anxieties about tomorrow, we must not forget Paul's statement, "And we know that all things work together for good to them that love God, to them who are the called according to his purpose" (Romans 8:28). God saw fit to not reveal the joys or the troubles of tomorrow to us TODAY. Please remember that. If the Lord had intended for us to take on all the worries and the troubles of tomorrow, then He would have equipped us in such a way that we could take care of these. But He did not see fit to reveal the joys of tomorrow or the troubles of tomorrow to us today. There is a curtain, shall we say, between us and then. God knows what is best and so He is saying, do not be overly anxious about tomorrow.

Some worry about tomorrow, but some put off until tomorrow what should be done today. To many people, the most dangerous word in all of our language is TOMORROW. Tomorrow paralyzes action and leaves duty undone. It is where failure lurks, and it is where destruction comes. It is like a mirage in the desert, and it deceives the soul of many a person. When Paul reasoned before Felix of righteousness, temperance, and judgment to come, Felix trembled (Acts 24:25). He shuddered at these thoughts as he considered his own condition; but in so far as we know, he lost his own soul when he said, "Go thy way for this time; when I have a convenient season, I will call for thee." Many a person has looked to another day as a convenient time to obey the Lord. But, unfortunately, that convenient "tomorrow" never did come, and he died without God and without hope in the world. Your heart ... your heart may be like Felix's and be tender only once and that may be today. Trusting in tomorrow could well cost you your soul, my friend. You may be like Agrippa the king, and be "almost persuaded" today, but unless you do something about it NOW, you may never have salvation TOMORROW.

Somewhere I read this little poem and I believe it is so worth considering. It pictures the condition of many a life. It says—listen:

> He was going to be all a mortal should be ... TOMORROW.
> No one would be better than he ... TOMORROW.
> Each morning he stacked up the letters he would write ... TOMORROW.
> It was too bad, indeed, he was too busy to see Bill, but he promised to do it ... TOMORROW.
> The greatest of workers he would have been ... TOMORROW.
> The world would have known him had he seen ... TOMORROW.
> But the fact is, he died and faded from view; and all that was left when living was through; was a mention of things he intended to do ... TOMORROW."

This picture is so true and so sad, in view of many, many a life who has put off for tomorrow the matter of obedience to the Lord.

But the question is, not so much—"What did you do yesterday?" or "What do you think you will do tomorrow?" The greatest question you can contemplate in your world today is, "What will you do with today?" This is the important question, and it will determine the reward of tomorrow. Today—remember this—today holds the key to tomorrow. Today is all the time you have. Yesterday is eternally gone. The past cannot be recalled; it is irrevocably lost. Tomorrow is yet to be and may never really come in your life upon this earth. Today is the day the Lord has given you. What will you do with today? How are you going to answer this question? You are doing something with it. I know that today, as you listen to me, you are doing something with today. But the question is ... is it worthwhile? How will it look when you look back on it? How will today look in the great Day of Judgment when you stand before God to "give an account of the deeds that have been done in the body." The answer to this question is about what you are doing or are planning to do TODAY? How will it appear in eternity?

David says, "This is the day which the Lord hath made; we will rejoice and be glad in it" (Psalm 118:24). God has made this day, and He has given it to YOU. He has lengthened your existence to this hour. Had He given us what we deserve, He would have cut us offlong before now in our iniquity. But by His grace, we have today. How are we going to use it? Will you, as the psalmist says, "rejoice and be glad in it"? Will you use this day for the God who made it and gave it to you? Think about it ... what are you willing to do today, for which you are willing to trade a day of your life ... a day that you will never recall ... a day that you will never be able to change. What are you planning to do today for which you are willing to trade one of your days—you do not have many. Will it be a time when you worship with the children of God in the Lord's house, the church of Jesus Christ? Or will you consume this day with pleasure or lust or selfishness or sin? Are you on your way to go fishing? ... and you forgot God today? Or are you placing something else above God today.

If you are not a Christian, consider the words of the Bible, "Behold, NOW"—listen to him—"NOW is the accepted time; behold, NOW is the day of salvation." This profound teaching is found in 2 Corinthians 6:2). And the writer of Hebrews adds urgency to this message: "To day if ye will hear his voice, harden not your hearts." (Hebrews 4:7). Jesus is calling you, tenderly calling you TODAY. He welcomes you to come to Him in full submission, believing in Him with all your heart, repenting of your sins, confessing your faith in Him as the Son of God, and being buried with Him in baptism for the remission of your sins. You may find all this teaching in Mark 16:16; Acts 2:38; Acts 8:36-38; Romans 10:10; Romans 6:4. You CAN obey Him today.

I do not know what you are planning to do today; but I know what you could do today. I know you could obey God. There is a gospel preacher, there is somewhere, a faithful Christian who stands ready and willing to help you obey the Lord. It is just as it was with Phillip who helped the Eunuch, as we read in Acts 8. Remember, "NOW is the accepted time, behold, NOW is the day of salvation." So, do not harden your heart and put off your obedience to the Lord. In the words of that old, old song, "Tomorrow's sun may never rise to bless thy long deluded sight, this is the time, O then be wise, be saved O tonight." Do not wait until tonight. Be saved TODAY through obedience to the gospel of Christ so that His love may wash away your sins (Acts 22:16).

Maybe you have already become a Christian. Maybe, as you listen to me this moment, you are already a Christian; but you have strayed from the path of service to the Lord. What we are concerned about is not so much what you did yesterday but what are you doing today? When we think about this question, we know that today is the time for you to come to yourself and to arise as the prodigal and go back home to your Heavenly Father and say, "Father I have sinned." As we read in Acts 8:22, he was told to "Repent therefore of this thy wickedness, and pray God, if perhaps the thought of thy heart may be forgiven thee." God's people are ready and willing to receive you and to help you this day to begin your life anew for God.

What about today's opportunities? Each day presents new opportunities for service for God and for others. Will you use those which are yours today? One writer has said:

> Many do with opportunities, as children do at the sea shore. They fill their little hands with sand; and they let all the grains fall thru their fingers one by one until they are all gone.

You remember the Greeks pictured opportunity as a woman having one forelock and the back of her head was shaven. If you would see that forelock, you must do so as she approaches, for once she has gone, once has escaped, not Jupiter himself, they would say, could catch her again. So, we must seize the privileges and opportunities for service ... when? ... TODAY for tomorrow they will be gone.

Do not waste this day. Rather, we should be redeeming the time (Ephesians 5:16; Colossians 4:5). What does he mean? Paul says "redeeming the time" means literally buying up the time for the days are evil. There is so much to be done and so little time to do it.

Mr. Edison once said, "Time is the most precious thing in the world." One greater than he says, "I must work the works of him that sent me, while it is day: the night cometh, when no man can work" (John 9:4). In the words of Solomon, "Whatsoever thy hand findeth to do, do it with all thy might; for there is no work, nor device, nor knowledge, nor wisdom, in the grave, whither thou goest" (Ecclesiastes 9:10). So, we would use the advice of this great man of God that we use every part of the day for good. Use it to God's glory, and use it as one who will give an account for it in the Day of Judgment. "For we must all appear before the judgment seat of Christ; that every one may receive the things done in his body, according to that he hath done, whether it be good or bad" (2 Corinthians 5:10). In James, we read:

> Go to now, ye that say, To day or tomorrow we will go into such a city, and continue there a year, and buy and sell, and get gain: Whereas ye know not what shall be on the morrow. For what is your life? It is even a vapour, that appeareth for a little time, and then vanisheth away. For that ye ought to say, If the Lord will, we shall live, and do this, or that. But now ye rejoice in your boastings: all such rejoicing is evil. Therefore to him that knoweth to do good, and doeth it not, to him it is sin (James 4:13-17).

One thing you have already learned ... your life is short, and the future is uncertain, but God has done one thing ... He has given you today. Use today for God. "Remember NOW" ... not tomorrow ... "remember NOW thy Creator in the days of thy youth" (Ecclesiastes 12:1).

You have no assurance of the future continuance of life and opportunity, so make up your mind to serve God TODAY. Talk to someone about Christ today. Use today to live for Jesus Christ.

Surely, we ought to think about that grand old song, "Take time to be holy, speak oft with thy Lord. Abide in Him always, and feed on His Word." Surely, we should stop to ponder the past, the present, and the future, and to realize that the only thing we hold is a little bit of TODAY. What will you do with it?

# *Encouragement*

Ladies and gentlemen, your attention is invited to the word of God. We are grateful to have you in our audience today as we talk about a subject that we feel should touch every person's life—the need for encouragement. Each one of us has his own weaknesses and times of discouragement. This statement is true regardless of how great or how good or how young or how old you may be. We have all experienced days when we stood in need of help either from others about us or from God; and often we long for help from both.

The word "encourage" means "to inspire with courage, to give hope, to animate, to hearten, and to cheer up another." Literally it means "to put courage in another." In Hebrews 3:13, the writer says, "Exhort one another daily." The word "exhort" means "to encourage." Mr. Williams' translation in the language of the people renders this passage: "But day by day, as long as today shall last, continue to encourage one another." It would be a wonderful thing if each one of us would strive to use each day to "continue to encourage one another."

There are many things that are wrong and harmful in and of themselves; and, of course, we must recognize that evil in any form should never have one ounce of our encouragement—especially is this true with a Christian. The Christian's influence must always be uncompromisingly AGAINST evil both in word and in manner of life. But it should be equally true that, as Christians, we will be very careful always to ENCOURAGE that which is good. Let us "be ready to every good work" (Titus 3:1). Often times good meets with great discouragement, and discouragement of good is wrong. It may be very harmful.

Many a person has intended to do what is right and good, but he has been defeated by the words of some of his fellows. Sometimes it seems that we meet more things to discourage us than we meet to encourage us. Some people either wittingly or unwittingly are given to spreading discouragement. Even the truth may be spoken in such a way as to discourage, when actually it should be used to encourage. The history of Israel is a good example. You recall that God had promised them the land of Canaan as a land "flowing with milk and honey"—a land of real abundance.

In the book of Numbers (chapters 13 and 14), we read about how Moses, at the direction of God, sent men to spy out the land as they were about to enter it. Twelve men were selected, one from each tribe of Israel. They were instructed to go and see the land, "And be ye of good courage, and bring of the fruit of the land" (Numbers 13:20). So, they went and brought back of the fruit and said, "Surely it floweth with milk and honey and this is the fruit of it" (verse 27). But ten of those men began to speak of the giants in the land saying, "We be not able to go up against the people; for they are stronger than we" (verse 31). It was true that strong men dwelt in the land of Canaan, but these men brought an "evil report" according to Numbers 13:32. I want you to notice that it was called an "evil report" because they discouraged the people. Joshua and Caleb said:

> If the Lord delight in us, then he will bring us into this land, and give it us; a land which floweth with milk and honey. Only rebel not ye against the Lord, neither fear ye the people of the land; for they are bread for us: their defence is departed from them, and the Lord is with us: fear them not (Numbers 14:8-9).

However, the discouraging words of the ten prevailed, and Israel murmured against Jehovah. Because of their murmurings, they wandered for forty years in the wilderness, and those of that generation perished. The ten evil spies had spoken even the truth in such a way as to discourage a mighty nation, and it caused more than 600,000 of them never to see the land that God had promised to them. Isn't that amazing? Just realize what a little discouragement can do! As it was with Israel, so often it is today. People are more inclined to listen to discouragement than encouragement. For some reason this situation is true. I have observed it year after year and time after time.

Let us never be guilty of discouraging that which is right and that which is good. God help us to be people who "encourage one another." In fact, it is our ever-present responsibility. The Bible has so instructed us in many passages. For example, in Romans 15:1, we are told, "We then that are strong ought to bear the infirmities of the weak, and not to please ourselves." This exhortation is true in a spiritual sense of those who are weak spiritually. Let us bear with them and help them to grow stronger. It is true of those who are weak physically and who need our patience and kindness and consideration that they might be encouraged in bearing their infirmities. Many, many a sick person has found new courage in the words of another, new strength to get well or new strength to bear the pain and suffering that they endure. In Acts 20:35, we are told "to support the weak, and to remember the words of the Lord Jesus, how he said, It is more blessed to give than to receive." In 1 Thessalonians 5:14, Paul exhorts us to "support the weak, be patient toward all men." If we would be followers of Christ, we must be mindful of the needs of others: the sick, the infirm, the needy, and those who are weak spiritually must never be overlooked. We must be ready to speak words to help them and to use the blessings that God has given us to minister to their needs.

Sometimes people are overtaken in wrong doing. They stumble and fall into sin. Let us not be more ready to censure than to help. It has been said that correction does much but encouragement does more. Encouragement after censure is as the sun after a shower. Paul gives this instruction in Galatians 6:1: "Brethren, if a man be overtaken in a fault, ye which are spiritual, restore such an one in the spirit of meekness; considering thyself, lest thou also be tempted." So, in gentleness and humility, with patience and meekness, let us undertake the restoring of the erring. No one should attempt to correct or to admonish another unless he can do it in the spirit of meekness, considering his own weakness and his own proneness to error. Tenderness and compassion should govern us in our dealings with others.

The Lord's rule is right—and remember this—not only is it right, it is always best. "Therefore all things whatsoever ye would that men should do to you, do ye even so to them" (Matthew 7:12). Let our attitudes and actions toward others be what we would like for theirs to be toward us is what He is saying. It would help us as we consider those words of Galatians 6:2, "Bear ye one anothers burdens, and so fulfill the law of Christ." All of us have our burdens. Many of them can be made much lighter by the encouragement and the help of others. So often just a kind word or a thoughtful deed can make a person's load much easier to bear. May we try, by God's help, to be ready and willing to help others in bearing their burdens. In so doing, we will find our own burdens are made lighter and easier for us to bear ourselves.

We have many examples of encouragement in the Bible. When Moses was old and about to die, he thought of Joshua who was to succeed him as leader of Israel. You remember God directed him to "encourage" Joshua and to "strengthen" him that he might lead the people of God (Deuteronomy 3:28). David, when he drew near the close of his life, spoke to Solomon, saying:

> I go the way of all the earth: be thou strong therefore, and shew thyself a man; And keep the charge of the Lord thy God, to walk in his ways, to keep his statutes, and his commandments, and his judgments, and his testimonies (1 Kings 2:2-3).

The Apostle Paul, even in the midst of the storm on the sea, spoke to those in the ship, saying, "Sirs, be of good cheer" (Acts 27:25). His letters are all letters of encouragement. To those at Philippi, who had suffered so much persecution, he wrote "Rejoice in the Lord alway: and again I say, Rejoice" (Philippians 4:4). Even as he wrote these words, he was himself a prisoner in Rome because of his obedience to the will of Christ. In all of his trials, he says, "I have learned, in whatsoever state I am, therewith to be content" (Philippians 4:11). In Acts 4, we are told of Joses whose name was changed to Barnabas who was so named by the apostles (his name means "son of consolation" or son of encouragement) because of the encouragement he gave his fellow Christians. We need many more people like Barnabas.

Christ our Lord set the greatest example of all. The scripture declares in Acts 10:38 that He "went about doing good." To the sick of the palsy, He says, "Son, be of good cheer" (Matthew 9:2). When John the baptist was in prison, Jesus sent words of encouragement to him (Matthew 11:4-5). Whereever He went, Jesus brought hope and cheer to the hearts of man. His compassion for all men meant His willingness to die for our sins that we might know the hope of eternal life. His sacrifice for us on Calvary, to every Christian, means He "bare our sins in his own body on the tree, that we, being dead to sins, should live unto righteousness: by whose stripes ye were healed" (1 Peter 2:24). Our Lord has invited all men to Him, saying, "Come unto me, all ye that labour and are heavy laden, and I will give you rest.

Take my yoke upon you, and learn of me; for I am meek and lowly in heart: and ye shall find rest unto your souls. For my yoke is easy, and my burden is light" (Matthew 11:28-30). Let us accept His invitation and obey His gospel.

My friend, have you accepted Christ as your Saviour? Have you had enough faith in Him to repent of your sins? Have you had enough faith in Him to confess the faith that you do have in Him? Have you had enough faith to be baptized in obedience to the Lord for the remission of your sins? If not, we pray that you will do so. We want to encourage you to obey the Lord and to stand up for Him. We believe that when you do, the Lord will become a tremendous source of strength to you. Paul says, "I can do all things through Christ which strengthenth me" (Philippians 4:13). He will give us courage to stand for the right and to be faithful in life, in worship, and in service.

He knows and understands our every need, and He will supply that which is best. By His help, we can overcome every temptation and withstand every trial. All the trials will be as James says: "The trying of your faith worketh patience. But let patience have her perfect work, that ye may be perfect and entire, wanting nothing" (James 1:3-4). We may not receive the help and the encouragement from our fellowmen that we expect. We may not receive the help and the encouragement that we think we deserve or that they should give us. But we must be careful not to let their failure to encourage us make us bitter in our attitude toward others or let it cause us to neglect our duty to encourage them or any of those about us. We have a greater source of courage than men. We have Christ, and we have our great God Jehovah from whom we can have courage as Christians. Let us rely upon them. The Psalmist David writes, "Cast thy burden upon the Lord, and he shall sustain thee: he shall never suffer the righteous to be moved" (Psalm 55:22).

Peter writes encouragement, saying, "Casting all your care upon him; for he careth for you" (1 Peter 5:7). The Lord can be our friend and the source of our encouragement at all times. In Psalm 42:5, the writer says, "Why art thou cast down, O my soul? and why art thou disquieted in me? hope thou in God: for I shall yet praise him for the help of his countenance." When David was greatly distressed, we are told in 1 Samuel 30:6 that "David encouraged himself in the Lord his God." So, we can find encouragement in our great God today, and this encouragement comes to us as we acquaint ourselves with the great promises in the word of God, the Holy Scriptures, and as we show our reliance upon Him through prayer.

May I remind you of this fact in closing, God's promises are sure. Our Lord will NEVER fail us. He knows and understands our hearts. He understands our burdens. He knows our trials. He takes note of our every need. We must ever be reminded that He who notes the sparrows fall surely has His eyes on us. In matters and moments of discouragement, let us never become despondent. God can take care of us. "He is able" the scripture declares; and "If God be for us, who can be against us?" I understand that teaching to mean this: that "If God is for us, who can successfully array himself against us?" (Romans 8:31).

The victory that can be ours is dependent upon our faith. If, indeed, we are looking for the victory, here it is: "This is the victory that overcometh the world, even our faith" (1 John 5:4). So, we beseech you today to accept Christ, to live for Him every day of your life, and through Him, you will have the strength to encourage one another. Indeed, we need to give more thought and more practice to supplying this great need. The Bible admonishes us "Encourage one another." May I read that translation to you once again: Mr. Williams' translation, "But day by day, as long as today shall last, continue to encourage one another."

# *Preach the Word*

Ladies and gentlemen, we invite your attention this morning to one of the most impressive exhortations in all of the Apostle Paul's writings. It is in 2 Timothy, 4:1-5, and it is a solemn charge in which he calls to witness both God and Christ. Paul reminds the young preacher Timothy that Christ is Lord and will be the judge of all, both the living and the dead, at the time of His coming. Let us turn to that place and read Paul's charge to the Timothy:

> I charge thee before God, and the Lord Jesus Christ, who shall judge the quick and the dead at his appearing and his kingdom; Preach the word; be instant in season, out of season; reprove, rebuke, exhort with all longsuffering and doctrine. For the time will come when they will not endure sound doctrine; but after their own lusts shall they heap to themselves teachers, having itching ears; And they shall turn away their ears from the truth, and shall be turned unto fables. But watch thou in all things, endure afflictions, do the work of an evangelist, make full proof of thy ministry (2 Timothy 4:1-5).

When we stop to really think about this passage and this great charge, we raise the question: Why did God place such stress upon preaching? The answer to this questions if found in many places in the Holy Scriptures. Let us notice a few.

In Romans 10:13-15, the Holy Spirit directs Paul to write:

> For whosoever shall call upon the name of the Lord shall be saved. How then shall they call on him in whom they have not believed? And how shall they believe in him of whom they have not heard? And how shall they hear without a preacher? And how shall they preach, except they be sent? as it is written, How beautiful are the feet of them that preach the gospel of peace, and bring glad tidings of good things!

This passage makes clear the means of salvation to all humankind. First, they must call upon the Lord to be saved. Secondly, in order to call upon the Lord, they must believe in Him. Thirdly, in order to believe in the Lord, they must hear about Him, as we read in Romans 10:17, "So then faith cometh by hearing, and hearing by the word of God." Therefore, God's word must be preached! Men must hear the gospel of peace, and they must learn the glad tidings of good things. There must be a preacher to preach the message of God so that men may hear, believe in the Lord, call upon the Lord in the Lord's appointed way, so that they may be saved. So, preaching is necessary! God's word must be preached now—today—if people are to be saved.

The spoken word has power, and it is not simply something that occurred in ages past—it has a power today! Preaching is not out of date. It is by the preaching of the gospel that men are led to Christ. Comparatively, few people learn God's truths without the help of some faithful teacher (Now it is certainly possible since we have the completed word of God). It is true that we have the written word ... it is true that as individuals we ought to search the scripture. Jesus says, "Search the scriptures; for in them ye think ye have eternal life: and they are they which testify of me" (John 5:39). We should be like those noble Bereans of whom we read in Acts 17:11: "They received the word with all readiness of mind, and searched the scriptures daily, whether those things were so." The gospel of Christ, containing God's plan of salvation, is found in the New Testament. That plan is so complete that men are not to add to it or take away from it (Revelations 22:18-19). Men are not to preach any other gospel or pervert or change the gospel of Christ, for the one who does so shall be accursed of God (Galatians 1:6-9).

All of us need to understand the gospel. It is not enough just to hear it, we need to understand it! Many times we are like the eunuch of Acts 8:30. When Philip asked him, "Understandest thou what thou readest?" he replied, "How can I, except some man should guide me? And he desired Philip that he would come up and sit with him." He desired Philip to teach the real meaning of the scripture. Notice as he realized he needed someone to guide him in understanding the word (verse 31). This is what we are looking at today! Christ must be preached, and one may not be saved without the gospel of Jesus Christ. May I ask those of you who are listening who are Christians, how did you learn about Christ? Did you read yourself into a knowledge of the truth, or did you have some faithful Christian to help you to learn the word of God? With most of us, our learning about Christ was because of the interest of some Christian who wanted to share with us the blessings of living for Christ—who wanted us to be saved through obedience to the gospel and who wanted us to have the hope of eternal life through Jesus Christ our Lord. It may have been a Christian mother or father who taught us. Perhaps we learned God's truth as preached from the pulpit or over the radio; but in whatever way, some devout follower of Christ impressed upon our hearts the word of God!

Paul has taught Timothy, and in turn Timothy was to teach others just as now it is our Christian responsibility to teach others (2 Timothy 2:2). So, what we are looking at this morning is this: Christ placed tremendous emphasis on teaching or preaching. He was the greatest teacher the world has ever known! He described His work saying, "Let us go into the next towns, that I may preach there also: for therefore came I forth" (Mark 1:38). Notice the priority! Notice the mission! "Therefore came I forth." He trained His apostles and sent them forth to teach. First, they went to the lost sheep of the house of Israel (Matthew 10:6). After the Lord's resurrection, He gave the command, "Go ye into all the world, and preach the gospel to every creature. He that believeth and is baptized shall be saved; but he that believeth not shall be damned" (Mark 16:15-16).

The apostles began their work as the witnesses of the Lord in preaching salvation. Notice they preached salvation through Christ on the day of Pentecost as recorded in Acts 2. Through the generations of the past, the gospel of salvation has come down to us and now it is ours! It is ours as the followers of Christ to share that solemn charge: Preach the word! We are to pass on to others the blessings that we enjoy in Christ, and this is to be done through preaching or teaching the word of God!

Now, let us notice another important part of the charge that Paul gave to the young preacher Timothy. Paul did not simply say, "Preach"— he says, "Preach the word." Notice, it is "the word," God's word, that is to be preached! Jesus says, "Preach the gospel to every creature." Therefore, we must conclude that the word is the gospel, and the gospel is the word. In Romans 1:16, Paul tells us that "the gospel of Christ is the power of God unto salvation to everyone that believeth." So, Christ is to be preached! When the gospel is preached, then Christ is preached.

Peter preached Christ on the day of Pentecost (Acts 2) to those who gathered in Solomon's porch. The apostles preached Christ in Jerusalem, even though the Jewish leaders forbade them and threatened them. It was for the preaching of Christ that Stephen was stoned to death, but Christ continued to be preached in the face of persecution and even death. When the disciples were scattered abroad because of the persecution, we are told, "Therefore they that were scattered abroad went every where preaching the word" (Acts 8:4).

Philip preached Christ to the Samaritans, to Simon, and to the eunuch. Peter preached Christ to the Gentiles at the house of Cornelius, according to Acts 10. Everywhere they went, they preached Christ! And they preached the word of God! So, it is evident that God wants us to hear Christ! The writer of the Hebrew letter says, "God, who at sundry times and in divers manners spake in time past unto the fathers by the prophets, Hath in these last days spoken unto us by his Son ... " (Hebrews 1:1-2). God says of Him, "This is my beloved Son, in whom I am well pleased; hear ye him" (Matthew 17:5).

Christ fulfilled the Old Testament scriptures; and having fulfilled them, He took out of the way the Law of Moses and it was nailed to the cross when Jesus died (Colossians 2:14). So, we now live under the law of Christ, and we must hear Christ. I am thinking of all those passages and also of the time in which we live, and think how tremendously the world needs Christ today! Wisdom of men cannot save us. God says:

> I will destroy the wisdom of the wise, and will bring to nothing the understanding of the prudent. ... for after that in the wisdom of God the world by wisdom knew not God, it pleased God by the foolishness of preaching to save them that believe (1 Corinthians 1:19-21).

So, Paul says, "But we preach Christ crucified." Now notice, Christ is the means of our salvation! Christ is our only Savior! It was Christ who died for our sins, according to the scripture (1 Corinthians 15:3). It was of Christ that Peter says, "He bare our sins in his own body on the tree, that we, being dead to sins, should live unto righteousness: by whose stripes ye were healed" (1 Peter 2:24).

The creeds of men will not save us! So many of them are so contradictory to the teachings of our Lord. Denominational doctrines and sectarian creeds have confused the minds of men—have divided the professed followers of Christ, and have caused untold thousands of people not to obey the gospel of our Savior. It is Christ that men need today! The Christ of the gospel—the Christ of God—as revealed to us in the word of God!

Many preach so many conflicting opinions and creeds that the world as a whole has remained in darkness, even though Christ, the light of the world, would shine into their hearts and give them salvation! No man has the right to declare his own wisdom or place his own statements of what he believes as the means of salvation! God has taught us: Preach the word! Have you ever thought about this: Insomuch as the scripture says, "Preach the word" nothing more, nothing less, then why should we be interested in anything else? The text says, "For the time will come when they will not endure sound doctrine; but after their own lusts shall they heap to themselves teachers, having itching ears; And they shall turn away their ears from the truth, and shall be turned unto fables" (2 Timothy 4:3-4).

Jesus says, "Men loved darkness rather than light, because their deeds were evil. For every one that doeth evil hateth the light, neither cometh to the light, lest his deeds should be reproved" (John 3:19-20). So, God's word is to be taught. Christians are to reprove, rebuke, and exhort with all long suffering and doctrine. Sin must be condemned! Men must learn to turn from sin in repentance, to confess Christ as God's Son, to be baptized into Christ, put on Christ in their lives, and to make not provision for the flesh to fulfill the lust thereof (Luke 13:3; Acts 2:38; Romans 13:13-14).

It is evident that the problem is that the world does not want to forsake sin! The majority of people would rather enjoy the pleasures of sin than to obey the gospel of Christ! They love darkness rather than light. Satan is on hand to deceive them into thinking they are all right. Pauls tells how can be done in the letter to the Thessalonians:

> After the working of Satan with all power and signs and lying wonders, And with all deceivableness of unrighteousness in them that perish; because they received not the love of the truth, that they might be saved. And for this cause God shall send them strong delusion, that they should believe a lie: That they all might be damned who believed not the truth, but had pleasure in unrighteousness (2 Thessalonians 2:9-12).

False teachers have had their part in this dilema. Paul says after their own lust shall they heap to themselves teachers, having itching ears. The false teachers set aside God's word; they preach things that would agree with the lustful ways of men. Error is always more popular than truth in the world of sin. So many love theory or speculation or some sort of fable in place of truth. Such things appeal to the ear, but they will not save the soul. Jesus says, "Ye shall know the truth and the truth shall make you free." Notice, Paul predicted they will turn away their ears from the truth! Jesus says, "Ye shall know the truth, and the truth shall make you free" (John 8:32).

False teachers fall into two classes: Some know they are false and deliberately deceive men; others do their work without knowing their doctrine is wrong; but both classes stand condemned before God, according to the Bible! It is evident that people need to be warned! Jesus says, "If the blind lead the blind, both shall fall into the ditch" (Matthew 15:14). John says, "Beloved, believe not every spirit, but try the spirits whether they are of God: because many false prophets are gone out into the world" (1 John 4:1). God has placed the responsibility upon the preacher to preach the word. Wherein he may err, the Lord will judge him in the Day of Judgment. Also, God has placed a responsibility on the hearer. Jesus says, "Take heed that no man deceive you" (Matthew 24:4). But hear the word of the Lord— search the scriptures. Do not take my word or the word of any man. Rather, we would point you to the truth of God and to the gospel. Believe in Christ as the Son of God, obey the gospel of Christ, and live for Christ. Let your faith not stand in the wisdom of men but in the power of God (1 Corinthians 2:5).

There has never been a time when this text was more needed than in our own generation. We will do well to let these words direct us to the blessings that are to be found in our Lord Jesus Christ. Remember, Jesus says, "I am the way, the truth, and the life: no man cometh unto the Father, but by me" (John 14:6). Let us make up our minds that we shall learn of Christ and walk in His ways so that we may have the full assurance of a faith that is based upon God's eternal truth. In so doing, we shall know the happiness of the Father's house in heaven.

We close with the desire and with the prayer that God may bless us all, that we may learn the word of God, that we may believe it, and that we may obey it so that by the grace of God we may be saved!

# *What Must I Do To Be Saved?*

Our subject today is "What must I do to be saved?" We would like to begin today with a study of the Great Commission. In carrying out the Great Commission of Mark 16:15-16 and Matthew 28:19-20, the apostles went to all men telling the story of salvation. In Acts 16, the jailer was told to believe on the Lord Jesus in order to obtain this salvation. In Acts 2, the people on Pentecost were told to repent and be baptized for the remission of sins. In Acts 9, Saul of Tarsus was told to arise and be baptized and wash away his sins. Seemingly, some have found it difficult to harmonize these answers given the question, "What must I do to be saved?" We have three different answers to the same question. But I feel the explanation is not difficult. (1) The jailer was an unbeliever. He was told to believe, and they preached to him for the purpose of producing faith. He then repented and was baptized (Acts 16). (2) The people on Pentecost did believe, so they were told simply to repent and be baptized for the remission of sins (Acts 2:38). (3) Saul was a believing, penitent man. He was simply told to be baptized and wash away his sins (Acts 22:16). (4) They were given different answers because they were at different places on the road to salvation. But they all did the same thing and all traveled over the same road of obedience.

In Mark the 10th chapter, the rich, young ruler asked, "Good Master, what shall I do that I may inherit eternal life?" (verse 17). Jesus did not begin by saying, "Keep the commandments." He knew the young man had done so; hence, there was no need to start at the beginning. Jesus began where the young man had traveled in keeping the commands of God. "One thing thou lackest:" Jesus says, "Go thy way, sell whatsoever thou hast, and give to the poor" (verse 21). But at this point someone points out that the scripture does not say in any one passage that an individual must hear, believe, repent, confess, and be baptized. Such reasoning, however, is not valid nor in harmony with God's wishes in rightly dividing the word of truth. In 2 Timothy 2:15, he insists that we must rightly divide or handle aright the word of truth. In other words, we must consider the whole in order to get the full truth. Let me illustrate. There is a story familiar to all in the

Bible concerning the time when Malchus, the servant of the high priest, had his right ear cut off by Peter and then restored by Jesus. Matthew 26, Mark 15, Luke 22, and John 18 all relate that story. Matthew and Mark tell the story but do not name the characters. John tells us the names of those involved. Luke tells us which ear was cut off. Thus, by harmonizing the full account by the four authors, we clearly see the whole story. When one views the story of salvation in the same light, he can see clearly the harmony that exists in saying that one must hear the gospel, believe it, repent of his sins, confess Christ to be God's Son, and be baptized for the remission of his sins in order to obtain salvation. **A refusal to accept faith as a condition of salvation is but a refusal to accept the Bible.**

I would like to begin today with a study of **faith**. While preaching in a small southern town, a gospel preacher taught that all drunkards, fornicators, idolators, etc. would not inherit the kingdom of God. His lesson was rightly based on 1 Corinthians 6. In the midst of his sermon, an elderly woman in the audience screamed. After the service, she came to the preacher and apologized. She related how her son had recently been killed while driving drunk; and she realized that he had lifted up his eyes in hell. Perhaps you and I would scream likewise were we to fully believe in God, not only in His goodness but in His severity as well. The multitudes that shall enter the broad way and the wide gate (Matthew 7:13) will do so because they fail to believe or have faith. Lot's wife turned to a pillar of salt because she did not fully believe God's word. King Saul lost the favor of the Lord because of his disobedience. Disobedience? Yes. Lack of faith? Yes. Had he fully believed in God, he would have never thought once of inserting his own way rather than God's. True faith prompts strict obedience. Weak, little, or no faith brings disobedience and opens the doors to hell. The absolute necessity of faith is emphasized from the beginning to the end of the Bible. It is absolutely indispensable to man's salvation. A refusal to accept faith as a condition of salvation is but a refusal to accept the Bible.

In Hebrews 11:1, we read that "Faith is the substance of things hoped for, the evidence of things not seen." Take the word "substance" and break it apart. "Sub" means "under" and "stance" means to "stand or support." Hence, we have "under support." Faith, then, is the undersupport of man's salvation. Without it, it is impossible to please God (Hebrews 11:6). Faith is childlike trust, wholehearted confidence, and active obedience. If you have faith, you will trust in

God and not in things material. You will place your confidence in Jehovah, knowing that "all things work together for good to those who love God" (Romans 8:28). And, finally, you will never falter in doing the commands of the Almighty.

But how do we acquire faith? "Faith cometh by hearing," the scripture states, "and hearing by the word of God" (Romans 10:17). In our homes we have the Bible that will unlock and unbar all closed doors through faith. We should read it to be holy, study it to be wise, and obey it to obtain salvation in that home prepared for the righteous.

The next step in God's plan of salvation is repentance. Probably the best question is: "What is repentance?" Repentance is far more than just an arbitrary step in the plan of salvation. It is, in many ways, the key that unlocks the door of conversion. In Acts 17:30, we learn that all men everywhere must repent. This command in the gospel age began to be preached in Jerusalem on Pentecost (Luke 24:47; Acts 2:38). Even though we shall perish unless we do repent—and I think we must realize that proper obedience enjoins upon us due penitence (Acts 3:19)—still so many people do not understand the scriptural definition of repentance. What is repentance? How is repentance brought about? What is the result of true repentance? What about death bed repentance? We shall strive to answer these questions in light of what the scriptures teach.

In the book of Matthew, we find the best clear-cut example and definition of repentance in the Bible.

> A certain man had two sons; and he came to the first, and said, Son, go work today in my vineyard. He answered and said, I will not: but afterward he repented, and went (Matthew 21:28-30).

What is repentance, then, according to the Bible? It is a change of mind or a change of decision. A man has decided to serve Satan and sin. He learns of the love of God and the terrible nature of sin and the hopeless condition he is in and the joys of serving the Lord. He changes his mind—decision—in regard to sin. He thus repents. No wonder we believe repentance is the real obstacle in the scheme of redemption. Show me an individual who will genuinely repent, and I will show you one who will not quibble over faith or repentance or baptism. Repentance is brought about by the love of God, the wrath of

God, and godly sorrow for sin. In Romans 2:4, we learn that the "goodness of God leadeth us to repentance." In Romans 11:22 and 2 Corinthians 5:11, we learn that the wrath of God should cause us to obey Him in this as well as other commands. In Luke 15, the prodigal son repented when he came to himself. He realized just how sinful he was and how wonderful his father was. Indeed, as 2 Corinthians 7:10 states, "Godly sorrow worketh repentance to salvation (or life) not to be repented of."

Now, what is the result of true repentance? Acts 2:38 and 3:19 show us that the result is a reformed life. Repentance is not just turning from sin. It is the decision to turn. Repentance is not a reformation of life, but it produces such. Faith changes our affections, repentance changes our will, baptism changes our relationship.

Deathbed repentance upon the part of an erring Christian, if genuine, would be acceptable. Only God knows, however. It takes more than repentance on the part of one who is out of Christ, and not a Christian, to remit sins (Acts 2:38; Mark 16:16). Too many people squander off a lifetime of opportunities and then call on God when it is too late. 2 Peter 3:9 tells us that God is "longsuffering to us-ward, not willing that any should perish, but that all should come to repentance." Question: Have you complied with this command yet?

Let us move to another factor in God's plan of salvation, and that is confession. Confessing Christ is more than a duty to be performed. We believe that it is a rare privilege that one obeying Christ must do. Jesus says "Whosoever therefore shall confess me before men, him will I confess also before my Father which is in heaven" (Matthew 10:32). He shows us the importance of this confession by commending Peter for making it in Matthew 16:18-19 and by witnessing it himself before Pontius Pilate (1 Timothy 6:12-13). We find it was a part of the plan of salvation given by the apostles in the beginning of the church. This confession, contrary to the belief of some, is not the confession of some doctrine or dogma but the simple confession of faith in Christ. Peter says simply, "Thou art the Christ, the Son of the living God" (Matthew 16:16). This is the only confession we are called upon to make. When the Eunuch requested baptism, he was told, if you believe, you may (Acts 8:37). When he answered, "I believe that Jesus Christ is the son of God," he was baptized. Thus the confession is a simple statement of belief in the divinity of Christ. This is the only question that one is asked when he comes to obey the Lord, and it is the only confession that is he is expected to make.

Let us consider another, and final, step in being saved from our past sins—and this is **baptism**. Scriptural baptism is the symbol of the series of events upon which Christianity is based. And that is the death, the burial, and the resurrection of Jesus Christ. To be a Christian, we must pattern our lives after the Saviour. As He died, was buried, and arose **literally**, we must do these things **spiritually**. To charge baptism as being unessential is to show a lack of understanding as to its significance. In the first place, God did not deal with non-essentials in His word. The Apostle Paul says to the Galatians that any change made in the gospel would render it void as the gospel of Christ. Baptism is testimony that the subject is dying to the world so that he might live unto God. It shows that the subject recognizes that he was worthy to die on the cross and live eternally in hell but that Christ died in his stead. Recognizing this fact, the person knows that he figuratively died with Christ 2,000 years ago when He was nailed to the cross. Please listen! Paul explains it in these words. "I am crucified with Christ: nevertheless I live; yet not I, but Christ liveth in me" (Galatians 2:20). This apostle says to the Colossians, "Ye are dead, and your life is hid with Christ in God" (Colossians 3:3). When was Paul crucified? He insists that "I am crucified with Christ." When did the Colossians die? Paul insists they are now "dead" and their life is hid with Christ in God. When did they die? I answer that the time at which they died was the time they were convicted and were baptized.

The truth is made known by Paul's word in. Please listen:

Know ye not, that so many of us as were baptized into Jesus Christ were baptized into his death? Therefore we are buried with him by baptism **into death**." Scriptural baptism involves a resolution on the part of the subject that he will be dead to the world of sin and alive unto God. Paul writes in the book of Romans:

> For in that he died, he died unto sin once: but in that he liveth, he liveth unto God. Likewise reckon ye also yourselves to be dead indeed unto sin, but alive unto God (Romans 6:3-4).

It is in this way that baptism is complementary to repentance. Baptism is also for the remission of sins, according to the Bible. We must be baptized if we desire to have God wash away or forgive our sins. Baptism is not an ordinance. It is not a sacrament. It is not a ritual. It is, rather, a command. In Acts 10:48, the Bible teaches us that they were **commanded** to be baptized. Acts 2:38, Acts 22:16, Mark 16:16, and other passages, show that baptism is necessary for salvation, according to God's word. There is no other way shown as to how one can get into Christ. Please read those passages and view them in the light of baptism being a command.

Baptism is the consummation of the new birth. In John 3:5 Jesus says one must be born of the water and of the Spirit if he is to be saved. Baptism is the last step of this birth. Paul teaches in Romans:

> Therefore we are buried with him by baptism into death: that like as Christ was raised up from the dead by the glory of the Father, even so we also should walk in newness of life (Romans 6:4).

Romans 6:3 says we are baptized into Christ and 2 Corinthians 5:17 states that in Christ we are new creatures. One cannot be born anew without being born of the water and of the Spirit. One cannot be in Christ without baptism; one cannot have his sins remitted without being baptized. These are not the words of men. This is simply the truth of God who loved us enough to give us His Son and then share with us what He wished for us to do.

I would like to mention as the last step in this great plan of salvation—the matter of endurance. All the world hates a quitter. From our earliest days, we are taught to finish what we start. To see any task through to fruition is considered an act of nobility, and it is even so with God and in the body of Christ. Jesus says, "He that shall endure unto the end, the same shall be saved" (Matthew 24:13). There are far too many who have begun the race of a Christian, only to turn back and to prove themselves unworthy of the crown of eternal life (2 Timothy 4:6-8). The Hebrew writer rebukes and reminds his brethren of this malady in Hebrews 6:1-15. In these forceful verses, the inspired writer emphasizes to the Hebrews who have been converted to Christ that they are to endure patiently that they might obtain the promise. Like them, we are not to be slothful; but through faith and patience, we shall inherit the promise of eternal life. After telling his brethren to remember the former days in which they were more zealous and consecrated, we find these words:

> Cast not away therefore your confidence, which hath great recompence of reward. For ye have need of patience, that, after ye have done the will of God, ye might receive the promise. ... Now the just shall live by faith: but if any man draw back, my soul shall have no pleasure in him. But we are not of them who draw back unto perdition; but of them that believe to the saving of the soul (Hebrews 10:35-39).

The writer passed along these words of encouragement and warning to these people who had converted to Christ but who were going through some discouraging times. He wants them to look to the reward and be stimulated to remain faithful to the end.

One of the saddest of all sad things will be the person in the judgment who had once been a faithful child of God but died out of duty in the beggarly elements of the world (Galatians 4:9-11). The Bible states it would be better for him if he had never been born.

One of the most beautiful portraits, however, is the picture painted by a devoted Christian. The older he grows the more like Christ he becomes and he blazes down the final lap of life in resplendent glory, steadfast, loyal, and enduring all the way. If at the end of time we truly can say, as the Apostle Paul did, "I have fought a good fight, I have finished my course and I have kept the faith," we can also expect that crown of righteousness that the Lord will give to those who remain faithful in His service.

Baptism, with faith, repentance, and confession, will put us into Christ but I will guarantee you it is endurance in the faith that will put us into heaven. We begin our spiritual walk with Christ by baptism. By remaining loyal to Him, we are ushered into that eternal rest with our Saviour.

I would like to remind you that we do have a heavenly prize. I fear that heaven does not mean as much to us today as it did to our forefathers. To them, going to heaven was the all-important goal of life. But to many in our generation, it is more like a fairy tale that we tell our children rather than a real and abiding hope. Some have suggested that we have made this old world such an attractive place that going to heaven does not seem much of an improvement for most of us, and this is one reason why we play at Christianity rather than realizing the serious thing that it actually is. But I think we must realize that heaven is an attainable goal, and this is the reason the Christian religion is so important to us—for it is the way of life that will cause us to inherit this heavenly prize that is called heaven itself. We want to thank you for listening today as we have studied together the plan of salvation.

# *Overcoming Difficulties*

Good morning, everyone. This morning we invite your attention to the subject, "Overcoming Difficulties." Every one of us, at some time or another, is faced with some kind of difficulty. The difficulty may be some problem that seems almost insurmountable or it may be some small and annoying circumstance that calls for extra patience and care to overcome. It seems that some people have more difficulties to come their way than others. Often the difference lies in the fact that the nature of some difficulties makes them more noticeable, or it may be that some individuals bear their problems on the inside and do not talk about them. But we may be certain that each person, in the normal course of life, has to face difficulties. Some of them will be small and others will be large and really try the soul. So the question today is not whether we shall have difficulties but whether we shall be able to overcome them.

Our attitude toward the problems that come before us will determine the success or the failure of our lives. It will determine the happiness or the sorrow that we will have. Will we overcome our difficulties or will we let them overcome us? Will we let them be hindrances or will they serve to help us and to strengthen us? Will they destroy us or will we destroy them? These are the questions we must face and that we must answer. In fact, each one of us must answer for himself, for each one of us must face the circumstances of his own life. So I guess we are simply asking, What is your attitude toward life? Are you a fatalist who thinks all things are determined by fate and there is nothing you can do to change them? Do you face life with the gloom and the despair of thinking your difficulties cannot be overcome? It seems to me that such an attitude would be a sad one indeed; yet there are many people who face life in such a way.

On the other hand, do you let the events of life make you bitter? Are you resentful toward the unpleasant things that come into your life? So often men and women let little things fill their lives with the bitterness that hides all the good and all the beautiful things about them. Bitterness will shut out all the rest, if only given the chance.

Are you a complainer? Some people are chronic complainers. They complain about everything and everybody. They think nothing good or worthwhile ever happens to them. They start each day with the attitude, What evil thing will befall me today? How much better it would be to begin each morning with the philosophy of a lady who began each day saying, "I wonder what good thing will happen to me today?" If we want to find something to be happy about, we usually can. If we want to find something to grumble and complain about, we can most certainly find it. Let us look for the good for which to be thankful, and in so doing we will not have the time or the interest to hunt out things about which we should complain.

On the other hand, we might raise this question. Is your condition worse than that of any one else? Do you consider your problems greater and worse than those about you? Someone, I am sure, has more burdens than you. It is so easy to become so absorbed in our own condition that we forget to look about us. I often think of the man who complained that he had no shoes until he met a man who had no feet. If you could see the plight of many in the hospitals of our cities or become acquainted with some of the problems of those who live not far from you, it would lead you to be so thankful for your own condition in life.

On the other hand, could we ask, "Are you a defeatist?" Some people are defeated without ever trying. They feel the task is impossible. They say there may be a way to overcome their difficulties, but they just cannot find it. They feel so frustrated that they do not even try to find a better way. Others have figured that all misfortune is sin, like the people in John the 9th chapter who asked the Master about the man who was born blind. They says, "Master, who did sin, this man, or his parents, that he was born blind?" (verse 2). They made a natural assumption that the sin of someone had caused this man to be blind. It isn't logical in this case as it isn't when we begin to reason in this way. How could his blindness was not caused by his own sins—he was born blind. And his parents were not to blame. Jesus says it was "that the works of God should be made manifest in him" (verse 3). The Lord used the blindness of that man to show His great power and to glorify God.

One of those who came professing to comfort Job in his trials vexed him rather than comforting him. Eliphas, the Temanite, had the attitude "who ever perished, being innocent? or where were the righteous cut off?" (Job 4:7). He was simply saying he thought all of Job's troubles had come upon him because of sin in Job's life. Of course, he was wrong; but in view of the serious problems Job was suffering, it seemed like a logical conclusion. Unfortunately, there are many like Eliphas who still live in our day. Many people blame God as soon as they suffer a problem in their lives. And many shift the blame to sin for all their troubles and all of their trials. It is true that sin often brings penalties that must be suffered, but all misfortune is not the result of our own sins.

According to the Bible, we don't have to be defeated because we deal with difficulties in our lives. We can be a person who turns our handicaps and misfortunes into blessings. It is just a matter of attitude. Paul, the apostle, is a good example. He had many things to befall him: there were trials and hardships and sufferings. It was while he was a prisoner that he wrote, "But I would ye should understand, brethren, that the things which happened unto me have fallen out rather unto the furtherance of the gospel" (Philippians 1:12). He had known plenty, and he had known how to be hungry; yet he says, "I have learned, in whatsoever state I am, therewith to be content" (Philippians 4:11). His source of strength was the Lord.  He says, "I can do all things through Christ which strengtheneth me" (Philippians 4:13).

Paul, you recall, had a thorn in the flesh. I do not know exactly what kind of affliction it was—the Bible does not tell us—but it troubled him exceedingly. He asked the Lord three times that it might be removed and the Lord answered him, "My grace is sufficient for thee: for my strength is made perfect in weakness" (2 Corinthians 12:9). The great apostle then added:

> Most gladly therefore will I rather glory in my infirmities, that the power of Christ may rest upon me. Therefore I take pleasure in infirmities, in reproaches, in necessities, in persecutions, in distresses for Christ's sake: for when I am weak, then am I strong (2 Corinthians 12:9-10).

It was through Paul's troubles that he learned the abundance of the Lord's grace. It was through the Lord's grace that he was able to overcome his difficulties and to turn them into blessings, both for himself and for the cause of Christ.

Cannot our difficulties also teach us that the Lord's grace is sufficient for us? Cannot our troubles teach us the real meaning of the words in James 4:8 where we read: "Draw nigh to God, and he will draw nigh to you"? Our difficulties and trials may cause us, as never before, to draw nigh to God. They may show us how wonderful the love is and how blessed we are to have the benefit of the providence of God, our loving Heavenly Father. James writes:

> My brethren, count it all joy when ye fall into divers temptations; Knowing this, that the trying of your faith worketh patience. But let patience have her perfect work, that ye may be perfect and entire, wanting nothing (James 1:2-4).

So then, according to this passage, why should we look upon trials with joy? Why should we be happy when in trouble? Is it not true that precious metal may be heated in fire to refine it, that the gold may have the dross separated from it? So the trying of our faith will make us pure and better before God. It will separate the waste from our lives and strengthen our hearts.

It is a fact that adversity has often resulted in good. This fact has been true in many different phases of life. It can be illustrated in almost any part of the history of man. Notice these examples:

> It was under the stress of necessity, in the time of war, that Robert Fulton gave to America the idea of the assembly line to change the whole course of the manufacturing industry.

> McCormick gave the farmers of America the first reaper and the first combine for harvesting grain because of the great need and the hardship of harvesting the grain with limited man power.

> You recall it was Hellen Keller who was deprived of both sight and hearing; but in overcoming these difficulties; she developed a success which few people have ever known. She became an inspiration to millions of people and an ambasador of good will in all the troubled nations of the earth.

> It was a young man by the name of Louis Braille who opened the door of learning to countless thousands of sightless people during the past one hundred thirty years. As a child of three he

lost his sight by accident. At the age of twenty, he invented the system of raised dots called Braille, which permitted the world's masterpieces of literature to be accessible to others who could not see. He prayed that life might become a blessing by being sightless. Even though he was only forty-three when he died, his work has been a blessing through all these years since 1829.

Martin Luther was virtually a prisoner in Wartburg Castle when he translated the New Testament and thus furthered the cause of the Reformation.

The Apostle Paul gave the world his prison epistles while chained to a guard as a prisoner in Rome. At the time of his imprisonment, the Holy Spirit directed him to write some of the very heart of the New Testament.

Many a person has turned affliction into opportunity. This situation has been true, I am sure, within your life, or at least in the life of some of your acquaintances. Perhaps as you listen today, you are a shut-in. May we pray that your condition will not overcome you but that you will use your condition in the service of God—that you will use your time for study and for prayer that the influence of your life will help others to know the will of God. Some of the happiest and the best people I have ever known have been physically handicapped. They have made others forget their handicaps in the glow of their faith and their sunny smiles and their happy dispositions.

May this lesson have real spiritual value? First, we understand that you may meet difficulties in becoming a Christian—in obeying the Lord. Maybe it is difficult for you to attend worship with regularity. It is for many. In fact, some go to worship under extreme difficulty. It may be a long distance you have to travel. You may have to make financial sacrifice or overcome some business arrangement that would hinder you from being faithful in worshiping God. If so, you can appreciate what the Lord meant when He says, "Seek ye first the kingdom of God" (Matthew 6:33). You can know the value of Christian fellowship and of praising God and keeping your appointment to eat the Lord's Supper with Him each Lord's Day.

I would like to ask you in closing, Are your burdens heavy today? You can take them to the Lord and know that He understands and that

He cares. Is your life filled with grief? Remember that God is a God of all comfort (2 Corinthians 1:3). The word of God contains His precious promises to sustain you in your every hour and in every trouble that you have to deal with in life.

# *Follow Thou Me*

The circumstance of the text of today's lesson is touching. Two of the most prominent of the Lord's disciples are the characters of our text— Simon Peter and John, both sons of Zebedee. Peter and John had been closely associated for many years. You recall they had been partners in the fishing business before the Lord called them to follow Him (Luke 5:10). Both of them learned about Jesus from John the Baptist. They were two of the first four to become apostles. They had traveled together with Jesus for more than three years. Indeed, they were of the inner circle of the apostles, as can be seen when Jairus' daughter was raised from the dead, at the transfiguration of Christ, and in the garden of Gethsemane. John gained Peter entrance at the palace of the high priest where Jesus was to be condemned before the Jews and, then, taken away to Pilate. They had seen Jesus crucified and had been to the empty tomb after the Lord's resurrection. Together they had talked with the risen Lord and had been with Him at many of His appearances. In the twenty-first chapter of John, we read of one of their very last times with the Lord.

They were by the shore of Galilee. The Master had asked Peter, "Simon, son of Jonas, lovest thou me more than these?" (John 21:15). Three times the question was asked, and three times Peter confessed his love for the Lord Jesus. Then the Lord says to Peter:

> Verily, verily, I say unto thee, When thou wast young, thou girdedst thyself, and walked whither thou wouldst: but when thou shalt be old, thou shalt stretch forth thy hands, and another shall gird thee, and carry thee whither thou wouldst not. This spake he, signifying by what death he should glorify God. And when he had spoken this, he saith unto him, Follow me (John 21:18-19).

Then Peter asked the Master about John saying, "Lord, and what shall this man do? Jesus saith unto him, if I will that he tarry till I come, what is that to thee? follow thou me" (verses 21-22).

Our Lord used the occasion to teach Peter an important lesson. No matter how close the relationship had been between Peter and John, the responsibility for Peter to consider was the statement of his Lord, "Follow thou me." His interest in John, no matter how close and tender and loving, was not to cloud the main issue. Jesus says to him, "Follow thou me." Christ was his Master. Peter had three times declared his love for Him; and now, regardless of what should happen to John, Peter was to follow the Lord Jesus Christ through hardship and sacrifice, even until he was old and another should gird him and lead him away to death. The will of Christ was to be his will. The Lord's work was to be his work, and the Lord was to be the standard of his life until the very end. This lesson to Peter is given for our good as we live for the same great Master and Leader. The Lord bids us to follow Him. To all of us He would say, "Follow thou me." The Lord and His teaching should be the standard for our lives.

The question today must be: "How much can we be interested in others? Can our interest in others hinder us in serving the Lord?" We must answer, "Sometimes it does." Sometimes our interest in others can hinder us in serving the Lord. Truly, as Christians, we should have some concern about the welfare of others in many ways. We should be interested in helping those who have need of our help. Jesus taught this lesson in the story of the Good Samaritan in (Luke 10). The physical needs of others should be taken care of as we realize what it is to love our neighbor as ourselves (Matthew 19:19). James says, "Pure religion and undefiled before God and the Father is this, To visit the fatherless and widows in their affliction, and to keep himself unspotted from the world" (James 1:27).

We should be interested in the salvation of the lost and do all we can to bring them to the "Lamb of God, which taketh away the sin of the world" (John 1:29). Even as Paul says, "My heart's desire and prayer to God for Israel is, that they might be saved" (Romans 10:1). So our heart's desire and prayer to God for the lost should be simply "that they might be saved." To this end, we should work and sacrifice and pray every day of our lives.

We should "love the brotherhood" (1 Peter 2:17). As John writes, "We know that we have passed from death unto life, because we love the brethren. He that loveth not his brother abideth in death" (1 John 3:14). Again, we are to "lay down our lives for the brethren" (verse 16). Our love for our fellow Christian should be deep and real and moving. It should move us to be kind and tender and forgiving. It should bind us with a cord that cannot be broken save by the hand of death itself. As we sing in that old song:

> Blest be the tie that binds
> our hearts in Christian love.
> The fellowship of kindred minds
> is like to that above.

But our interest in others should never cause us to forget that Jesus says, "Follow thou me." The Lord's commandments are to rule our entire lives. Friendships and fleshly ties should never sway us or deter us from doing the Master's Will. Our interest in and concern for others should be the means of doing the will of Christ. Our love for one another should be our expression of our love for Christ. Our ministry to those who are God's children should be governed by the words of Christ, "Inasmuch as you have done it unto one of the least of these my brethren, ye have done it unto me" (Matthew 25:40).

We are creatures who are much too inclined to follow other people. Peter allowed the presence of the enemies of Jesus to cause him to deny his Lord three times. At another time he permitted the coming of some from Jerusalem to cause him to separate himself from faithful Gentile Christians at Antioch. Paul says, "I withstood him to the face, because he was to be blamed" (Galatians 2:11). The Christians at Corinth were so torn in their concern for even good men that some said, "I am of Paul; and I of Apollos; and I of Cephas; and I of Christ" (1 Corinthians 1:12). They divided the church of our Lord at Corinth. Paul rebuked them saying, "Is Christ divided? Was Paul crucified for you? or Were ye baptized in the name of Paul?" So the church of the Lord today is sometimes divided because men are inclined to take men as their standard instead of Christ. The unity of Christ's people should be our aim as we all follow the example of Christ. Jesus taught that following Him should be more important than family ties and family traditions. He says:

> If any man come to me, and hate not his father, and mother, and wife, and children, and brethren, and sisters, yea, and his own life also, he cannot be my disciple (Luke 14:26).

The word "hate" is used in the sense of "love less." Our love for fleshly ties should be, at all times, less than our love for the Lord. So many people use family traditions and family conceptions of religion as the standard for their lives instead of the teachings of Christ. My friend, may we ask you these pointed questions:

Why are you what you are religiously?

Can you read in the Bible the things you practice in religion?

> Do you love the Lord enough to obey Him even when it means breaking away from family traditions and practices in your obedience to the teachings of Christ?

> Would you love Christ enough—listen—would you love Christ enough to be a New Testament Christian and a member of the Lord's church instead of a member of a religious organization that is not taught in the New Testament?

> If you, through a careful study of the Bible, find that you have not obeyed the Lord's teachings and you are not a member of the Lord's church as revealed in the New Testament, do you love Christ enough and have enough faith in Him to repent and to be baptized for the remission of your sins? (Acts 2:38)

> Will you let the Lord add you to His church (Acts 2:47) and then be faithful in life and worship and in service to Him as a Christian?

These are some heart-searching questions that face thousands of good and conscientious people today. In considering them, we may think of what Paul gave up to make Christ his standard for his life. Paul says:

> What things were gain to me, those I counted loss for Christ. Yea doubtless, and I count all things but loss for the excellency of the knowledge of Christ Jesus my Lord: for whom I have suffered the loss of all things, and do count them but dung, that I may win Christ (Philippians 3:7-8).

Christ became all in all to Paul, even to such an extent that he wrote, "For me to live is Christ, and to die is gain" (Philippians 1:21). For through Christ, in death, he would gain the blessings of heaven. May we make Christ our life so that death may be "gain" to us.

Others make material value their standard for life. We are living in an age of material prosperity that is unequalled and in the most prosperous nation in all the world; too often we are allowing these material things to cause us to distort their proper values and standards in life. We are too involved in the tearing down of barns and building greater barns and houses. We are so obsessed with the kind of house we have or the kind of car we drive or the modern conveniences we own or the kind of clothes we wear or the size of our income, that we forget that some of these days we are going to leave it all behind. We must realize that we cannot take one little particle of it when we die. The Lord says, "A man's life consisteth not in the abundance of the things which he possesseth" (Luke 12:15).

Christ gave us the story of "The Rich Fool" in Luke 12 to remind us that some of these days God may say to us, "Thou fool, this night thy soul shall be required of thee: then whose shall those things be, which thou hast provided? So is he that layeth up treasure for himself, and is not rich toward God"(verses 20-21). People are so interested in their businesses and their professions and their possessions that they are forgetting their own souls and the souls of their own boys and girls. They are forgetting that our lives on this earth are short, that this earth is but a cosmic school system in which we are to prepare for the never ending eternity which follows this life. Parents are training their children so that they can make more money instead of training their souls for eternity. The dollar sign is so often more important than the cross of Christ. Financial matters are taking precedence over the welfare of the soul. Men are paying a passing allegiance to Christ while they bow at the altar of material idols.

Let us stop and let us think, "What are we doing?" and "Where are we headed?" Have we forgotten the teachings of Christ when He says, "For what shall it profit a man, if he shall gain the whole world, and lose his own soul? Or what shall a man give in exchange for his soul?" (Mark 8:36-37). One day—listen—one day in heaven will be worth more than all the wealth of the world. The time in eternity is not measured by our earthly days and years, for eternity knows no end. It is forever and ever and ever. What about your soul and the soul of your son or the soul of your daughter? Where are you going to spend eternity? Will it be in the eternal Paradise of God in heaven or are you letting the devil lead you downward toward hell and the everlasting fire that is prepared for the devil and his angels? (Matthew 25:41). You are going to make the decision. It is up to YOU. Christ has provided the way to heaven. He has told us plainly, "In my Father's house are many mansions." He has described something of their happiness and glory and He has told us, "I am the way, the truth and the life: no man cometh unto the Father, but by me" (John 14:6). He leads the way to heaven and has provided the proper standard for our lives that we may enter that wonderful City.

"Christ also suffered for us, leaving us an example, that ye should follow his steps" (1 Peter 2:21). But each one of us must decide for himself to hear Him as He says, "Follow ... thou ... me." What is your standard for life? Is Christ your standard? Is the Bible your Guide Book? Do you read the word of God and let its teachings rule your life? Christ came to do the will of God. Of Him it is said, "Lo, I come (in the volume of the book it is written of me,) to do thy will, O God" (Hebrews 10:7). He was "obedient unto death, even the death of the cross" (Philippians 2:8). If Christ is the pattern and example for our lives, the Bible will be our sole authority in the whole of our lives as we walk in the steps of our Master.

What is important enough—think about this—what is important enough or valuable enough in all this world to cost us our souls happiness in eternity? We must never let the influences of men—no matter how strong they may be—to be our standard for life. The shortcomings and criticisms and neglect and hypocrisy of all the world should never be permitted to hinder us in our determination to follow Christ. All of the wealth of the world or any part of it should never come between us and our service to the Lord. The pleasures and lusts and allurements of the world are as nothing and should never blind us to the brightness of the glory of the example of holiness that is found in our Lord and Saviour Jesus Christ.

Make up your mind to follow Christ. Listen to Him as He says, "Follow THOU me." Are you?

# *We Have Not Passed This Way Heretofore*

In the book of Joshua, we read of the time when the children of Israel had come to the river of Jordan. They were ready to enter the land of Canaan. They had spent forty years wandering in the wilderness; now the time had come to cross over Jordan. You remember that the leaders of Israel had passed through the company to tell them that the ark of the covenant would go before them to show them the way to go. They, according to chapter three, verse four, were admonished, "Ye have not passed this way heretofore." Israel did not know which way to go. Before them, lay the land of Caanan; and the land was new and strange. The enemies were many and their cities were strong. But Jehovah would guide them and be with them. His presence would give them victory in the way that He would lead them.

I think it is interesting that at this particular time of the year we stand in a similar circumstance. As we come to speak to you today on the last day in this year, we are at the threshold of a New Year. We are crossing over the Jordan into the conquest of a new land—a new year. Behind us lie the wanderings of past years; indeed, we have not passed this way heretofore. We know not what this year will hold, not even for a day. We do not know of ourselves which way we should go; God alone knows what lies beyond our Jordan. Like Israel, we need God to go before us and to lead us in the way we should go and to give us strength for every conflict and the wisdom for every hour.

It is good for us to stop for reflection, to think of the way we have come—of the year now past. God has blessed us. But for God's grace we might be like millions on earth today who are hungering, suffering, dying without God or opportunities and blessings that are so bountifully showered about us. We are spared monuments, living monuments of His goodness, His grace, and His mercy.

It is so true that time rapidly passes and that it does so even with greater rapidity as you grow older. It seems but yesterday that the past year was just beginning. It makes us realize the meaning of the words of Job, in chapter fourteen, verses 1 and 2, "Man that is born of a woman is of few days, and full of trouble. He cometh forth like a flower, and is cut down: he fleeth also as a shadow, and continueth not."

We need the exhortation found in James, when he says:

> Go to now, ye that say, To day or to morrow we will go into such a city, and continue there a year, and buy and sell, and get gain: Whereas ye know not what shall be on the morrow. For what is your life? It is even a vapour that appeareth for a little time, and then vanisheth away. For that you ought to say, If the Lord will, we shall live, and do this, or that (James 4:13-15).

Some of us will not live to see the shadows of this year gather and depart. Some who listen this day will not be numbered among the living when the year is gone. Others will fall in the hours of temptation. There will be new work to be done and new joys to be shared and new burdens to be born. There will be new sorrows to tear at our hearts. Some days will be filled with sunshine and into some, indeed, the rain will fall. But how will we face the future? It is inevitable that we face it. The question is, "HOW will we face it?" Surely we will not face it alone. Even the bravest and strongest feel the need of someone greater and stronger than we. This is a good time to think of that need and to realize that Jehovah is God and the source of our strength and that Christ wants to be our Saviour and to lead us in the way we should go. He says, "I am the way" (John 14:6). Let us learn to walk in that way.

Many have made resolutions for the New Year. I am sure some will soon be forgotten, but some will be remembered. Solomon says, "Better is it that thou shouldest not vow, than that thou shouldest vow and not pay" (Ecclesiastes 5:5). Let us keep our vows and resolutions before God and be sure they meet with His approval. As the steward of Luke 16:4, let us say, "I am resolved what to do" and then arise and do it. Soon our stewardship on this earth will come to an end. We must resolve and act today that we might be received into the everlasting habitations. May I present five resolves? Let us weigh them seriously and make them a part of our lives. I think they are worthy. Let us consider them carefully:

First of all, I am resolved that I will have a greater faith. John says, "This is the victory that overcometh the world, even our faith" (1 John 5:4). Hebrews 11:6 states: "But without faith it is IMPOSSIBLE to please him." One of the great needs of our day is more faith. May we say?—I will have greater faith in God as my Maker, my Creator, and my Preserver. He is the one from whom all blessings flow. It is in Him that we live and move and have our being. I cannot face the future without Him. I will remember how much He has loved me and what all He has done for me and how abundantly He has blessed me, and what all He is able to do for me now. I will have greater faith in Christ as my Saviour, who died that I might live. By His blood, I can be made whole and have my sins all washed away, by becoming a Christian and living the Christian life. He can lead me as my Shepherd and be the Giver of my strength. May I be able to say with Paul, "I can do all things through Christ which strengtheneth me" (Philippians 4:13); so that we may boldly say, "The Lord is my helper, and I will not fear what man shall do unto me" (Hebrews 13:6). I will walk with Him that He may walk with me and lead me to life eternal.

Furthermore, I will have greater faith in my fellowmen. Sometimes we are keenly disappointed in our fellows. Many are unfaithful, the days are evil, sin is ever present, Satan's influence is strong, and it is deceptive. Men sometimes betray the confidence we have placed in them. Sometimes we may be inclined to be like Elijah, simply sit down under our juniper tree and say, "I, even I only, am left; and they seek my life, to take it away" (1 Kings 19:10). But, God showed Elijah there were seven thousand people who had not bowed unto Baal. So there are many faithful, good, God-fearing people today who have faith in us. Let us seek them out and walk with them and do not let others be disappointed in us. The world needs men with greater faith in their fellowmen, who can extend loving hearts and helping hands in their time of need. Let us be kind and considerate and charitable to others. With the judgment we judge others, we shall be judged. Let us make up our minds that we will visit the sick, encourage the weak, and lift up the fallen. May God help us to remember, "If a man be overtaken in a fault, ye which are spiritual, restore such an one in the spirit of meekness; considering thyself, lest thou also be tempted" (Galatians 6:1). Your help or mine may save a soul. "Brethren, if any of you do err from the truth, and one convert him; Let him know, that he which converteth the sinner from the error of his way shall save a soul from death, and shall hide a multitude of sins" (James 5:19-20). Let us never forget the words of our Master, "He that is greatest among you shall be your servant" (Matthew 23:11). As we have faith in one another, we will serve and help one another.

Not only this, but I am determined to have greater faith in myself. God made me. I am a living soul, more precious than all the wealth of the world. God has a purpose for me, a work for me to do. He will give me the power to do it. Shall I have less faith in me and in my worth and ability than God has. We are not worthless—none of us is too weak or too small or too poor or too old, but that we can do something for God and for others. God has not asked that which is impossible. Let us resolve to exercise more faith in ourselves. It will surprise you what God can do ... THROUGH YOU.

Again, let us resolve: I will commune with God—I will make Him my daily companion. His word, the Bible, will be my daily reading—the food for my soul. "Man shall not live by bread alone, but by every word that proceedeth out of the mouth of God" (Matthew 4:4). Through the Bible, God can speak to me and tell me what He wants me to KNOW and to DO. I need to remember that prayer is my privilege as a Christian. I can talk with God. Every child of God who has been born into God's family—born of water and of the Spirit, baptized into the church of our Lord and the family of God (John 3:5)—has this exalted privilege. We can approach God's throne of grace through Christ as our High Priest. Daily communion with God will help me to trust His providence. He who clothes the grass of the field and who notes the fall of the sparrow will surely take care of me. He is able to make "all things work together for good to them that love God, to them who are the called according to his purpose" (Romans 8:28). My people, what the future holds, God alone can see. But He will suit the thing that is best as we trust Him. Let us pray, Lord "give us this day our daily bread" (Matthew 6:11). Let us live each day with God—live it to the fullest as though it were our last. Then when we lay our armor down, He will bid us come up higher where we can commune with Him and worship Him forever and ever. So let us resolve we will have greater faith in God, and we will commune with God.

I think, thirdly, we should resolve to confess Christ at all times. By the words that I say, I will confess Him. Let my speech be nothing but good. May we say—I will avoid as the plague all evil words, all idle words in joking or jesting, all evil or smutty jokes and tales and filthy stories, and never speak lightly of things divine or sacred? Let us not forget that "every idle word that men shall speak, they SHALL give account thereof in the day of judgment. For BY THY WORDS"—listen—"BY THY WORDS thou shalt be justified, and BY THY WORDS thou shalt be condemned" (Matthew 12:36-37). I think we should resolve to talk more about Christ, to tell others how He loves them, too, and He wants to save them. I will tell them how they can believe in Him as their Saviour, how He can lift them out of the practice of sin in repentance, how they can confess Him before men, and how He can wash away their sins as they are baptized in obedience to Him and how He will lift them up from the watery grave of baptism that they might walk with Him and be blessed as they live for Him and worship Him (Mark 16:15-16). May we be able to say, I will confess Christ not only with my tongue but in the way that I live. All the habits and all the ways of my life will be Christ-like and show that I have been with Jesus. There is never a time for wrong acts or evil deeds. May we make up our mind that it will never be right to do wrong; life is too short, living for our Christ is far too important. In the things that I do, may God help me to ask, "Is it right? Will it do me good? What influence will it have on others? Will it draw me nearer to God and make me more like Christ?"

Next, may we resolve, I will remember that someone is watching, following me. It may be a brother or a sister or a husband or a wife or a son or a daughter. Or it could be some girl or some boy, some friend, someone at work or at play, or even a stranger I have not noticed. Someone—someone has faith in me. Someone is using my life for a pattern. Someone is resting his faith in me, and someone is reading my life each day. If I stumble or become unfaithful, he or she may do the same thing. Would not it be a terrible thing to miss heaven ... and even worse to lead someone else to hell? It may be someone dear to me or someone dear to you. Let us be faithful to this trust and reaching back, take him who follows by the hand and lead him home to God. God is counting on you. I do not think you should be allowed to forget that—God is counting on YOU. He wants YOU to help lead someone to the place that is called heaven. Life will be sweeter and heaven's hope will be brighter.

Next and last, may we resolve that I will place God first in every thing I do. Every day is filled with problems and choices; even in the little things of life, we must make decisions. Can we say I will place God

FIRST—first in thought, first in the whole of my life? In this New Year, may I place His worship first above all other things. Today and every Lord's Day, may I worship Him, "not forsaking the assembling of ourselves together" (Hebrews 10:25). When we come to the end of this year, this new year, may we be able to say I was never absent from worship except when I was physically unable to be there. May I place the study of the word of the Lord first. May I in my business place God first. My gifts to God should come first; my business should be operated for Him. I am God's steward; I will give an account to Him. Let me lay by in store today and each Lord's Day as God has prospered me, and let the increase from my business be used for Him. May God help me to see how abundantly He can bless me. In my home may God's will reign supreme. Let my home, your home, be according to the pattern of God, that His love may fill our hearts and make us happy both for time and eternity.

In conclusion, may God help us—each one of you who now listen and each one of us who bring these programs to you—that every day of this year may bring us nearer and nearer to God, closer to each other, and nearer the great blessings that heaven holds in store for those who love God and those who serve Him.

# *Why the Church of Christ? #1*

This morning we turn your attention now to another question, and that question simply is: Why the Church of Christ? Every once in a while, someone raises that question; and I think it is perfectly good to ask the question: Why the Church of Christ? Why these Christians? Why the Lord's church? In fact, I think we will take several topics or this will be our topic of study for several times in the future broadcasts. Let us give our attention to this study and see what the Bible answer is on this matter. In a topic so near and dear to us, I think we sometimes lose sight of the reasons for: Why the Church of Christ? For such an examination, we should use the only reliable source that we have and that is the word of God. The Bible states that all scripture is given by inspiration of God and is profitable for doctrine, for reproof, for correction, for instruction in righteousness. So we want to turn to the inspired scripture (2 Timothy 3:16), and we want to turn to the truth (John 17:17). Paul further states that the church is the pillar and the ground of the truth (1 Timothy 3:15). To this truth, we will resort. It will be the court of final appeal to us because we have no other way of knowing the mind of God than to turn to the scripture. So our answer must come from the Holy Scripture. This truth is God's divine message to the human family, revealing the Christ and the glorious church that He built. Where, then, does any have the authority to alter by adding to or taking away from this inspired revelation? We dare not do that. What I say, what any man says, what any creed book or books may say, none of these are good enough. Only God's truth is going to do, and this is the only answer that should be acceptable to you or to me.

Let us take a look at this question: Why the Church of Christ? We want to look at the right builder of the church. If indeed, the Church of Christ is here on earth, then someone built the church. Let us listen to the Lord's words in Matthew 16:18 when He says, "Upon this rock, I will build my church." How such a beautiful simple statement as this can be so misunderstood is quite amazing. Notice the limiting concepts within His word. He says, "Upon this rock." Now this statement clearly denotes one particular rock, one firm foundation, one way, and no other is going to do—upon this rock, one fixed and firm standard that cannot be denied, when truth has its free course within our lives. Notice He says upon this rock, "I will build," I, Jesus Christ, will build it. No one else has the authority. No one else can. Then He tells us what He is going to build, He says, "I will build my church," a personal possession of our Lord, as the bride of the Lamb, so is the church to Jesus Christ (Revelation 21:2; 1 Corinthians 12:20). Now each one of these points we are going to examine a little later on in the broadcast. But it should be obvious to any thinking person, that the words "I" and "my," used in reference to Jesus Christ, limit the builder or the founder to one person, and one person only, and that is Jesus Himself. Remember, all scripture is inspired, not of man but of God. Jesus says He would build it and it was His. This declaration eliminates forever any organizations built on anything that adds to truth or takes away from truth for its teaching or for its foundation. Human builders such as Calvin, Wesley, Joseph Smith, Martin Luther, Charles Rutherford, C.T. Russell, and Joseph Rutherford and thousands of others cannot possibly be of truth because you simply do not find these people in scripture.

Some have erroneously declared John the Baptist—that is—John the baptizer, as the founder. John clearly states, "I am not the Christ" (John 1:19-20). He further states, "He that cometh after me is mightier than I, who shoes I am not worthy to bear" (Matthew 3:11). Notice please Matthew 14:10, where Herod sent and beheaded John in prison. John is dead. Now listen to Jesus' words in Matthew 16:18, "Upon this rock, I will build my church." So Jesus points to the establishment of the church as a future event. This event, the church, Acts 2:47, was so important that Jesus says, "He that is least in the kingdom of heaven," that is the church, "is greater than he," as He spoke of John the baptizer (Matthew 11:11). Now one might wonder, why did Jesus say that—why does He say that here is one of the greatest men ever born among women, and yet He says the least in the kingdom is greater than he? The reason is that Jesus had not yet gone to Calvary and given Himself, the innocent for the guilty. He had not been buried, He had not arisen victorious over death, hell, and the grave, and He had not ascended back to the Father. When these events have occurred, the least in the kingdom, the least member, the one whose faith in the gospel message would bring about the complete surrender and submission to His plan, this person, He says, would be greater than the greatest man who had been born of women. This person was John, the forerunner of Jesus Christ. In other words, the kingdom had not yet been established; otherwise it is a nonsensical statement to say that John is one of the greatest of those born among women, and a believer under the New Covenant would be the least in the kingdom. It is evident the kingdom was not there because if it had been there, John would have been in the kingdom. John is dead; and after his death, Jesus says, "Upon this rock, I will build my church."

The penalty that Jesus declares for institutions built by men, calling themselves the church, not authorized by God, is, "Every plant"— "every plant, which my heavenly Father has not planted, shall be rooted up" (Matthew 15:13). They have no authority for existence, and they shall die, being rooted up. Jesus says, "I will profess unto them, I never knew you" (Matthew 7:23). The psalmist declares, "Except the Lord build the house, they labor in vain that build it" (Psalm 127:1). It is vain for any to assume the authority of God in building an institution other than the one Jesus says He will build. "I will build," He says. Peter then writes, "Holy men of God spake as they were moved by the Holy Ghost" (2 Peter 1:21). So, no one can claim any authority except as we find it in the Holy Scripture.

Now, let us talk about the foundation of the church. Foundation is exceedingly significant, whether you are talking about the house or about a church or whatever building you are talking about—the foundation is of utmost importance. By definition, a foundation is the prepared ground upon which a structure is raised. Jesus proclaims, "Upon this rock I will build my church" (Matthew 16:18). Therefore, for a structure to be sound, it needs a firm foundation, which will withstand any storm that may assail it. It also needs a worthy chief cornerstone, one selected and chosen because it is the best to be found. Notice these words in 1 Peter 2:4-10, where Jesus Christ, God's only begotten Son, the very best that could be found, is spoken of as being, "chosen of God, and precious." Now, why the best?— listen—Jesus declares the Father is always with Him, for He says, "For I do always those things that please him" (John 8:29). Again, "As the Father gave me commandment, even so I do" (John 14:31). In His obedience to the Father, Jesus Christ was the best, the best and only cornerstone to be found.

As we look at Jesus' statement, "upon this rock," let us listen to Paul's words: "For other foundation can no man lay than that which is laid, which is Jesus Christ" (1 Corinthians 3:11). Thus, with Paul's statement, we can be assured that whatever "this" is, He says, "upon this rock, I will build my church." Whatever "this" is, it must include Jesus Christ as the foundation or the rock. Since all scripture is inspired, Paul's words must be true. Remember Jesus questions, "Whom do men say that I the son of man am?" (Matthew 16:13) and "Whom say ye that I am?" (Matthew 16:15). Peter answers, "Thou art the Christ, the Son of the living God" (Matthew 16:16). Now, here we have a truth proclaimed that is firm, true, and unchangeable, a firm truth confessing Jesus to be the Christ, the Son of the living God. Men may have tried to explain that confession away. Atheists may attack it and shout their denial. Intellectuals of modern thought may seek something new. Groups abominable in God's sight may declare their rights, yet God's word reads "the same yesterday, and to day, and for ever" (Hebrews 13:8). Truth does not change. How wonderful that we do not have to get up in the morning and wonder what changed during the night. Do we have some new truth, how is this going to stand with the other truths, and how is this going to alter things that are in motion? Truth never changes. Jesus Christ remains the only begotten Son of God, and all who attack this glorious truth shall at last be repelled. This basic, yet sure, tenant was to be the firm foundation upon which the church would be established, which even the gates of hell could not prevail against. It is this truth that Jesus says must be confessed by man, "Whosoever therefore shall confess me before men, him will I confess also before my Father which is in heaven" (Matthew 10:32).

The term used as Peter confesses Jesus Christ to be the Son of God is greatly significant. It sets God apart from the lifeless idols of wood and stone, which many bow to even till this day in idol worship. God throughout the Old Testament tells His followers not to make any graven images, of anything, and then bow before them. Yet, in Paul's letter to the church in Rome, he writes of some who would change the glory of the incorruptible God, into an image. Paul's words—listen—Paul's words that proclaim Jesus Christ to be the foundation, sure and unshakable, should be sufficient; yet some declare that the church was built by Peter, that the church was built upon Peter, instead of upon what he confessed. When you go back to examine what is said in Matthew 16:13-19, the Lord built the church, not upon a fallible man such as Peter, He built the church upon the confession that Peter made, "Thou art the Christ, the Son of the living God" (verse 16). So the bedrock foundation of the church is Jesus Christ Himself. Jesus was the prepared one, by His firm stand against Satan (Matthew 4). By His complete submission to do the Father's will, He stands as the solid rock. Peter displays weaknesses as he denies Jesus three times (Matthew 26:26-72). Again, Peter in his usual haste, declares upon the Mount of Transfiguration, "Let us build here three tabernacles, one for Thee, one for Moses, and one for Elijah" (Matthew 17). But God would not let that go. God declares, "This is my beloved Son, in whom I am well pleased; hear ye him" (Matthew 17:5).

Isaiah writes, "Behold, I lay in Zion a foundation." Where did He lay this foundation? Zion is Jerusalem. The Lord is going to build His house, His church in Jerusalem. He says, "Behold, I lay in Zion for a foundation a stone, a tried stone, a precious cornerstone, a sure foundation" (Isaiah 28:16). In Matthew's account, Jesus applies this prophecy to Himself: "Did ye never read in the scriptures, The stone which the builders rejected, the same is become the head of the corner: this is the Lord's doing, and it is marvellous in our eyes?" (Matthew 21:42). Peter also applies the prophecy to Jesus when he says, "This is the stone which was set at nought of you builders, which is become the head of the corner" (Acts 4:11). So, what a wondrous thing to know that the house of God, the church, rests upon a solid foundation and that foundation is the great truth that Jesus is the Christ, the Son of the living God.

Now we turn to Daniel chapter 2, as we pursue this question: Why the Church of Christ? In Daniel 2, Daniel prophesies the rise and fall of world empires and then makes a statement about the church. He says it will always be on the earth. We may not know when the Lord will come again; in fact, no one does except God Himself. What we do know is that when He comes, His church will be here: He will not bring it here, but it will be here because He says the kingdom in Daniel 2 will never be destroyed. Since this is the case, if we follow this prophecy, we can see it fulfilled in the New Testament exactly as the Old Testament prophets said it would be. Daniel 2 is talking about Babylon, a worldwide empire, then taken over by the Medes and Persians, then taken over by Alexander and the Macedonians, and then taken over finally by Rome. Now, when he considers these last-mentioned kings, the Roman kings, the God of heaven will set up a kingdom that will never be destroyed. We can go into the New Testament and see the fulfillment of this prophecy. For some 4,000 years, God guided humanity through the Patriarchal and the Mosaic age and finally brought about the glorious blood-bought institution over which Christ became the head (Ephesians 1:22, 5:23). Jesus says, "All power is given unto me in heaven and earth" (Matthew 28:18).

We have the honor and the privilege of becoming adopted sons and daughters of God and serve in that institution, the church, which was in the mind of God from the dawn of time itself. According to Ephesians chapter 3, it was in the mind of God even before that time. Take a good look at Ephesians 3. The church, the kingdom of God, the kingdom of heaven, is called by several terms in the scripture. People wonder sometimes why it is not simply called by one term rather than several. Its perspective determines its use. For example, it is called the kingdom of heaven (Matthew 16:18-19), where Jesus says, "Thou art Peter, and upon this rock I will build my church; and the gates of hell shall not prevail against it." He then tells Peter He is going to give him the keys to the kingdom of heaven. In one verse, Jesus speaks of His church and in the next verse He talks about the kingdom—two different approaches, two different words. He speaks of the church. He speaks of the kingdom. The way to determine what He is talking about is to look at the context.

The context must always be used to determine usage. There are readings that refer to the kingdom in the eternal sense, as the heavenly abode of the soul; for example 2 Timothy 4:1, 4:18; and then there are many times when the kingdom simply refers to the church, as it exists in the world—the church that began in the city of Jerusalem and continues until this day (Matthew 13:24-33). The church is not described in scripture as a democracy where man can make or change rules and practices, decide what the people are going to believe or not believe. As members of His church, the kingdom of God, we have absolutely no say whatsoever in making the laws to govern the church. In terms of the laws of the church, it is truly a kingdom because it is a monarchy. Jesus is the absolute Supreme Ruler of this kingdom and in Him is vested all the departments of power, the legislative, the executive, the judicial, are all in Jesus Christ. Even while Jesus was here on earth, He said, "For in him dwelleth all the fullness of the Godhead bodily." In Matthew 28:18, Jesus says, "All authority," that is all power, "is given unto me"—where?— "in heaven and on earth." What a tremendous thing to know what the church is. I hope that this answers some of the question of: Why the Church of Christ? We will begin right here next time and continue this study; and we would be very happy to hear from you in regard to any of it. Thank you for listening, and we will speak to you again next Lord's Day at this same time.

# *Why the Church of Christ? #2*

Last Lord's Day, we talked about answering the question: Why the Church of Christ? We would like to continue that subject today. Last Lord's Day, we laid the foundation that we must resort to the scriptures for answers because all we know about what pleases God is what we find in the scriptures. Scriptures come by inspiration of God, so we know they are the truth. Paul also declares that the church is the pillar and ground of truth (1 Timothy 3:15). We have talked about the fact that the Lord Jesus Christ Himself is the right builder of the church because He says in Matthew 16:18, "But upon this rock **I will build my church**; and the gates of hell shall not prevail against it." We talked about the foundation of the church. Paul writes to the Corinthians, "Other foundation can no man lay than that which is laid, which is Jesus Christ" (1 Corinthians 3:11). The foundation was not the Apostle Peter, according to Matthew 16, but it was the truth that he confessed that Jesus is the Christ, the Son of the living God.

We then talked about the church in prophecy by going back to the book of Daniel where the prophet said that in the days of certain kings the God of heaven would set up a kingdom that will never be destroyed. The Bible tells us that from the perspective of government the church is properly called a kingdom. So, if the writer is referring to the government of the church, he will likely refer to the church as the kingdom of heaven or the kingdom of God. The reason is that the church's government is not like the United States or any state where man is said to have a voice in making and establishing His laws to govern him in a democracy. One of the great truths of the Bible is that the church, the kingdom of God, is not a democracy. Certainly, it is for the people, but it is not of the people.

In terms of organization, the church is called a body. In Ephesians chapter 5, Paul declares the body of Christ to be the church of the Lord Jesus Christ; and he views the church in terms of its organization. In an analogy, he likens the church to the human body.

The head gives direction and authority to the members of the physical body, even as Christ directs His church. We, in His church, are all members of that one body (Ephesians 5:30). And our authority comes from Jesus Christ, our Supreme Head in heaven, through the word that He left. People, therefore, look upon us strangely when they ask us where our headquarter, the home office of the church, is; and we tell them that we do not have an earthly headquarters—that our headquarters is in heaven, because that is where the Head of the church is. We have no governing body here upon this earth that is handing down rules and laws for the Church of Christ. Usually, when we explain this situation to a person, he will say Yes, but where is your earthly headquarters located? Jesus Christ, our head, rules supreme. He left us His last will and testament to rule and to govern us here on this earth. "His word is truth" (John 17:17). It is the only, and the supreme, law by which members of His body, the church, shall and must be governed.

Now, in relationship with the world, the kingdom is properly called the church. The word, church, in the Bible comes from the Greek word, *ecclesia*, "*ec*" meaning out of and "*clesia*" meaning a calling, which simply means "the called out." The word church means the called out, a company of the redeemed, and all members of the church of the Lord Jesus Christ are called out of darkness, sin. Members are called into this total monarchy over which Jesus is the Supreme Head. Those who hear His voice (Revelation 3:20) and obey and follow Him are the called out. They become a separate people and are distinctively different. People in the world and those who work around us may think that we are strange because we no longer walk as we once did or as they walk. We can no longer go to places that are even questionable. We do not follow our lust into doing wrong. We are more careful of the things that we say or even listen to; and we attempt to control our thoughts so that we will not dwell upon evil. And truly, if we live according to the dictates of King Jesus, people are going to think we are a little odd, a little backward, a little old-fashioned.

We cannot continue to do as the world does and still be separate. If we do so, we are failing to obey the command in 2 Corinthians 6:17, where Paul says, "Come out from among them and be ye separate"? It just will not work, continuing to behave like the world. We are to be different when we become Christians, and we can thank the Lord for that. It is so important that we understand what the church is.

Some religious groups teach that the church existed prior to New Testament times, such as in the days of Abraham or in the days of Moses or in the days of Solomon. It would not have been possible. Listen to Paul's words in Hebrews where he says:

> For where a testament is, there must also of necessity be the death of the testator. For a testament is of force after men are dead: otherwise it is of no strength at all while the testator liveth (Hebrews 9:16-17).

We have the testament of the Lord Jesus Christ today, that is the New Testament, and it teaches there is an organization that operates strictly under the rules of the New Testament and not under the Old. The New Testament further provides proof that somebody died to set it all in force. Since the only rules and regulations for the church are found in the New Testament, it becomes immediately clear that the church could not have existed under the Old Testament. The church exists today—listen—the church exists today because of the death of the testator, whose death set in force the New Covenant, the New Testament in which we find guidelines for the church that belongs to Christ.

In Hebrews, Paul contrasts this New Covenant—and this is important—he contrasts this New Covenant with the Old. The Old did not provide the lasting spiritual benefits as the New because the New is established on better promises. Listen to his words:

> If that first covenant had been faultless, then should no place have been sought for the second. For finding fault with them, he saith, Behold, the days come, saith the Lord, when I will make a new covenant with the house of Israel and with the house of Judah: Not according to the covenant that I made with their fathers ... This is the covenant I will make ... I will put my laws in their mind, and write them in their hearts: and I will be to them a God, and they shall be to me a people: And they shall not teach every man his neighbor, and every man his brother, saying, Know the Lord: for all shall know me, from the least to the greatest. For I will be merciful to their unrighteousness, and their sins and their iniquities will I remember no more. In that he saith, A new covenant, he hath made the first old. Now that which decayeth and waxeth old is ready to vanish away (Hebrews 8:6-13).

Paul says, let the Old Testament go. Jesus has replaced it with something better. We no longer have Moses as a mediator, nor the Ten Commandments as a covenant. Let go of all of that. The New Covenant has new promises and a new mediator, Jesus Christ, who has better things in store for us.

The covenant under which the church exists and operates is quite different from the Old Testament. A casual reading of the Bible will certainly teach us that. On the day of Pentecost, a Jewish feast day, after the death, burial, and resurrection of Jesus Christ, the church was established; and three thousands souls were added to it (Acts 2:41-42). "The Lord added to the church daily such as should be saved" (Acts 2:47). Who were those who should be saved from their past sins? It is those who had obeyed the Lord.

Now I want to go back to this prophecy in Daniel chapter 2, that we mentioned last week. You remember that Daniel was just a boy when he was captured by the Babylonians. Nebuchadnezzar was allowed by the providence of God to enter into the land of Judah and to take as captives some of God's prized young men. Only the best had been brought in order to enrich the Babylonian empire. They were to be fed with the king's meats or, in other words, they were going to be fed with the finest food that was available. But Daniel and three of the Hebrew children, Shadrach, Meshack, and Abednego refused to eat the food, saying they wanted to be given only vegetables. They wanted no part of the foods the king wanted them to eat.

Even though they were strongly encouraged to eat the king's meat, they would not. Daniel insisted they put them to a test to prove that they could survive on their own food. His plan was for them to eat vegetables for ten days and then check them to see if their countenance was fair; if it were not, they could deal with them. The test was given. Their countenance was fairer than anyone. For three years, they were there; and God blessed them with wisdom and skill. Daniel was allowed to remember and interpret dreams and became known as one of the wise men of Babylon.

In the second year of Nebuchadnezzar's reign, the king had a special dream that is given in Daniel chapter 2. He saw an awful image, an awful thing standing before him, which was so upsetting that it awakened him. Though he knew he had dreamed this awful dream, he could not remember the dream. So, Nebuchadnezzar calls the magicians, telling them of his dream and telling them to interpret it. They said, "O king, live forever. Tell thy servants thy dream and we will show the interpretation." The king explained to them that the dream was gone from him. They responded that there was not a man upon the earth who could show the king his dream except the gods. Since the wise men could not tell the king his dream, he sent out a decree ordering that all the wise men of Babylon were to be destroyed. So, the king's guards sought Daniel and his fellows to be slain with the others. Daniel told them he would tell the king his dream and its interpretation (Daniel 2:30). Daniel went on to explain, "Thou, O king, sawest, and behold a great image" (verse 31), "and the form thereof was terrible. This image's head was a fine gold. His breast and his arms were of silver, his belly and his thighs of brass, his legs of iron, his feet part of iron and part of clay." Daniel continued that the king was the head of gold. Scholars relate that this is the record of the decline of man as each kingdom gave way to another kingdom. These were world empires, and each was inferior to the preceding one.

Daniel also says, "Thou sawest that the stone was cut out of the mountain without hands, that it break in pieces the iron, the brass, the clay, the silver, and the gold" (Daniel 2:45). The stone that was cut out was Jesus Christ. Daniel says, "The dream is certain, and the interpretation thereof sure." Now remember Daniel told the king of Babylon that he was the head of fine gold. The chest and arms of silver represent the Medo Persian Empire (536 BC). The belly and thighs of brass represent Alexander, the Great, with the Syrian and the Egyptian empires. The legs of iron were the Roman Empire. And the feet and toes of iron and clay were the time of the Caesars and the Herods. At the time that the church was established, the Caesars were on the throne and the Herods, plural, over Palestine. Daniel says, "In the days of these kings, shall the God of heaven set up a kingdom, which shall never be destroyed." He said the church and the kingdom would not be left to other people. This kingdom is not like other kingdoms, for it would never be replaced by another. In fact, he used these words, "it shall stand for ever" (verse 44). All other kingdoms would come and go. They would decay, but this kingdom would be so strong that even the gates of hell would not prevail against it (Matthew 16:18).

The stone cut out without hands was showing the miraculous nature of Jesus and His church—they would fill the whole earth. It needed no hands to accomplish its purpose because the foundation and chief corner stone of the church would be the Lord Jesus Christ Himself. In the days of these kings, also there came along a man named John the Baptist. He was announcing that the kingdom of God was nigh, meaning it is at hand. Isn't that interesting? At the very time that Daniel says the kingdom that would never be destroyed would come to pass, John says it is nigh (Matthew 3:2), it is at hand. Later, when John's work was done and John was in prison, Jesus taught His disciples to pray. After this manner pray ye, "Thy kingdom come" (Matthew 6:9-10). The time was right, and they were looking for the coming of the kingdom.

In Matthew 16:13-19, in the days of the Herods, Jesus declares, "I will build my church," and He gave to Peter the keys of the kingdom of heaven (verse 19). Peter was the keeper of the gate, not the rock of its foundation. He possessed keys that he and the other apostles would use to swing wide the doors to the Jews on the day of Pentecost. On that day, three thousands souls submitted to baptism, were added to the kingdom, the church. Peter would once more use those keys some ten years later at the conversion of Cornelius and his house when the doors were opened to the Gentiles. The firm truth that Jesus Christ is the Son of God and the gospel message is God's plan for salvation through obedience swung wide the doors that no man can close, for they were opened by the authority of Jesus Christ.

In Mark 9:1, there is an amazing prophecy from the Lord. Now remember Jesus says, "Upon this rock I will build my church." To Peter, "I am giving you the keys to the kingdom." Here in Mark 9:1, He says, "Verily I say unto you, That there be some of them that stand here, which shall not taste of death, till they have seen the kingdom of God come with power." Now that is an amazing prophecy. It was at the time of the Caesars and the Herods that Jesus says some of those who were living would not die until they saw the kingdom come. For those who believe the kingdom is something still yet to come after two thousand years, they have a problem. Either we have some very old people, like two thousand years old, or the kingdom is here now. John says the kingdom is nigh, is at hand, and some standing there would see it come with power, and it would come with power.

In Luke 24:49, Jesus tells His disciples to "tarry ye in the city of Jerusalem, until ye be endued with power from on high." In Acts 1:8, we find the disciples all waiting as Jesus had told them to do. Wait there until they received the power. This was the time when the Holy Spirit would come and give them the power (Acts 1:8). Jesus says the kingdom would come with power. If we can learn where the Spirit came, we can also know when the power came; and if we know when the power came, we can also know when the kingdom came. Notice, the power came as a rushing mighty wind, and they were all filled with the Holy Spirit (Acts 2:1-4). Evidence proclaims the kingdom, the establishment of the glorious church, His church, the Church of Christ. It was to occur in the days of these kings (Daniel 2:44). Christ's disciples were to await the power from on high in Jerusalem (Luke 24:49). On the day of Pentecost, the power came (Acts 2:1). When the power came, the kingdom came, the church came.

In the church, today, if the singing, the teaching, the communing together, the praying, and the giving of our means, (the fellowship) can all be documented as the scriptural practice of the early church, then we can know that we are members of the church or the kingdom prophesied by Daniel. In Acts 2:47, for the first time, we find people being added to the church. Up until this time, Pentecost AD 33, we read of the church as a future happening; but from this time on, the church exists. It all happened just as it was prophesied that it would. God's word is unmistakably clear. It is an amazing thing. We can all be members of Christ's church through acceptance and obedience of truth, God's holy word.

It is important that we recognize that people can be members of the Lord's church. In accordance with Ephesians 5:23, Christ is the Savior of the body, His church (Colossians 1:18; Matthew 16:18). Therefore, it is necessary to be in Christ, His body, to be saved. How do we get into Christ? How did those people back in those days get into Christ? What we have seen is that they were told to repent and be baptized in Jesus' name for the remission of their sins; and when they did so, the Lord added them to the church. So, it is evident that we must hear the word of God, we must believe it, we must repent of our sins and we must be willing to confess our faith in Jesus Christ. You remember in Acts 8, the Ethiopian nobleman said, "I believe that Jesus Christ is the Son of God" (Acts 8:37). The fifth step is to be baptized into Christ, His body (Galatians 3:26-27). It is for the remission of sins, and you are promised the gift of the Holy Spirit (Acts 2:38). Jesus says, "He that believeth and is baptized shall be saved" (Mark 16:16). Baptism is a burial, immersion, in water (Romans 6:3-5; Acts 8:36-38). One of the wonderful things to know about the church is that all of those things were done so that we can be saved; it is important to know that we can be a part of this glorious institution and that it is so essential.

All who obey the gospel are saved by the Lord. The Lord adds to His church, the body, all who should be saved (were being saved) as we have noted in Acts 2:47. Now, these steps into Christ are steps we must take to receive the benefit of the great sacrifice that Jesus made for us. Jesus can save us only, if we are willing to obey Him. These steps into Christ come from the Bible and not from man. What a wonderful study. This is in response to the question: Why the Church of Christ? Excellent question! I hope that as you study these things, you will come to the conclusion that this is what the Book says. Remember we are here not to sell, not one thing. We are here to help you, in any way we can, to understand what the church is. Until this time next Lord's Day, we bid you one and all a very pleasant good day.

# Why the Church of Christ? #3

We will turn our attention now to the topic at hand and that is, Why the Church of Christ? In our past studies, for several Lord's Days now, we have talked about the church from the standpoint of the builder. Jesus says, in Matthew 16:18, "And upon this rock I will build my church; and the gates of hell shall not prevail against it." We have also considered not only the builder but the foundation. Since the Bible describes the church as the house of God, that house would rest upon a foundation and that foundation was the right confession Peter made when he said Jesus Christ is the Son of God. We have also taken a look in the last two Lord's Days about the church in prophecy, when holy men of God spoke as they were moved by the Holy Spirit; and they looked down the stream of time telling us that a part of God's eternal purpose certainly involved the church.

This morning, I am going to turn your attention to the name. The question that was asked was simply, why the Church of Christ? Or, why do we call ourselves Christians? These are excellent questions. Let us take a look at some of the answers from the word of God. When God created the first man, He called him Adam, a name that means literally red earth. Now this fact is significant because man was made from the elements of the earth. Then God created a help meet for Adam, and she was called woman. Notice in the word woman appears the word man. As Adam proclaims, "She shall be called Woman, because she was taken out of Man" (Genesis 2:23). "And Adam called his wife's name Eve; because she was the mother of all living" (Genesis 3:20).

Names have always been significant throughout the Bible. God has always called His people by name. The Old Testament tells of a man named Abram whom God renamed Abraham. This action takes place after Genesis 17:5; it will always be Abraham and not Abram. With Abram, God made a covenant, "Neither shall thy name anymore be called Abram, but thy name shall be Abraham; for a father of many nations have I made thee." Also, God renamed his wife: her name was Sarai, and God renamed Sarah (Genesis 17:15).

God's people were given a special name when Jacob's name was changed to Israel. This name, Israel, exalted the name of God because EL meant God in Hebrew. It is important to note that the people of God wore one name, not only was it given by God, but it meant that they were His people. God declares, "You shall have no other gods before me." Daniel by inspiration proclaims, "Thy people are called by thy name" (Daniel 9:19). In your studies you might also take a look at Exodus 20:3. The prophets began to speak of a new name that would come, and the Bible declares that God's people would be called by this new name at some point in time. In Isaiah 65:15, we have such a prophecy. Isaiah says, "And you shall leave your name for a curse unto my chosen: for the Lord God shall slay thee, and call his servants by another name." In Isaiah 56:5, Isaiah says, "Even unto them will I give in mine house and within my walls a place and a name better than of sons and of daughters: I will give them an everlasting name, that shall not be cut off." It is exceedingly significant that it will not just be a common name of some individual here in this world or some important reformer or a person who has lived in days past. But He says I will give them a name that is better than that of sons and daughters.

The prophet Isaiah says:

> For Zion's sake will I not hold my peace, and for Jerusalem's sake I will not rest, until the righteousness thereof go forth as brightness, and the salvation thereof as a lamp that burneth. And the Gentiles shall see thy righteousness, and all kings thy glory: and thou shalt be called by a new name, which the mouth of the Lord shall name (Isaiah 62:1-2).

Now there is irrefutable evidence when we read these scriptures that a new name would be given to God's people. Notice where it will be: this new name was to be given in God's house. This name would be an everlasting name that shall not be cutoff or changed. This name would be given to God's people, both Jew and Gentile. It would be better than any other name, and God would be the one who would give it. Notice He says also, in Isaiah 62:2, "And the Gentiles shall see thy righteousness." We see his fulfillment at the conversion of the house of Cornelius (Acts 10). Upon this occasion Peter declares, "Of a truth I perceive that God is no respecter of persons: But in every nation he that feareth him, and worketh righteousness, is accepted with him" (Acts 10:34-35). The scripture says a new name will be given and it will be given by God Himself. Now in Acts 9:15, we are told by an inspired word that Paul is going to quote, "Bear my name"—listen—"bear my name before the Gentiles, and kings, and the children of Israel." A short time later we find Paul in Antioch, Jews and Greeks, also translated Gentiles, being present and he, Paul, taught much people. The scripture says, "And the disciples were called Christians first in Antioch" (Acts 11:19-26). A new name had been given to the disciples, given in the house of God. This name had not been known before either in the sacred or in profane history.

Paul, God's spokesman to the Gentiles, delivers a beautiful name, one honoring Christ, the Savior of the world from its sins, the name Christian. The name given to Christ's followers is above every name (Philippians 2:9). Peter commands, "Repent, and be baptized every one of you in the name of Jesus Christ for the remission of sins" (Acts 2:38). Paul then tells those at Colossae, "Whatsoever you do in word or deed, do all in the name of the Lord Jesus" (Colossians 3:17). Peter later declares, "Yet if any man suffer as a Christian, let him not be ashamed" (1 Peter 4:16).

It seems almost beyond belief that anyone can declare that there is nothing in a name when you go back and see God changing peoples' names. You are seeing God giving a new name after 1,500 years of biblical history. All of these things insist that there is something in a name. God's people wore the name Israel and worshiped in Jerusalem because that is what God expected and that is what He commanded under the Old Testament. Today, His disciples wear the name Christian because the scripture says, "Of whom the whole family in heaven and earth is named." Named after whom? After Jesus Christ (Ephesians 3:14-15). Jesus declares of the church at Philadelphia, "I know thy works ... thou has kept my word, and hast not denied my name" (Revelation 3:8).

Today we are only Christians, nothing more, nothing less, and nothing else. Obedience, that is, keeping His word, offers to all men salvation. Thankfully, the Bible says, "Neither is there salvation in any other: for there is none other name under heaven given among men, whereby we must be saved" (Acts 4:12). Jesus declared the church to be His. In Matthew 16:18, He says, "And upon this rock I will build my church." The church is the bride of Christ and the bride of the Lamb, which is the Lord Jesus (Revelation 19:7). You can also read that in Revelation 21:2. God has not changed in His expectations.

Christ's bride will wear His name; now that makes a great deal of sense to us, doesn't it? If the church is the bride of Christ, it should wear His name. The bride's name is the Church of Christ. It belongs to Him. We may scoff at this point; but when we examine it with an open heart, I think we will see that is all it can mean. We wear His name with honor. As Christians, we have been added to the church, the Lamb's bride.

Names are important. There is no doubt about it. For us to pick up the thought that there is nothing in a name that some promote is foolish. The idea is just simply the case, even in human dealings, and so why would it be true when you come to the word of God? Names are important, even as in the beginning, "we have been given power to become the sons of God" (John 1:12) and to be "added to the church" (Acts 2:47). The Bible says, the "Lord added to the church daily such as were being saved." The church is Christ's church, it is His bride; and it is the same church about which Jesus says, "I will build" (Matthew 16:18). It is the church that Jesus calls, "My church," in Matthew 16:18. He calls it "the bride" in Revelation 22:17. The Church of Christ about which Paul speaks collectively of all who wear Christ's name and worship and declare only Bible truths when he says, "The churches of Christ salute you" (Romans 16:16).

Today, many want to be His bride but refuse to wear His name. Many want to be called Christians but refuse to obey His commandments. May I say to you, it will not work. It will not work according to this book. Today the church and Christians, that is the disciples of the gospel of Jesus, declare the same message of salvation that was delivered nearly 2,000 years ago. We can declare no more, we can declare no less, than what the Master has given. Salvation is for all who will hear and obey Him. Jesus says in Matthew 11:28, "Come unto me, all ye that labor and are heavy laden, and I will give you rest." He also says, "And whosoever will, let him take the water of life freely" (Revelation 22:17). Remember Jesus says, "I am the way" (John 14:6). He did not say, I am one of the many thousands of ways. He says, "I am the way, the truth, and the life, no man comes to God but by me." How absolutely important that we study these things and study them carefully.

But let us talk some more about the church in answering the question, why the Church of Christ or what is this that is referred to as the church? How do they serve Him, how do they worship Him? Let us talk a little bit about the way we worship. The Bible is our only creed. We have no creed book. We simply have the word of God, and we must look to it for our every practice. Paul says, "All scripture is given by inspiration of God, and is profitable for doctrine, for reproof, for correction, for instruction in righteousness: That the man of God may be perfect, thoroughly furnished unto all good works" (2 Timothy 3:16-17). Paul says all good works that are to be done for doctrine as we worship and serve Him, they are furnished, and they are given to us. Where are they? They are in inspired scripture that has been given by God, by His Holy Spirit, who guided and directed his writing. God's word was and is far too important to leave for any man to write on his own or to change as some would do today. Listen to Peter's words:

> We have also a more sure word of prophecy; whereunto ye do well that ye take heed, as unto a light that shineth in a dark place, until the day dawn, and the day star arise in your hearts: Knowing this first, that no prophecy of the scripture is of any private interpretation. For the prophecy came not in old time by the will of man: but holy men of God spake as they were moved by the Holy Ghost (2 Peter 1:19-21).

The scriptures were penned as the Holy Spirit directed these men to write them—every word of them. Remember Paul says, "All scripture is given by inspiration of God," all scripture was literally God breathed.

So when we come together on the first day of the week to worship God, we have things we are told to do. Acts 2:42 says, "And they continued steadfastly in the apostles' doctrine and fellowship, and in breaking of bread, and in prayers." All of these things were done in the early church, when the apostles were living, and in many cases where apostles were present in their assembly, such as in Acts 20:7. Oftentimes, someone raises the question: when the Church of Christ comes together to worship, why does it not use mechanical instruments of music in the assembly like everyone else? I think that is a good question. The Bible says we must be ready and able to give an answer to every person who asks a reason of the hope that is in us, and we are to do it with meekness and with fear. But if we simply go to the scripture and consider nothing more, nothing less than what do you see being done in the worship of the early church? Remember all we know about it, all we know about what pleases God, is what He has told us. So we turn to the scriptures; and we find that, indeed, a part of the worship was their singing. What a wonderful thing that the Lord has made singing a part of our worship. In Hebrews 2:12, the apostle says, "In the midst of the church will I sing praise unto thee." It is very evident that when the church came together to worship, they would sing. The Bible tells us they were to speak one to another in psalms and hymns and spiritual songs, singing with grace in their hearts unto the Lord.

When we come together as a congregation, we sing without the aid of any instrument of music, we teach one man at a time in an undivided assembly, we have one cup on the Lord's table containing the fruit of the vine (which is juice of the grape) and one loaf of unleavened bread in the communion. We give as we have been prospered and as we have purposed in our hearts, and we pray in the name of Jesus Christ. Why? The reason we do all the things is that we find scripture for such a practice. There is a Bible reason for it. Our worship is structured to the very best of our ability according to the pattern that we have in the word of God. This is the reason we have to make up our mind, either we are going to go according to the pattern or we simply are not and we will do whatever we please to do. One thing is evident in the scriptures: God is a God of law. He is a God of pattern, and it is for this reason that anything practiced or used that is newer than the New Testament is too new. We are concerned with what God's word commands through words spoken by the Lord Jesus, and through the writings of the apostles and the holy men of New Testament times. What any man or any man-made organization since that time may have said, or given approval to, just is not enough. We cannot perform any action unless God's word authorizes it.

The scriptures will direct us into all good works—remember—he has given us everything that pertains to life and godliness and so everything that is good, everything that pertains to life and godliness, is found in the scriptures. If something is not found in the scriptures, then let us leave it alone and do only what we find authority for in the word of God. As we begin to talk about singing and about why we do not use mechanical instruments in our worship, I want you to remember the words of Jesus. Jesus says, "But the hour cometh, and now is, when the true worshipers shall worship the Father in spirit and in truth: for the Father seeketh such to worship him. God is a Spirit: and they that worship him must worship him in spirit and in truth" (John 4:23-24). He declares that the true worshiper shall worship with both the right spirit and according to truth. Now we cannot leave either one of these out. We cannot exalt one of these over the other. This scripture clearly implies the possibility of false worship. Jesus emphasizes this point in Matthew 15:8-9 when He calls the worship done according to man's commands and precepts as being vain worship—listen to His words—Jesus says, "But in vain do they worship me."

Is it possible for people to worship God in vain? Jesus says so. They are worshiping God, the right person to worship, but Jesus says, "It is in vain." Well, what would make that true? Why? Because He says, "They are teaching for doctrine the commandments of men." Therefore, a man may come and go through all the motions of worship to God, but fail in his efforts it he does not either seek truth or be in the right spirit when he worships; both are declared to be vain worship. It is so important that we recognize that worshiping God is not some little thing. Worshiping God is not some game we play—it is not child's play. It is a very serious matter. It is a serious occasion when we come together and offer worship unto God.

Paul states in Colossians 3:17 "And whatsoever you do in word or deed, do all in the name of the Lord Jesus." These are strange words in this day in which we live. I can assure you that those words are like a voice crying in the wilderness, in a wilderness of a time, when compared to the order of our day. I think it is sad when we just listen to the word of God and then just say, whatever, in other words, we can do what we want, when we want, how we want, and with whatever regularity we want or do not want. When the Book says— listen—the Book says, whatsoever you do, in word or deed. Now, word is simply our preaching or teaching, our deeds are our practice; so whatever we teach, whatever we practice, he says, you do all this in the name of the Lord Jesus. Now, does this mean we can simply toss off the name of Jesus and say well then that makes anything and everything okay? No. What it means is by His authority. Paul stresses the importance of everything we do being done in the name of Jesus, that is, by His authority. In John 5:27, we see the authority was given into Jesus' hands because He is the Son of man. In Matthew 28:18, Jesus says, "All power"—that is, all authority—"is given unto me in heaven and in earth." What an amazing degree of authority. It was this same Jesus who declared God's word to be truth (John 17:17), so our authority must be based upon a thus saith the Lord or it is written. The New Testament is our only basis of authority for every practice.

Now, a little bit more about that, in the name: you remember that case in Acts 4 when they brought Peter and John before the magistrates because they had healed the crippled man at the beautiful gate? They brought them and set them in their midst and asked them, "And by what power or by what name have you done this?" So when we are talking about the name, it is the same as if someone were to knock on your door and say, Open up in the name of the law. So as we talk about "in the name" we are saying the same thing as "by His authority," that is, by His power. So Paul says, whatever we do in our teaching or in our practice, we must do everything by the authority of Jesus Christ. Well, how do we know what the authority of Jesus Christ is? We have to turn to the word of God. We want to close there and we will pick up here again next Lord's Day if it be His will. We look forward to studying with you. We look forward to hearing from you. Until that time, I bid you a very pleasant good day.

# *Why the Church of Christ? #4*

When we closed our last study, we were talking about the church in prophecy. I would like this morning to continue this subject as we talk about those who looked down through the stream of time and by inspiration told of the coming days. Jacob's ladder is only one of the many prophecies in the Old Testament that foreshadows an event that was fulfilled in the New Testament age. In Hebrews 10:1, the Apostle Paul tells us, "For the law having a shadow of good things to come, and not the very image of the things." So, a shadow is a rough image or outline of the things that are foreshadowed. Thus, from the shadow, it may difficult to discern what the fulfillment of the prophecy will be; but when you see the fulfillment of it, it becomes quite clear.

In Genesis 28, we have this account that tells of a great vision that Jacob had while on his way to get married. Jacob was the grandson of Abraham, and it was common for a young man to be sent by his parents to a place where he could find the right kind of woman. Jacob was told to go down to the land where his uncle Laban, his mother's brother, dwelt; and there take himself a wife of his daughters. It was likely that he never had seen them before, as they lived a great way off. On his way there, the Bible says that he stopped along the roadside for the night and gathered some rocks for a pillow. It was on this occasion that a wonderful dream or vision came to him. He saw a ladder set on the earth; the top of it reached to heaven, and the angels of God were ascending and descending upon it (Genesis 28:12). That must have been an impressive sight, listen to the passage: "And, behold, the Lord stood above it" (verse 13), with angels climbing up and down on this ladder. Jacob must have realized this vision pictured a special event. Jacob heard God say, "I am the Lord God of Abraham thy father, and the God of Isaac: the land whereon thou liest, to thee will I give it, and to thy seed; And thy seed shall be as the dust of the earth" (Genesis 28:13-14). He also tells Jacob, "I am with thee, and will keep thee in all places whither thou goest, and will bring thee again into this land; for I will not leave thee, until I have done that which I have spoken to thee of" (verse 15).

God made this promise Himself; therefore, it was certain, even though it may not occur for hundreds of years. But it will come to pass as surely as God is. The only times He did not do as He promised was when His people were disobedient. His promises are so sure that Paul refers to Him as "the Lord, the righteous judge" (2 Timothy 4:8) because God cannot lie (Hebrews 6:18; Titus 1:2). When Jacob awakened from his dream, he declared the place to be the house of God (verse 17), and he says, "And I knew it not." Jacob poured oil upon the rocks, and it became a hallowed spot. This is the land of Bethel, just north of where Jerusalem would be built and where the house of God would come to dwell. It was the vicinity where Isaac was figuratively offered on Mount Moriah. Scholars believe this is the very spot where Jesus Christ the Son of God was crucified. So without a doubt, it was a special place, and it was here that Jacob saw the ladder.

When we think of a ladder, we obviously think of using it to get from one place to another, from the ground to the top of something. When Jacob saw the ladder, he saw a way from earth to heaven; and that way had never been manifested to anyone before this time, even though now it was only in a visionary sense that Jacob saw it. Jacob had no idea how God would bring all this to pass upon the earth, but he was certain God would do it. The same promise, made many years before to Abraham, was now made to him and to his descendents. It was through this genealogy that eventually Jesus Christ would be born. The bloodline began with Adam, came down to Abraham and Isaac, then to Solomon, then to Christ, and the other over to Nathan and then to Christ. These are recorded for us in Matthew 1:1-17 and Luke 3:23-38. These give the bloodline of Jesus and were the promise made to Abraham, "And in thee shall all families of the earth be blessed" (Genesis 12:3). All the families, certainly meant more than just a few, more than just the descendents of Jacob. Of course, you remember Jacob's real name was changed to Israel, so his sons were the fathers of the twelve tribes of the children of Israel. So by his promise God says the whole world would be blessed through Abraham's seed someday.

Now, if we are going to examine Jacob's ladder and see the image fulfilled in New Testament times, we need to look for a passage of scripture in which we find heaven open. We need to find a ladder or something that can take the place of a ladder, and we need to see the angels of God ascending and descending upon that ladder. Now, remember in Hebrews 10:1 Paul says, "For the law having a shadow of good things to come" implies that a dream or a vision is often quite different from the real thing; but whatever the ladder represented, it must be pictured with heaven open and angels ascending and descending upon it. It is my understanding that the ladder represents the church; and, thus, contrary to many beliefs, it could not have existed in the days of John, the immerser. Notice if you will, in John 1:51, where Jesus responds to a statement by Nathaniel who says, "Thou art the Son of God, thou art the King of Israel." Jesus says—listen—"Verily, verily, I say unto you, Hereafter ye shall see heaven open, and the angels of God ascending and descending upon the Son of man" (John 1:51). Here it is, AD 30 or 31; the work of John the Baptist is over, and we hear the words of Jesus declared. Hereafter, the very thing we are looking for shall come to pass. John's work is over. Heaven has not been opened. Jesus says, it would be after this time; therefore, the ladder that Jacob saw could not have existed during John's time. Paul then confirms this point as he writes in the book of Hebrews:

> The Holy Ghost this signifying, that the way into the holiest of all was not yet made manifest, while as the first tabernacle was yet standing: Which was a figure for the time then present, in which were offered both gifts and sacrifices, that could not make him that did the service perfect, as pertaining to the conscience (Hebrews 9:8-9).

Twice every day, the common priest went into the holy place to officiate for the sins of the people at 9 a.m. and 3 p.m. Then, once a year on the Day of Atonement, the high priest went into the most holy place and there offered sacrifices for the sins of himself and for all the congregation. Remember Paul says, "The way was not yet manifest into the holiest of all," in reference to heaven.

No one knew how to get from earth to heaven while the first tabernacle yet stood; that is an Old Testament situation. Why? It is really quite simple because until Jesus died, the tabernacle and the law that governed it were still in effect, that is, the Old Testament law. Recall please that on the day that Jesus died, the time of His crucifixion was 9 a.m., the third hour of the day and He died at 3 p.m., the ninth hour of the day. This is so significant because the very times when the common priest would be in the Temple hurriedly offering sacrifices directly before the veil is the time when Christ was crucified and when He died. If the priest were where he should have been, he was right there when the veil was ripped from top to bottom; he represented the Christian today in the holy place. This priest hurriedly went about all his duties without sitting down and then quickly left. Yet Jesus, our High Priest, entered into the most holy place and there offered the one sacrifice that would be good for all time; then the scripture says He sat down at the right hand of God. His work was complete; the fact that He sat down shows that His work was finished and that no further sacrifice would ever be needed. Whereas, the common priest under the Old Testament, who never sat down, indicated that his work was continual. Sacrifice after sacrifice was needed to be offered. Jesus, when He died on the cross offered the only sacrifice that would ever be needed. In Matthew 27:51 we read, "And, behold, the veil of the temple was rent in twain from the top to the bottom" and for the first time ever, the way between earth and heaven was made known to the ordinary priest. It was no longer a mystery, but rather all could see it and understand and know the way to be saved.

When Peter preached the first gospel sermon on the day of Pentecost, he made known for all time the way for sin to be forgiven. Paul says that when Jesus died, the ordinances were taken out of the way; nailing them to the cross. Under the old law there was no forgiveness of sins except in the ceremonial sense. Paul points out that if this were true today then continual sacrifice would still have to be made.

On the other hand, if forgiveness were possible under the old law, then sacrifices once made would erase forever those sins; however, under the Old Testament system, the cycle of sacrifice had to be repeated each year. I think it is interesting that the ladder could not have existed until Jesus died on the cross because we know the tabernacle, the Old Testament Tabernacle, stood until He died about AD 33. It was nine o'clock in the morning, on the first day of the week when Peter stood up and preached the first gospel sermon and three thousand souls were added to the church (Acts 2:41). When we stop and examine the facts, man needed a ladder that he might reach God. Man, who is fault ridden, prone to sin, must continually be asking God for forgiveness, over and over again, because of his sins. On the one hand, we have the imperfection, a man who needs to be reunited with God. who is perfect. On the other hand, we have the Son of God, an infinite and perfect God. These are opposite extremes. A way needed to be found to connect a finite and imperfect man with a perfect God if man were ever going to attain heaven. Is not that what a ladder is supposed to do—connect? There needed to be a way to make it possible for one to reach the other.

Sometimes the connection seems impossible; and if left in man's hand to accomplish, it would be. In God's plan was the miracle needed to connect man to God when Jesus Christ appeared on the scene. When Jesus was born, He had with Him the deity, the glory, and the power of God. He was God, with God, and was God in the very beginning. The Bible says, "All things were made by him; and without him was not any thing made that was made" (John 1:3). He tells us in John 1, "And the Word was made flesh, and dwelt among us, (and we beheld his glory, the glory as of the only begotten of the Father)" (John 1:14). He took upon Himself the seed of man. Paul says about Him:

> Seeing then that we have a great high priest, that is passed into the heavens, Jesus the Son of God, let us hold fast our profession. For we have not a high priest which cannot be touched with the feeling of our infirmities; but was in all points tempted like as we are, yet without sin (Hebrews 4:14-15).

Every temptation that we have ever had, Jesus had to put up with the same. He was tempted in all points like as we are; yet in this tabernacle of clay dwelt the glory, the power, and the deity of God. In Jesus Christ was available all that the Godhead held. So, with one hand this man Jesus could reach up and take hold of the hand of God, and with the other hand He could reach down to man; and thus these two opposites were joined. The miracle was performed and man could now find peace with God through Jesus Christ. In 2 Corinthians 5:19, the Bible says, "To wit, that God was in Christ, reconciling the world unto himself, not imputing their trespasses unto them; and hath committed unto us the word of reconciliation." Is not that interesting? Paul tells us that God was reconciling the world unto Himself and in that same verse He says God was in Christ. In John 14:6, Jesus says, "I am the way, the truth, and the life: no man cometh unto the Father, but by me."

Evidently, the ladder is Jesus Christ, the way is the church, and now if anyone desires to be saved, to reach the Father, it can be done, but only through and by Jesus Christ. To reach God, the ladder must be used. Jesus says in John 1:51, "Hereafter, (or after this time) ye shall see heaven open." Heaven will be open in the sense that man now has access to it and the way is clear for all who have eyes to see. And the servants of God, the angels, are seen climbing up and down this ladder, Jesus Christ. That is what Jacob saw so very long ago. What a wonderful thing to be able to look at it through the eyes of inspiration, through the eyes of the scripture.

Yet, to get from earth to heaven, we have to get on the ladder, don't we? Jesus says, I am the way, the truth, and the life; but we must get in the way, that is, onto the ladder, if you will, that is, if we are going to go to God (Ephesians 1:20-23). Another way of expressing it that we must get into Christ, which is the same as getting into the body of Christ. To be in the body and to be in the church are one in the same thing. Jesus is the head of the body, the church (Colossians 1:18). In Ephesians 4:4, Paul says, "There is one body," and so, we are talking about the Lord's church. Why the Church of Christ? Because, it belongs to Him, and He says, "I am the way, the truth, and the life; no man cometh to the Father, but by me." Obedience and submission to Christ in baptism puts us into Christ. In Galatians 3:27, the Bible says, "For as many of you as have been baptized into Christ have put on Christ." So to get on the ladder, is to obey the gospel plan of salvation: believing (Hebrews 11:6), repenting of our sins (Luke 13:3), confessing Jesus Christ to be the Son of God (Matthew 10:32, Romans 10:9-10), and being baptized for the remission of our sins (Acts 2:38).

Is not this what Jesus says in the Great Commission? He tells His apostles that they are to go into all the world and preach the gospel to every creature; and then He stipulates that anyone who believes and is baptized shall be saved. He goes on to say that those who do not believe not shall be condemned. It is the same message that Peter gives on the birthday of the church when the people cried out, Men and brethren, what shall we do? He tells them to "repent, and be baptized every one of you in the name of Jesus Christ for the remission of sins." Paul has a similar message in the book of Romans where he says:

> Know ye not, that so many of us as were baptized into Jesus Christ were baptized into his death? Therefore we are buried with him by baptism into death: that like as Christ was raised up from the dead by the glory of the Father, even so we also should walk in newness of life (Romans 6:3-4).

These steps put us on the ladder, if you will, they put us into Christ. Peter says in his second epistle:

> And beside this, giving all diligence, add to your faith virtue; and to virtue knowledge; And to knowledge temperance; and to temperance patience; and to patience godliness; And to godliness brotherly kindness; and to brotherly kindness charity. For if these things be in you, and abound, they make you that ye shall neither be barren nor unfruitful in the knowledge of our Lord Jesus Christ. But he that lacketh these things is blind, and cannot see afar off, and hath forgotten that he was purged from his old sins (2 Peter 1:5-9).

We have come to call these characteristics Christian graces. When we add them to our life in Christ, we are giving an example of obedient faith. If one does add them, he will never fall, according to the Apostle Peter. If he fails to add them, he will fall.

Indeed, we climb this ladder differently from the way we climb any other ladder. As we climb, we carry with us each characteristic of that ladder step-by-step until we complete our Christian journey. That is the reason he says we get on the ladder through our obedient submission. Then we add to our faith virtue and we take another step up and add virtue to knowledge and to knowledge, temperance and to temperance, patience and to patience, godliness. Then take another step and add godliness to brotherly kindness and brotherly kindness to charity. We are taking these steps, if you will, toward heaven. In 2 Peter 1:11, Peter says, "For so an entrance shall be ministered unto you abundantly into the everlasting kingdom of our Lord and Savior Jesus Christ." The gates of heaven shall open wide, granting what Peter calls an abundant entrance to the Christian. He doesn't say it is going to be barely—he says it will be ministered unto all the faithful abundantly.

What a wonderful thing to contemplate. The child of God has no reason to be afraid. Jesus died for us. His great sacrifice cleanses us as we serve Him, confess our sins, and pray fervently unto God. Hundreds of years before Jesus came to earth to live as the Son of Man, to suffer the cruel treatment by mankind, to go to Calvary that man might be saved, and to build His church as He promised, God gave this vision to Jacob; and it fits the church so beautifully.

Thank you for listening. What a pleasure to be with you today and to study with you the scriptures. We appreciate your statements, your questions, your concerns, and we are happy to hear from you. It does not matter whether you agree or disagree, we are happy to hear from you and to know what your needs may be. Until this time next Lord's Day, we bid you one and all a very pleasant good day.

# *Why the Church of Christ? #5*

Once again, we turn our attention to the scripture and to the question we have been considering in recent broadcasts. This is the fifth broadcast in which we have responded to this question: What is the Church of Christ or why the Church of Christ? These are good questions, and we ought to be able to give an answer of the reason for the hope that is in us with meekness and with fear. During these last broadcasts, those of you who have been listening and studying with us, we have been talking about the builder of the church, and that, of course, is Jesus. He is the one who said, "Upon this rock I will build my church." We talked about the foundation of the church, which is the confessed truth that Jesus is the Christ the Son of the living God. Paul states, "That other foundation can no man lay than that which is laid, which is Jesus Christ." We have talked about the church in prophecy, predictive prophecy, and the fulfillment of prophecy as regards the church. We talked about the name that we wear. We talked about the worship, and this morning we would like to talk about teaching the word of God.

As we said in the opening part of the broadcast this morning, it is our responsibility to preach the word of God. In fact, we are under a divine charge to:

> Preach the word; be instant in season, out of season; reprove, rebuke, exhort with all long-suffering and doctrine. For the time will come when they will not endure sound doctrine; but after their own lusts they will heap to themselves teachers, having itching ears; And they shall turn away their ears from the truth, and shall be turned unto fables (2 Timothy 4:2-4).

When the apostle called the elders of the church at Ephesus in Acts 20, you remember he says to this group of men, "Take heed therefore unto yourselves, and to all the flock, over which the Holy Ghost hath made you overseers, to feed the church of God, which he hath purchased with his own blood" (Acts 20:28). The Lord's church recognizes and accepts the authority of Jesus to rule, and His church realizes that any commandments that were given were given out of deep love for God's children. Commandments were not just arbitrarily given. They are there for our good whether we understand the purpose or not.

Before our Lord left here, He says, "I go to prepare a place for you. And if I go and prepare a place for you, I will come again, and receive you unto myself; that where I am, there ye maybe also" (John 14:2-3). Jesus says, "All power is given unto me in heaven and in earth" (Matthew 28:18). Jesus says, "Keep my commandments" (John 14:15). Jesus is coming again, and He is coming to take God's children home to live forever.

The source of influence that God established to produce believers is the gospel. Paul says, "For I am not ashamed of the gospel of Christ: for it is the power of God unto salvation to every one that believeth; to the Jew first, and also to the Greek" (Romans 1:16). Not only has the gospel been given to man, but He has also given mankind the ability to believe and to obey it or to reject it. He is "not willing that any should perish, but that all should come to repentance" (2 Peter 3:9). Now, it is evident that all are not going to come to repentance, but the Lord is not willing that any should perish. It is His will that we all turn around and come to Him. The scriptures teach that the choice of obedience and service is left with man. All of the evidence needed to arrive at truth is available in the Bible. Man, by his sins, is worthy of death; but the gospel tells us how we can be saved through the blood of the Lord Jesus Christ (Romans 3:25; Ephesians 1:7).

Jesus says, "Come unto me, all ye that labor and are heavy laden, and I will give you rest" (Matthew 11:28). We can know what to do to be saved. Jesus says in John 8:31-32 that, "If you continue in my word, then are ye my disciples indeed; And ye shall know the truth, and the truth shall make you free." The scripture declares—listen—the scripture declares that if a man comes to know God, so that his soul can be saved, it will be through "the foolishness of preaching" (1 Corinthians 1:20-21). In all of our secular knowledge and wisdom, we will never know God. Only by God's word, the Bible, can we come to a knowledge of Him. In 1 Corinthians 3:19, Paul says, "For the wisdom of this world is foolishness with God." When man foolishly attempts to worship God outside the prescribed way, the scripture says, "But in vain do they worship me, teaching for doctrines the commandments of men" (Matthew 15:9).

The truth of God's word **must** be preached, it **must** be preached, declaring how Christ came to the world, how He lived His life doing good, how He was tried by cruel men and crucified, how He was buried, upon the third day rose again, and then ascended back to the Father. Christ sits at the God's right hand and mediates our prayers to the Father at this very moment. The world views the preaching of the cross to be foolishness (1 Corinthians 1:18). It pleases God by the foolishness of preaching—it does not please God by foolish preaching. But what the world perceives to be the foolishness of preaching will save those who believe. Many who proclaim a religion put God's word aside and decide it is just as well to have lectures on the problems of the day or talk about, you name it, whatever makes the speaker feel good because that is what the people want to hear. But the apostle says, "Preach the word"—"preach the word … For the time will come when they will not endure sound doctrine" (2 Timothy 4:1-3). Also, in connection with your study read 1 Timothy 4:1-3. Clearly, this passage proclaims that preaching and teaching are empty unless it is the Christ-centered gospel. Jesus says, "Go ye into all the world, and preach the gospel to every creature" (Mark 16:15). He further says, "Teaching them to observe all things whatsoever I have commanded you" (Matthew 28:20).

The gospel is so powerful that it can separate the old man of sin from our lives. The sinner who will turn and serve can be saved by the glorious gospel of Jesus our Lord. Now this message is what the lost world needs to hear: a message that gives them hope—hope through Christ for salvation, that is, for eternal redemption. Peter says in his writings, "Men and brethren, ye know how that a good while ago God made choice among us, that the Gentiles by my mouth should hear the word of the gospel, and believe" (Acts 15:7). Notice the way he puts it: that they should, by his mouth, hear the word of the gospel and believe. Paul says:

> How then shall they call on him in whom they have not believed? And how shall they believe in him of whom they have not heard? And how shall they hear without a preacher? And how shall they preach, except they be sent? (Romans 10:14-15).

When the gospel is preached and it is heard and understood by a receptive heart, it will produce a believer who is ready to become obedient and serve and follow the lead of the Master. It was that power, the power of the gospel, that convicted 3,000 souls when Peter stood up and preached the first gospel sermon. You will find this record in Acts 2.

Peter speaks to the Jews who have condoned the crucifixion of the Son of God; and by his preaching the Bible says, "they were pricked in their heart," that is, they were convicted and they cried out "Men and brethren what shall we do?" To this cry, Peter responds, "Repent and be baptized" (Acts 2:38). The scripture says, "They that gladly received his word were baptized" (verse 41). The church was established right there. We know it was because the scripture says, "they were added to them." Luke goes on to talk to us about this event, and he writes it like this: "And the Lord added to the church daily such as should be saved" (Acts 2:47).

In the parable of the sower—which is one of the great, great sermons of the Bible—the personal sermon of our Lord Jesus Christ—the parable of the sower stresses several valuable points that I will just touch on briefly; but we need to remember how we are to open our hearts. The Bible says, "A sower went out to sow." The second thing it says, "he sowed only good seed." The next thing it states is that seed went where ever it was cast and came to rest somewhere. Some seed did not even germinate, for it was quickly stolen away. Some germinated and quickly died for lack of depth of soil, which is the heart. Some grew and was then choked out by the thorns, the stones, or lack of proper soil; but some of the seed produced a harvest of fruit for the Master's use. The seed sown by the sower is the word of God. Luke 8:11 tells us, that the word of God is the seed of the kingdom. In other words it is the means by which it will produce a new life, a new way. Now this being the case, the seed was the glorious truth given, that men might hear it, believe it, and obey it since God's word is truth (John 17:17). Good seed and only good seed must be sown.

The picture that Jesus portrays about the sower shows that the seed is being broadcast and it fell wherever it would. A good sower covers the entire field as he moves about slowly, being sure no place has been missed by the seed because until the seed is sown nothing good is going to happen. The field is the world (Matthew 13:38). The field is the world into which the word needs to be sown. God's word is powerful and sharper than any two-edged sword; and within the prepared soil or heart, it will bring forth the results, or the fruit, that God desires.

Now, He also states that some of the seed fell by the wayside (Matthew 13:19). In fact, He puts it like this: when anyone hears the word of the kingdom and understands it not, "Then cometh the devil, and taketh away the word out of their hearts, lest they should believe and be saved" (Luke 8:12). The word comes upon those who do not recognize that they are standing guilty in sin or that they are lost because their hearts are so hardened by the evil influence of the world—they just do not understand. The wicked one sends his ministers in the shape of evil thoughts and worldly lusts, stealing away the very words of salvation.

Now, he also says, as the sower went forth to sow, some seed fell by the wayside on hardened earth, earth that was so hard the seed could not penetrate. The hardened earth represents a heart that is so hard the word of God cannot not get within it. He continues that some of the seed fell on stony places where there was not much earth (Matthew 13:5). Now, the picture here is truly a sad one: the life and the heart have hardened into a selfish will and desire, but a small part whispers the need for salvation and a desire for it. The word is received and begins to grow quickly, but the commitment is not there. When times get hard, when something arises that conflicts with what a person desires, the young plant withers away because it had no depth of earth.

But then some of the seed fell among thorns (Matthew 13:7). Nothing is mentioned here of the lack of soil but rather the growth of two plants in the same space. It is apparent from the growth described that the thorns are growing as well as, if not better, than the good seed. The scripture declares that no man can serve two masters (Matthew 6:24). How tragic is this case because the soul pictured may worship and even be a leader for years while attempting to hold on to position, worldly friends, worldly possessions, the cares of the world, the deceitfulness of riches. Jesus says they choke the word, and it becomes unfruitful (Matthew 13:22).

Our commitment, our conviction, our devotion must be to serve God. Anything that is placed above our God in service eventually is going to lead us to spiritual death. But what a wonderful thing to know that when the sower went forth to sow that not all seed fell by the wayside, upon stony ground, or among thorns; thankfully some fell into good ground (Matthew 13:8).

Seekers of the truth will find it, according to Matthew 7:7. And when the truth of God's word enters into that fertile soil, it can spring forth to produce fruit for the harvest. Our Lord concludes this great sermon, the parable of the sower, with these words: "Who hath ears to hear, let him hear" (Matthew 13:9). Now one cannot believe until he has heard the gospel, so we need to broadcast it, we need to preach it, we need to be telling the story. People in all nations need to hear the gospel of Jesus Christ. It can prick the hearts of people today as it did nearly 2,000 years ago. It can save anyone who will give up his life of serving sin and deliver him into the Master's hands where he can serve daily in the kingdom of God by doing His will. Our Lord says, "Go ye into all the world, and preach the gospel to every creature" (Mark 16:15). Yes, this message was spoken to the apostles, but it resounds to us even today. And Jesus left an example for us to follow in that He went about preaching and teaching—and He commands all of us to "follow me" (John 12:26). So, we, too, must be willing to give the gospel to anyone and to everyone who will listen.

It is evident from this sermon, and from many other places in the word of God, the message that needs to be taught. When Jesus approaches the time of His departure from this world, His return to the Father, He speaks these words:

> So when they had dined, Jesus saith to Simon Peter, Simon, son of Jonas, lovest thou me more than these? He saith unto him, Yea, Lord; thou knowest that I love thee. He saith unto him, Feed my lambs. He saith to him again the second time, Simon, son of Jonas, lovest thou me? He saith unto him, Yea, Lord; thou knowest that I love thee. He saith unto him, Feed my sheep. He saith unto him the third time, Simon, son of Jonas, lovest thou me? Peter was grieved because he said unto him the third time, Lovest thou me? And he said unto him, Lord, thou knowest all things; thou knowest that I love thee. Jesus saith unto him, Feed my sheep (John 21:15-17).

You will recall that Matthew records these words:

> Go ye therefore, and teach all nations, baptizing them in the name of the Father, and of the Son, and of the Holy Ghost: Teaching them to observe all things whatsoever I have commanded you: and, lo, I am with you alway, even unto the end of the world. Amen (Matthew 28:19-20).

Now the stress in each of these statements has focused upon the teaching and the purpose of the teaching. In last week's study, we dealt with giving the gospel—the good news—to those who were lost in sin so that they might be saved and so that his sins could be blotted out (Acts 3:19). Or as it is stated in the book of Acts, so that his sins could be washed away (Acts 22:16). Surely this is the heart of Jesus' message: He said to go teach all nations and to baptize them (Matthew 28:19).

But now there is another message that all who teach and all who hear must recognize. Matthew continues by saying, "teaching them." Teaching them what? "Teaching them to observe," that is. to do or to keep, "all things whatsoever I have commanded you." The Lord does not leave any doubt, does He? He has the authority to command; and what He commands, we are to keep and we are to do. The apostles were told to teach what He had personally given them. He says, for this is the will of God. Jesus declares to these men, whom He had chosen to carry the gospel to all the world—listen to what He says to them—He says, "I will pray the Father, and he shall give you another Comforter" (John 14:16). "But the Comforter, which is the Holy Ghost, whom the Father will send in my name, he shall teach you all things, and bring all things to your remembrance, whatsoever I have said unto you" (John 14:26). Jesus goes on to say:

> But when the Comforter is come, whom I will send unto you from the Father, even the Spirit of truth, which proceedeth from the Father, he shall testify of me: And ye also shall bear witness, because ye have been with me from the beginning (John 15:26-27).

"When he, the Spirit of truth, is come, he will guide you into all truth: for he shall not speak of himself; but whatsoever he shall hear, that shall he speak" (John 16:13).

Our Lord chose these men who were with Him from the beginning of His short ministry on earth. He told them they would be given special guidance, and this guidance would be by the Comforter whom God would send. This Comforter would give to these men inspired words from God, literally, God-breathed words. For the early church, for Christians, for the salvation of souls, nothing is so important as the truth being given. Anything so important as truth would not be left to chance or to the opinions of men. The words written to the churches of Christ by the apostles came from God through the Holy Spirit; and because of this important fact, Paul could write to Timothy, "All scripture is given by inspiration of God and is profitable" (2 Timothy 3:16-17). If all is inspired and we are to teach all things commanded, and the New Testament is our authority for the church and for Christian living, then what are we to teach? It really does not take a genius to figure it out, does it? I think we all know that we need to "go into all the world, and preach the gospel to every creature. He that believeth and is baptized shall be saved; but he that believeth not shall be damned" (Mark 16:15-16). This is the message that we have from Him: that we take the gospel to the world. How good it is to be with you this morning and to study with you the scriptures and to attempt to answer this question from the scripture of why the church? We invite you to continue with us as we will continue this study; and so until this time next Lord's Day, we bid you a very pleasant good day.

# *Why the Church of Christ? #6*

Beautiful words indeed in our song this morning. They beheld His glory, speaking of the resurrection of the Lord Jesus Christ. Our very salvation depends upon the fact that He did rise again from the grave. Turning our attention here this morning to another study, and this is a part of the series that we have been studying about, possibly our last one in this series. When someone raised the question: Why the Church of Christ and what is the Church of Christ, and why do they worship as they worship? Turn your attention to this topic this morning. We have considered with you what the church is; we have talked about the builder of the church, that is, Jesus Himself; we have studied about the foundation of the church, which is Christ; we spent two or three lessons speaking about the church in prophecy; we have studied about the name we wear; and then we began to study in regard to the worship. Last Lord's Day we talked about the importance of teaching the word of God when we come together into one place.

This morning, I turn your attention to one of the things we are taught to do and that is to break bread. The Bible states in Acts 2:42 "And they continued steadfastly in the apostles' doctrine and fellowship, and in breaking of bread, and in prayers." Then in Acts 20:7, the scripture says, "And upon the first day of the week, when the disciples came together to break bread, Paul preached unto them." So, there is no doubt that the early church did observe the Lord's Supper and that they observed it on the Lord's Day, which is the first day of the week; and, of course, every week has a first day. So, let's talk about this bread that we break. What is its significance? Is it really important? Is it something the Lord has commanded us? In 1 Corinthians 10, Paul talks about the bread. In 1 Corinthians 11:1, he says, "Be ye followers of me, even as I also am of Christ." He goes on to say in 1 Corinthians 11, "That the Lord Jesus the same night in which he was betrayed took bread: And when he had given thanks, he brake it, and said, Take, eat: this is my body, which is broken for you: this do in remembrance of me." That is 1 Corinthians 11:23-24.

Matthew writes, in Matthew 26 saying, "And as they were eating, Jesus took bread, and blessed it, and brake it, and gave it to the disciples, and said, Take, eat; this is my body" (Matthew 26:26). Luke writes, "And he took bread, and gave thanks, and brake it, and gave unto them, saying, This is my body which is given for you: this do in remembrance of me" (Luke 22:19). That which our Lord did was to establish an example that those who came after could practice and be assured that the form of their worship was correct. If we observe in the spirit, we have prepared our minds by examining ourselves and bringing into captivity every thought to the obedience of Christ. Our worship must be in spirit and in truth as God's pure and holy word directs so that we as His children are strengthened each time we commune together. Not only that, but we proclaim the Lord's death until He comes. So, this is an ordinance of the church that we must observe, and we must do it until the Lord comes or until we come to the end of our days.

The Lord has a pattern in Matthew 26, Mark 14, Luke 22, and 1 Corinthians 10 and 11. The pattern that He establishes here was done during the feast of unleavened bread (Matthew 26:17). Upon this occasion Jesus commands His disciples, "Go into the city to such a man, and say to him, The Master saith, My time is at hand; I will keep the passover at thy house, with my disciples" (Matthew 26:18). Passover week was special, and it was a strict time under Jewish custom when no leaven was to be found in their houses. Please notice the scripture says:

> Seven days shall there be no leaven found in your houses: for whosoever eateth that which is leavened, even that soul shall be cut off from the congregation of Israel, whether he be a stranger, or born in the land. Ye shall eat nothing leavened; in all your habitations shall ye eat unleavened bread (Exodus 12:19-20).

Now the Lord commanded, "No meat offering, which ye shall bring unto the Lord, shall be made with leaven" (Leviticus 2:11). No yeast or leavening agents of any kind were to be used.

Jesus clearly tells us that He came to fulfill all the law (Matthew 5:17-18). Thus, to even assume that our Lord would have used elements with leaven would be a contradiction to God's word. When you have an opportunity, read Leviticus 2. It is very revealing on this matter. It does not give a recipe for unleavened bread, but it does give that which we have the authority to include. It names flour and oil (verses 1-2) and salt (verse 13). Using what is authorized is always the acceptable and the best way to go and indeed is the only way to go. God's word has the authority to command, and we have the obligation to obey if we love Him (John 14:15). God's word of truth is so very clear when we get our opinions out of the way. It is difficult for us to get our opinions out of the way, but we must. In fact, the Bible says we are to examine ourselves; we are to prove all things and hold fast to that which is good.

One might ask What is wrong with using a different kind of bread? Or one may say it does not say not to use a different kind of bread. Or one may say well I think it is all right to use a different kind of bread. Or one might say, Everybody else is doing it, why can't we? Or it is so much more convenient or sanitary or pretty. If God had left the plan of salvation in our hands, and He did not, we would be free to design our own plan for the Lord's Supper or for any other matter in Christianity. But, he didn't, so we need to listen to His words not our own. Isaiah wrote, and this is God speaking, "For my thoughts are not your thoughts, neither are your ways my ways, saith the Lord. For as the heavens are higher than the earth, so are my ways higher than your ways, and my thoughts than your thoughts" (Isaiah 55:8-9). According to God's word, the Holy Scripture, it is given that we might come to a knowledge of the truth. What do we find when we turn to the accounts? Really, there are not many accounts. One might think in view of what we hear about communion that must be everywhere in the Bible; but, really, in the New Testament, we simply have Matthew 26, Mark 14, Luke 22, 1 Corinthians 10, and 1 Corinthians 11.

What we learn when we isolate and look at these records that we have, the scripture says that Jesus took bread and He "break" it (1 Corinthians 11). He took bread, He blessed it, He gave it, and He says, this, is my body (Matthew 26:26). Consistently, throughout the scripture relative to the church, there is a thread of unity declared in the singularity and oneness of the church and its practice. Why is it that we think we can improve upon God's perfect system? Not only is God's way complete, but there is no room left for change. For nothing can be improved upon that God has set in place. How could it? He is perfect. God is a perfect God. He cannot set forth an imperfect revelation and imperfect revelation is not going to set forth an imperfect plan. So, it must follow, perfect God, perfect revelation, and perfect plan. He has given us His plan or His pattern so we will know what to do.

In regard to the Lord's Supper, Paul says, "For whatsoever things were written aforetime were written for our learning, that we through patience and comfort of the scriptures might have hope" (Romans 15:4). From the inspired writings of the Old Testament, we should be able to discover a shadow of things to come (Colossians 2:17) concerning the Lord's Supper. Paul writes the church at Corinth, saying, "Christ our passover is sacrificed for us" (1 Corinthians 5:7). John says concerning our Lord, "Behold the Lamb of God" (John 1:29, 36). In the Old Testament, God permits us to see the Passover lamb was a type of Christ; and Moses says, "Your lamb shall be without blemish, a male of the first year" (Exodus 12:5). Peter says about the Christ, "Who did no sin, neither was guile found in his mouth" (1 Peter 2:22). Now concerning the Passover lamb—listen—concerning the Passover lamb the Lord commanded "neither shall you break a bone thereof" (Exodus 12:46). When Jesus Christ our Passover was crucified, the scripture says, "But when they came to Jesus, and saw that he was dead already, they brake not his legs" (John 19:33). You see, there was a picture, there was a pattern, there was a foreshadowing of that event, even as specific as breaking the bones of the Lamb or in this case of Jesus.

God also commanded Israel to "take to them every man a lamb, according to the house of their fathers, a lamb for a house" (Exodus 12:3). Now that seems simple enough, doesn't it? One lamb for one house—Jesus Christ is indeed the Lamb of God. He is our one lamb in the communion of the body of Christ. Thus, He speaks at the celebration of the Passover with His disciples when He says, "Take, eat, this is my body." How beautifully and how simply the Old Testament foreshadowed the new. Notice, the Passover lamb was a picture of Jesus Christ, the Lamb of God. The one lamb of the Passover is a picture of the one bread or the one loaf on the Lord's Table: the one house, the one congregation; the one church, the church of Jesus Christ.

Now, something else we notice in this study. He commands in regard to the Passover, saying, in one house shall it be eaten (Exodus 12:4). Now literally thousands and thousands of lambs were killed in Israel for the Passover, but one and only one for each house. Is not that amazing? God is so specific here about what He wants done and certainly He has the right to tell us how He will be worshiped. Here He is telling Israel how they will worship Him. He says there will be one lamb for each house. Many congregations shall assemble just as many kindred families assemble to celebrate the Passover, and each congregation shall have one loaf, my body, as they focus upon the one Christ, the Lamb of God, that they may maintain the simple example that was established.

The Bible says in John 4:23-24, "the true worshippers,"—listen to the emphasis here—Jesus says, "The true worshippers shall worship the Father in spirit and in truth." In John 4, He is telling us that when we observe the Lord's Supper, it must be in the same simple form the truth has authorized. What it authorizes, if you to go back and look at the record, is one loaf of unleavened bread on the Lord's Table. In the communion, each disciple breaks from the loaf and eats his portion and he passes it to the next disciple. What does he pass to him? That one loaf of unleavened bread that symbolizes the unity of the one body about which the Lord Jesus Christ prayed, saying, "This is my body."

At the institution of the Lord's Supper, Jesus says, "With desire I have desired to eat this passover with you before I suffer: For I say unto you, I will not any more eat thereof, until it be fulfilled in the kingdom of God" (Luke 22:15-16). Then He went on to say, "This is my body which is given for you: this do" (Luke 22:19). Not only does the Lord give the example, He then gives the command, "this do"; in other words, you do what I have done. So, the example was given; and it seems so clear when He says, "this do." Did Jesus participate in the eating? Yes, else could He have said, "I will not anymore eat of this" and then He says, "this do," as He showed the disciples the way to go. We dare not alter the pattern that has been given to us by God's truth in any way.

One of the things we noticed in past studies is that three thousand souls responded to the first gospel call issued on the day of Pentecost when Peter commanded, "Repent, and be baptized every one of you in the name of Jesus Christ for the remission of sins" (Acts 2:38). "Then they that gladly received his word were baptized: and the same day there were added unto them about three thousand souls. And they continued steadfastly in the apostles' doctrine and fellowship, and in breaking of bread, and in prayers" (Acts 2:41-42). The entire communion is referred to, as the breaking of bread. The scripture says, "And upon the first day of the week, when the disciples came together to break bread, Paul preached unto them" (Acts 20:7). The disciples came together to break bread, that was to do what? To "take, eat this is my body." Paul says, "For we being many are one bread, and one body: for we are all partakers of that one bread" (1 Corinthians 10:17).

As followers of Christ who through obedience were called Christians first in Antioch (Acts 11:26), let this simple plan of God's word hold forth the only light that we follow. Remember, we believe in speaking where the Bible speaks and in being silent where the Bible is silent. God's word is truth, and it is always right. Let not any person's ways pervert the true worship. We must remember Jesus' words: "This people draweth nigh unto me with their mouth, and honoreth me with their lips; but their heart is far from me. But in vain they do worship me, teaching for doctrines the commandments of men" (Matthew 15:8-9). He says, "Let us hold fast the profession of our faith without wavering; (for he is faithful that promised)" (Hebrews 10:23).

Not only do we break bread in the Lord's Supper but we also partake of the cup of blessing. Listen again to Paul:

> And as they were eating, Jesus took bread, and blessed it, and brake it, and gave it to the disciples, and said, Take, eat; this is my body. And he took the cup, and gave thanks, and gave it to them, saying, Drink ye all of it; For this is my blood of the new testament, which is shed for many for the remission of sins. But I say unto you, I will not drink henceforth of this fruit of the vine, until that day when I drink it new with you in my Father's kingdom (Matthew 26:26-29).

Listen to Mark's account:

> And as they did eat, Jesus took bread, and blessed, and brake it, and gave to them, and said, Take, eat: this is my body. And he took the cup, and when he had given thanks, he gave it to them: and they all drank of it. And he said unto them, This is my blood of the new testament, which is shed for many. Verily I say unto you, I will drink no more of the fruit of the vine, until that day that I drink it new in the kingdom of God (Mark 14:22-25).

Now listen to Luke's account, it helps to listen to the different accounts that we have. Luke 22:19-20: "And he took bread, and gave thanks, and brake it, and gave unto them, saying, This is my body which is given for you: this do in remembrance of me. Likewise also the cup after supper, saying, This cup is the new testament in my blood, which is shed for you."

Now listen to Paul in 1 Corinthians 10:16-17: "The cup of blessing which we bless, is it not the communion of the blood of Christ? The bread which we break, is it not the communion of the body of Christ? For we being many are one bread, and one body: for we are all partakers of that one bread."

Finally, the last account we have is in Paul's first letter to the Corinthian church: he tells us, "Be ye followers of me, even as I also am of Christ" (verse 1). Then he says:

> For I have received of the Lord that which also I delivered unto you, That the Lord Jesus the same night in which he was betrayed took bread: And when he had given thanks, he brake it, and said, Take, eat: this is my body, which is broken for you: this do in remembrance of me. After the same manner also he took the cup, when he has supped, saying, This cup is the new testament in my blood: this do ye, as oft as ye drink it, in remembrance of me. For as often as ye eat this bread, and drink this cup, ye do show the Lord's death till he come (1 Corinthians 11:23-26).

Now these are all of the accounts that we have in the scripture in regard to the Lord's Supper. It ought to become a studied art with us to find out what Jesus meant when He says, "This do." He, evidently, is demonstrating and saying "what I have done," "you do." The readings of the Bible accounts of the Lord's Supper given here are so important because they outline for us which way to go. All we can do, then, is to follow the direction that is given, even if we think we should do it another way. We must be mindful of what Paul told the young evangelist Timothy. He says, "All scripture is given by inspiration of God, and is profitable for doctrine, for reproof, for correction, for instruction in righteousness: That the man of God may be perfect (now that means complete), throughly furnished unto all good works" (2 Timothy 3:16-17). We never have to wonder how to be complete as a Christian or how to serve properly in our worship because the scripture, the truth, has come to us from God. It does not require any altering to be more complete or more up to date. God gave man the perfect plan to follow so that he could be saved. It is for us—for every person—then to accept the Lordship of Christ, for Jesus says, "If ye love me, keep my commandments" (John 14:15).

I want you to notice that He took the cup and He gave it to them, in all of these accounts. The inspired writers use the words, the cup or this cup. These last two writers have clearly indicated the cup as being the New Testament. The scripture says, He gave it to them. That certainly does not take a lot for us to figure out that the Lord picked up the cup and He blessed it and its contents, the fruit of the vine. Then He gave the cup to them to drink from. In every case, the inspiration of the Holy Spirit caused Paul and the other inspired writers of the New Testament to write in the singular case. Why was this? The Holy Spirit was not wrong. We certainly are not more intelligent or smarter than these inspired men. We must not allow our wishes or our pride to rule in this matter. We simply must say, Speak Lord, thy servant heareth.

Thank you for listening. it was a pleasure to be with you today. We invite you continue with us. We welcome your questions, your concerns, whatever it may be. Until this time next Lord's Day, we bid you a very pleasant good day.

www.ingramcontent.com/pod-product-compliance
Lightning Source LLC
Chambersburg PA
CBHW030916090426
42737CB00007B/210